Philosophy
Gone
Wild

Philosophy Gone Wild

Essays in
Environmental
Ethics

Holmes Rolston III

Prometheus Books
Buffalo, New York

Published 1986 by Prometheus Books
700 East Amherst Street, Buffalo, New York 14215

Library of Congress Catalog Card Number: 86-60106
ISBN 0-87975-329-3
Printed in the United States of America

Contents

Preface

Nature is perhaps the most ancient philosophical category, yet few others are of greater current relevance. Still, a quarter century back, not even the most astute observer would have predicted a wild turn in philosophy. There has been no more surprising philosophical development than the recent, serious reconsideration of the human relationship to the ecosystemic Earth. The questions come in many forms: Have we any duties *to* natural things at all, or merely duties *to* persons *concerning* natural things? What sort of human dominion over nature is proper? In what senses can or should humans follow nature? Have we duties to animals, perhaps at least to sentient animals? Have we duties to endangered species, or, again, only duties to persons concerning rare species?

Is nature only a resource for human needs, natural things accordingly having merely instrumental value? Or are there intrinsic values in ecosystems, apart from human concerns? Are these to be located in organic individuals or in their biological communities, the whole of which the organism is a part? Are the values associated with nature subjective or objective? Precisely what are these values carried by natural things? How are they to be traded off against other human values, against the legitimate and not-so-legitimate demands of industry, business, development? How much nature do we destroy in order to benefit the poor? How much nature do we owe to future generations? How does the present debate about valuing nature reconnect with longstanding issues within philosophy such as the (so-called) naturalistic fallacy, that of moving from an *is,* describing nature, to an *ought,* prescribing an ethic? How does it relate to the Darwinian portrait of nature red in tooth and claw? What, after all, is the nature of nature, and what experiences encountering nature are appropriate in the light of contemporary bioscience and of philosophical criticism? The essays that follow discuss the environmental turn in philosophy.

I. ETHICS AND NATURE

No one will deny that we have duties to others that may involve natural things. Persons are greatly helped or hurt by the condition of their environment, and this in complex ways. Thus, the extinction of the grizzly bear would impoverish the wilderness experiences of numerous vacationers, now and for generations to come. But this involves an environmental ethic in a secondary, humanistic sense. Can there be an environmental ethic in a primary, naturalistic sense, one where natural things are morally considerable in their own right? How is such an ethic to divide or integrate its concern between individual organisms and the ecosystems out of which they evolved and in which they still flourish? How far is such an ethic divided between the prosperity of humans and the prosperity of the ecosystem and its other natural members? We seem to need an ethic for partners with entwined destinies.

No one will deny that we can and ought to be prudent in our use of natural resources. But when philosophy takes this wild turn, ought nature in some sense to be followed? Can it be a tutor of human conduct? What, if anything, do we learn in nature that forms character? The mainstream Western paradigm, characterized a century ago by John Stuart Mill, urges us to study nature and finds this the first principle of intelligent action. But humans so study nature in order to amend and repair it. They seek to use it resourcefully. Is there any further studying of nature that appreciates its wildness, its spontaneous generative powers, its beauty? Is there a nature that we can and ought to love?

Such questions in the essays that follow open out to wider horizons, and we conclude this section asking how to form a worldview of this earthen ecosystem that has borne and that continues to bear up the natural and human histories. Perhaps the most basic duty of all is to the great river of life, past, present, and future.

1

Is There an Ecological Ethic?

The Ecological Conscience[1] is the arresting title of a representative environmental anthology. The puzzlement lies neither in the noun nor in the by now familiar modifier, but in their operation on each other. We are comfortable with a Christian or humanist ethic, but the moral noun does not regularly take a scientific adjective: a biological conscience, a geological conscience. In a celebrated survey, *The Subversive Science*,[2] where ecology reaches into our ultimate commitments, Paul Sears entitles an essay "The Steady State: Physical Law and Moral Choice." To see how odd, ethically and scientifically, is the conjunction, replace homeostasis with gravity or entropy.

The sense of anomaly will dissipate, though moral urgency may remain, if an environmental ethic proves to be only an ethic—utilitarian, hedonist, or whatever—*about* the environment, brought to it, informed concerning it, but not in principle ecologically formed or reformed. This would be like medical ethics, which is applied to but not derived from medical science. But we are sometimes promised more, a derivation in which the newest bioscience shapes (not to say, subverts) the ethic, a resurgent naturalistic ethics. "We must learn that nature includes an intrinsic value system," writes Ian McHarg.[3] A *Daedalus* collection is introduced with the same conviction: Environmental science "is the building of the structure of concepts and natural laws that will enable man to understand his place in nature. Such understanding must be one basis of the moral values that guide each human generation in exercising its stewardship over the earth. For this purpose ecology—the science of interactions among living things and their environments—is central."[4] We shall presently inquire into the claim that an ecological ultimacy lies in "The Balance of Nature: A Ground for Values." Just what sort of traffic is there here between science and morality?

The boundary between science and ethics is precise if we accept a pair of current (though not unargued) philosophical categories: the distinction between

Reprinted by permission from *Ethics: An International Journal of Social, Political, and Legal Philosophy* 85 (1975):93-109. Copyright © 1975 by the University of Chicago Press.

descriptive and prescriptive law. The former, in the indicative, marks the realm of science and history. The latter, including always an imperative, marks the realm of ethics. The route from one to the other, if any, is perhaps the most intransigent issue in moral philosophy, and any who so move will be accused of the naturalistic fallacy. No set of statements of fact by themselves entails any evaluative statement, except as some additional evaluative premise has been introduced. With careful analysis this evaluation will reappear, the ethics will separate out from the science. We shall press this logic on ecological ethics. Environmental science describes what is the case. An ethic prescribes what ought to be. But an environmental ethic? If our categories hold, perhaps we have a muddle. Or perhaps a paradox that yields light on the linkage between facts and values.

We find representative spokesmen for ecological morality not of a single mind. But the multiple species can, we suggest, be classified in two genera, following two concepts that are offered as moral sources. *(A)* Prominent in, or underlying, those whom we hear first is this connection of homeostasis with morality. This issues largely in what we term an ethic that is secondarily ecological. *(B)* Beyond this, surpassing though not necessarily gainsaying it, is the discovery of a moral ought inherent in recognition of the holistic character of the ecosystem, issuing in an ethic that is primarily ecological.

But first, consider an analogue. When advised that we ought to obey the laws of health, we analyze the injunction. The laws of health are nonmoral and operate inescapably on us. But, circumscribed by them, we have certain options: to employ them to our health, or to neglect them ("break them") to our hurt. Antecedent to the laws of health, the moral ought reappears in some such form as, "You ought not to harm yourself." Similarly, the laws of psychology, economics, history, the social sciences, and indeed all applied sciences describe what is (has been, or may be) the case; but in confrontation with human agency, they prescribe what the agent must do if he or she is to attain a desired end. They yield a technical ought related to an if-clause at the agent's option. So far they are nonmoral; they become moral only as a moral principle binds the agent to some end. This, in turn, is transmitted through natural law to a proximate moral ought. Let us map this as follows:

Technical Ought	*Natural Law*	*Antecedent If-Option*
You ought not to break the laws of health	for the laws of health describe the conditions of welfare	if you wish not to harm yourself.

Proximate Moral Ought	*Natural Law*	*Antecedent Moral Ought*
You ought not to break the the laws of health	for the laws of health describe the conditions of welfare	and you ought not to harm yourself.

Allow for the moment that (in the absence of overriding considerations) prudence is a moral virtue. How far can ecological ethics transpose to an analogous format?

A.

Perhaps the paramount law in ecological theory is that of homeostasis. In material, our planetary ecosystem is essentially closed, and life proceeds by recycling transformations. In energy, the system is open, with balanced solar input and output, the cycling being in energy subsystems of aggradation and degradation. Homeostasis, it should be noted, is at once an achievement and a tendency. Systems recycle, and there is energy balance; yet the systems are not static, but dynamic, as the forces that yield equilibrium are in flux, seeking equilibrium yet veering from it to bring counterforces into play. This perpetual stir, tending to and deviating from equilibrium, drives the evolutionary process.

1. How does this translate morally? Let us consider first a guarded translation. In "The Steady State: Physical Law and Moral Choice," Paul Sears writes: "Probably men will always differ as to what constitutes the good life. They need not differ as to what is necessary for the long survival of man on earth. Assuming that this is our wish, the conditions are clear enough. As living beings we must come to terms with the environment about us, learning to get along with the liberal budget at our disposal, promoting rather than disrupting those great cycles of nature—of water movement, energy flow, and material transformation that have made life itself possible. As a physical goal, we must seek to attain what I have called a steady state."[5] The title of the article indicates that this is a moral "must." To assess this argument, begin with the following:

Technical Ought	Ecological Law	Antecedent If-Option
You ought to recycle	for the life-supporting ecosystem recycles or perishes	if you wish to perserve human life.

When we replace the if-option by an antecedent moral ought, we convert the technical ought to a proximate moral ought. Thus the "must" in the citation is initially one of physical necessity describing our circumscription by ecological law, and subsequently it is one of moral necessity when this law is conjoined with the life-promoting ought.

Proximate Moral Ought	Ecological Law	Antecedent Moral Ought
You ought to recycle	for the life-supporting ecosystem recycles or perishes	and you ought to preserve human life.

The antecedent ought Sears takes, fairly enough, to be common to many if not all our moral systems. Notice the sense in which we can break ecological law.

Spelling the conditions of stability and instability, homeostatic laws operate on us willy-nilly, but within a necessary obedience we have options, some of which represent enlightened obedience. To break an ecological law means, then, to disregard its implications in regard to an antecedent moral ought.

Thus far ecological morality is informed about the environment, conforming to it, but is not yet an ethic in which environmental science affects principles. Antecedent to ecological input, there is a classical ethical principle, "promoting human life," which, when ecologically tutored, better understands life's circulations, whether in homeostasis, or in DDT, or strontium 90. Values do not (have to) lie in the world but may be imposed on it, as humans prudently manage the world.

2. Much attention has focused on a 1968 address, "The Tragedy of the Commons," given by Garrett Hardin to the American Association for the Advancement of Science. Hardin's argument, recently expanded to book length, proposes an ecologically based "fundamental extension in morality."[6] While complex in its ramifications and deserving of detailed analysis, the essential ethic is simple, built on the model of a village commons. Used by the villagers to graze cattle, the commons is close to its carrying capacity. Any villager who does not increase his livestock will be disadvantaged in the market. Following self-interest, each increases his herd; and the commons is destroyed. Extended to the planet, seen as a homeostatic system of finite resources, the model's implication of impending tragedy is obvious. (The propriety of the extrapolation is arguable, but not at issue here.) The prescription of an ecological morality is "mutual coercion, mutually agreed on" in which we limit freedom to grow in order to stabilize the ecosystem to the mutual benefit of all.

To distill the ethics here is not difficult. We begin as before, with ecological law that yields options, which translate morally only with the addition of the life-promoting obligation.

Technical Ought	*Ecological Law*	*Antecedent If-Option*
We ought to stabilize the ecosystem through mutually imposed limited growth	for the life-supporting ecosystem stabilizes at a finite carrying capacity or is destroyed	if you wish mutually to preserve human life.

Proximate Moral Ought	*Ecological Law*	*Antecedent Moral Ought*
We ought to stabilize the ecosystem through mutually imposed self-limited growth	for the life-supporting ecosystem stabilizes at a finite carrying capacity or is destroyed	and we ought mutually to preserve human life.

To clarify the problem of mutual preservation, Hardin uses an essentially Hobbesian scheme. Every man is an ego set over against the community, acting in his own self-interest. But to check his neighbor's aggrandizement, he compromises and enters a social contract where, now acting in enlightened self-interest, he limits his own freedom to grow in return for a limitation of the encroaching freedom of his competitors. The result is surprisingly atomistic and anthropocentric, recalling the post-Darwinian biological model, lacking significant place for the mutual interdependence and symbiotic cooperation so prominent in recent ecology. In any event, it is clear enough that Hardin's environmental ethic is only a classical ethic applied in the matrix of ecological limitations.

Typically, ecological morality generated by population pressure resolves itself into a particular case of this kind, as for instance in the analysis by Paul Ehrlich in *The Population Bomb*. This is an ethic of scarcity, but morality since its inception has been conceived in scarcity.

3. Let us pass to a more venturesome translation of homeostasis into moral prescription, that of Thomas B. Colwell, Jr. "The balance of Nature provides an objective normative model which can be utilized as the ground of human value. . . . Nor does the balance of Nature serve as the source of all our values. It is only the *ground* of whatever other values we may develop. But these other values must be consistent with it. The balance of Nature is, in other words, a kind of ultimate value. . . . It is a *natural* form, not a product of human convention or supernatural authority. It says in effect to man: 'This much at least you must do, this much you must be responsible for. You must at least develop and utilize energy systems which recycle their products back into Nature.' . . . Human values are founded in objectively determinable ecological relations with Nature. The ends which we propose must be such as to be compatible with the ecosystems of Nature."[7]

Morality and homeostasis are clearly blended here, but it is not so clear how we relate or disentangle them. Much is embedded in the meanings of "ground of human value," "ultimate value," the mixed moral and physical "must," and the identification of a moral norm with a natural limit. Let us mark out first a purely technical ought, followed by an antecedent moral ought that may convert to a proximate moral ought.

Technical Ought	*Ecological Law*	*Antecedent If-Option*
You ought to recycle	for the value-supporting eco-system recycles or perishes	if you wish to preserve the ground of human value.

Proximate Moral Ought	*Ecological Law*	*Antecedent Moral Ought*
You ought to recycle	for the value-supporting eco-system recycles or perishes	and you ought to preserve the ground of human value.

The simplest reading of Colwell is to hold, despite his exaggerated terms, that the "ground of human value" means only the limiting condition, itself value-free, within which values are to be constructed. Homeostasis is not "an ultimate value," only a precondition of the value enterprise, necessary but not sufficient for value. But then it is misleading to say that "human values have a root base in ecological relationships." For homeostasis, like scarce resources, or the cycling seasons, or soil characteristics, or the conservation of matter-energy, is a natural given, the stage on which the value-drama is played.

If, seeking to manage my finances wisely, I ask, "How shall I spend my money?" and you counsel, "You ought to balance your budget," the advice is sound enough, yet only preparatory to serious discussion of economic values. The balanced budget is necessary but not sufficient for value, a ground of value only in an enabling, not a fundamental sense; certainly not what we would ordinarily call an ultimate value. It is true, of course, that the means to any end can, in contexts of desperation and urgency, stand in short focus as ultimate values. Air, food, water, health, if we are deprived of them, become at once our concern. Call them ultimate values if you wish, but the ultimacy is instrumental, not intrinsic. We should think a person immature whose principal goal was just to breathe, to eat, to drink, to be healthy—merely this and nothing more. To say that the balance of nature is a ground for human values is not to draw any ethics from ecology, as may first appear, but only to recognize the necessary medium of ethical activity.

Thus far, ecological ethics reduces rather straightforwardly to the classical ethical query now advised of certain ecological boundaries. The stir is, to put it so, about the boundedness, not the morality. The ultimate science may well herald limits to growth; it challenges certain presumptions about rising standards of living, capital, progress, development, and so on; convictions that, though deeply entrenched parameters of human value, are issues of what is, can, or will be the case, not of what ought to be. This realization of limits, dramatically shift ethical application though it may, can hardly be said to reform our ethical roots, for the reason that its scope remains (when optimistic) a maximizing of human values or (when pessimistic) human survival. All goods are human goods, with nature an accessory. There is no endorsement of any natural rightness, only the acceptance of the natural given. It is ecological secondarily, but primarily anthropological.

B.

The claim that morality is a derivative of the holistic character of the ecosystem proves more radical, for the ecological perspective penetrates not only the secondary but also the primary qualities of the ethic. It is ecological in substance, not merely in accident; it is ecological per se, not just consequentially.

Return, for instance, to Colwell. He seems to mean more than the minimal interpretation just given him. The mood is that the ecological circumscription of value is not itself amoral or premoral, neatly articulated from morality. Construct values though humans may, they operate in an environmental context where they must ground their values in ecosystemic obedience. This "must" is ecologically descriptive: certain laws in fact circumscribe humans and embrace their value enterprises. And it is also morally prescriptive: given options within parameters of necessary obedience, humans morally ought to promote homeostasis. But here, advancing on the preceding argument, the claim seems to be that following ecological nature is not merely a prudential means to moral and valuational needs independent of nature but is an end in itself; or, more accurately, it is within human relatedness to our environment that all human values are grounded and supported. In that construction of values, humans doubtless exceed any environmental prescription, but nevertheless our values remain environmental reciprocals. They complement a homeostatic world. Human valuations, like other human perceptions and knowings, are interactionary, drawn from environmental transactions, not merely brought to it. In this environmental encounter, humans find homeostasis a key to all values—the precondition of values, if you will—but one which, for all that, informs and shapes other human values by making them relational, corporate, environmental. But we are passing over to moral endorsement of the ecosystemic character, and to a tenor of argument that others make clearer.

Perhaps the most provocative such affirmation is in a deservedly seminal essay, "The Land Ethic," by Aldo Leopold. He concludes, "A thing is right when it tends to preserve the integrity, stability, and beauty of the biotic community. It is wrong when it tends otherwise."[8] Leopold writes in search of a morality of land use that escapes economic expediency. He too enjoins, proximately, recycling, but it is clear that his claim transcends the immediate context to teach that we morally ought to preserve the excellences of the ecosystem (or, more freely as we shall interpret him, to maximize the integrity, beauty, and stability of the ecosystem). He is seeking, as he says, to advance the ethical frontier from the merely interpersonal to the region of humans in transaction with their environment.

Here the environmental perspective enters not simply at the level of the proximate ought which, environmentally informed and preceded by homocentrist moral principles, prescribes protection of the ecosystem. It acts at a higher level, as itself an antecedent ought, from which proximate oughts, such as the one earlier considered, about recycling, may be derived.

Proximate Moral Ought	Ecological Law	Antecedent Moral Ought
You ought to recycle	for recycling preserves the ecosystem	and you ought to preserve the integrity of the ecosystem.

Note how the antecedent parallels upper-level axioms in other systems (e.g., "You ought to maximize human good," or "You ought not to harm yourself or others," or "Love your neighbor as yourself"). Earlier, homeostatic connectedness did not really alter the moral focus; but here, in a shift of paradigms, the values hitherto reserved for humans are reallocated to humans in the environment.

Doubtless even Leopold's antecedent ought depends on a yet prior ought that one promote beauty and integrity, wherever one finds it. But this, like the injunction that one ought to promote the good, or that one ought to keep his promises, is so high level as to be, if not definitional or analytic, so general as to be virtually unarguable and therefore without any real theoretical content. Substantive values emerge only as something empirical is specified as the locus of value. In Leopold's case we have a feedback from ecological science which, prior to any effect on proximate moral oughts, informs the antecedent ought. There is a valuational element intrinsically related to the concepts utilized in ecological description. That is, the character of what is right in some basic sense, not just in application, is stated postecologically. Doubtless too, the natural course we choose to preserve is filtered through our concepts of beauty, stability, and integrity, concepts whose origins are not wholly clear and that are perhaps nonnatural. But, perspectival though this invariably is, what counts as beauty and integrity is not just brought to and imposed on the ecosystem but is discovered there. Let us map this as follows:

Proximate Moral Ought	Ecological Law	Antecedent Moral Ought	Ecosystemic Evaluation
You ought to recycle	for recycling preserves the integral ecosystem	and you ought to preserve the integrity of the ecosystem	for the integral ecosystem has value.

Our antecedent ought is not eco-free. Though preceding ecological law in the sense that, given this ought, one can transmit it via certain ecological laws to arrive at proximate oughts, it is itself a result of an ecosystemic appraisal.

This evaluation is not scientific description; hence not ecology per se, but metaecology. No amount of research can verify that the right is the optimum biotic community. Yet ecological description generates this evaluation of nature, endorsing the systemic rightness. The transition from "is" to "good" and thence to "ought" occurs here; we leave science to enter the domain of evaluation, from which an ethic follows. The injunction to recycle is technical, made under circumscription by ecological necessity and made moral only by the presence of an antecedent. The injunction to maximize the ecosystemic excellence is also ecologically derived but is an evaluative transition that is not made under necessity.

Our account initially suggests that ecological description is logically (if not chronologically) prior to the ecosystemic evaluation, the former generating the latter. But the connection of description with evaluation is more complex, for the description and evaluation to some extent arise together, and it is often difficult to say which is prior and which is subordinate. Ecological description finds unity, harmony, interdependence, stability, etc., and these are valuationally endorsed, yet they are found, to some extent, because we search with a disposition to value order, harmony, stability, unity. Still, the ecological description does not merely confirm these values, it informs them; and we find that the character, the empirical content, of order, harmony, stability is drawn from, no less than brought to, nature. In post-Darwinian nature, for instance, we looked for these values in vain, while with ecological description we now find them; yet the earlier data are not denied, only redescribed or set in a larger ecological context, and somewhere enroute our notions of harmony, stability, etc., have shifted too and we see beauty now where we could not see it before. What is ethically puzzling, and exciting, in the marriage and mutual transformation of ecological description and evaluation is that here an "ought" is not so much *derived* from an "is" as discovered simultaneously with it. As we progress from descriptions of fauna and flora, of cycles and pyramids, of stability and dynamism, on to intricacy, planetary opulence and interdependence, to unity and harmony with oppositions in counterpoint and synthesis, arriving at length at beauty and goodness, it is difficult to say where the natural facts leave off and where the natural values appear. For some observers at least, the sharp is/ought dichotomy is gone; the values seem to be there as soon as the facts are fully in, and both alike are properties of the system.

While it is frequently held that the basic criterion of the obligatory is the nonmoral value that is produced or sustained, there is novelty in what is taken as the nonmoral good—the ecosystem. Our ethical heritage largely attaches values and rights to persons, and if nonpersonal realms enter, they enter only as tributary to the personal. What is proposed here is a broadening of value, so that nature will cease to be merely "property" and become a commonwealth. The logic by which goodness is discovered or appreciated is notoriously evasive, and we can only reach it suggestively. "Ethics cannot be put into words, " said Wittgenstein, such things *"make themselves manifest."*[9] We have a parallel, retrospectively, in the checkered advance of the ethical frontier recognizing intrinsic goodness, and accompanying rights, outside the self. If we now universalize "person," consider how slowly the circle has been enlarged fully to include aliens, strangers, infants, children, Negroes, Jews, slaves, women, Indians, prisoners, the elderly, the insane, the deformed, and even now we ponder the status of fetuses. Ecological ethics queries whether we ought again to universalize, recognizing the intrinsic value of every ecobiotic component.

Are there, first, existing ethical sentiments that are subecological, that is, which anticipate the ecological conscience, and on which we might build? Second, is the ecological evaluation authentic, or perhaps only a remodeled traditional humanistic ethic? Lastly, what are the implications of maximizing the ecosystem, and what concept of nature warrants such evaluation?

1. Presumably the evaluation of a biotic community will rest partly on the worth of its elements, if not independently, then in matrix. We have a long-standing, if (in the West) rather philosophically neglected, tradition that grants some moral ought to the prevention of needless animal suffering: "A righteous man has regard for the life of his beasts" (Proverbs 12.10). Consider what we oddly call "humane" societies or laws against cockfighting, bear baiting, and (in

our nation) bullfighting, and (in most states) steer busting. We prohibit a child's torture of a cat; we prosecute the rancher who carelessly lets horses starve. Even the hunter pursues a wounded deer. That one ought to prevent needless cruelty has no obvious ecological foundation, much less a natural one, but the initial point is that animals are so far endowed with a value that conveys something like rights, or at least obligates us.

More revelatory is the increasingly common claim that one ought not to destroy life, or species, needlessly, regardless of suffering. We prevent the wanton slaughter of eagles, whether they suffer or not. Even the zealous varmint hunter seems to need the rationalization that crows rob the cornfield. He must malign the coyote and wolf to slay them enthusiastically. He cannot kill just for fun. We abhor the oilspills that devastate birdlife. The Sierra Club defends the preservation of grizzlies or whooping cranes on many counts as means to larger ends—as useful components of the ecosystem, for scientific study, or for our children's enjoyment. (We shall return to the integrated character of such argument.) But sufficiently pressed, the defense is that one ought not destroy a life form of beauty. Since ecosystems regularly eliminate species, this may be a nonecological ought. Yet it is not clearly so, for part of a species' evaluation arises as it is seen in environmental matrix. Meanwhile, we admit they should continue to exist, "as a matter of biotic right."[10]

This caliber of argument can be greatly extended. A reason given for the preservation of Cades Cove in the Great Smoky Mountains National Park is the variety of rare salamanders there. Certain butterflies occur rarely in isolated hummocks in the African grasslands. Formerly, unscrupulous collectors would collect a few hundred then burn out the hummock to destroy the species, and thereby drive up the price of their collections. I find myself persuaded that they morally ought not do this. Nor will the reason resolve into the evil of greed, but it remains the needless destruction of even a butterfly species. At scattered occurrences of rare ferns in Tennessee I refused to collect, not simply to leave them for others to enjoy, but morally unwilling to imperil a species. Such species are *a fortiori* environmentally pressed, yet they remain, and even prosper, in selected environmental niches, and their dispatch by human whim seems of a different order from their elimination by natural selection—something like the difference between murder and death by natural causes.

This respect enlarges to the landscape. We preserve certain features of natural beauty—the Grand Canyon, or Rainbow Bridge, or the Everglades. Though it seems odd to accord them "rights" (for proposals to confer rights on some new entity always sound linguistically odd), we go so far as to say that, judged to be places of beauty or wonder, they ought to be preserved. Is this only as a means to an end, that we and others may enjoy them? The answer is complex. At least some argue that, as with persons, they are somehow violated, even prostituted, if treated merely as means; we enjoy them very largely for what they are in themselves. To select some landscapes is not to judge the omitted ones valueless. They may be sacrificed to higher values, or perhaps selected environments are judged sufficiently representative of more abundant ones. That we do preserve any landscape indicates our discovery of value there, with its accompanying ought. Nor are such environments only the hospitable ones. We are increasingly drawn to the beauty of wilderness, desert, tundra, the arctic, and the sea. Planetary forces ever reshape landscapes, of course, and former environments are now extinct; nevertheless, we find in extant landscapes an order of beauty that we are unwilling to destroy.

2. Do we perhaps have, even in this proposed primary ecological ethic, some eco-free ought? If Leopold's preserving the ecosystem is merely ancillary to human interests, the veiled antecedent ought is still that we ought to maximize human good. Were we so to maximize the ecosystem we should have a corporate anthropological egoism, "human chauvinism," not a planetary altruism. The optimum ecosystem would be but a prudential means to human welfare, and our antecedent ought would no longer be primarily ecological, but, as before, simply a familiar one, incidentally ecological in its prudence.

Even when richly appreciative of nature's values, much ecological moralizing does in fact mix the biosystemic welfare with an appeal to human interests. Reminiscent of Leopold, Réné Dubos suggests extending the Decalogue with an eleventh commandment, "Thou shalt strive for environmental quality." The justification may have a "resources" cast. We preserve wilderness and the maximally diverse ecosystem for reasons scientific and aesthetic. Natural museums serve as laboratories. Useless species may later be found useful. Diversity insures stability, especially if we err and our monocultures trigger environmental upset. Wild beauty adds a spiritual quality to life. "Were it only for selfish reasons, therefore, we must maintain variety and harmony in nature. . . . Wilderness is not a luxury; it is a necessity for the protection of humanized nature and for the preservation of mental health."[11]

But the "were it only . . ." indicates that such reasons, if sufficient, are not ultimate. Deeper, nonselfish reasons respect "qualities inherent" in fauna, flora, landscape, "so as to foster their development." Haunting Western civilization is "the criminal conceit that nature is to be considered primarily as a source of raw materials and energy for human purposes," "the crude belief that man is the only value to be considered in managing the world and that the rest of nature can be thoughtlessly sacrificed to his welfare and whims." While holding that man is the creature who humanizes nature, the ecological conscience is sensitive to other worth. Indeed, somewhat paradoxically, it is only as man grants an intrinsic integrity to nature that he discovers his truest interests. "An enlightened anthropocentrism acknowledges that, in the long run, the world's good always coincides with man's own most meaningful good. Man can manipulate nature to his best interests only if he first loves her for her own sake."[12]

This coincidence of human and ecosystemic interests, frequent in environmental thought, is ethically confusing but fertile. To reduce ecological concern merely to human interests does not really exhaust the moral temper here, and only as we appreciate this will we see the ethical perspective significantly altered. That alteration centers in the dissolution of any firm boundary between humans and the world. Ecology does not know an encapsulated ego over against his or her environment. Listen, for instance, to Paul Shepard: "Ecological thinking, on the other hand, requires a kind of vision across boundaries. The epidermis of the skin is ecologically like a pond surface or a forest soil, not a shell so much as a delicate interpenetration. It reveals the self ennobled and extended, rather than threatened, as part of the landscape, because the beauty and complexity of nature are continuous with ourselves."[13] The human vascular system includes arteries, veins, rivers, oceans, and air currents. Cleaning a dump is not different in kind from filling a tooth. The self metabolically, if metaphorically, interpenetrates the ecosystem. The world is my body.

This mood frustrates and ultimately invalidates the effort to understand all ecological ethics as disguised human self-interest, for now, with the self expanded into the system, their interests merge. One may, from a limited perspective, maximize the systemic good to maximize human good, but one can hardly say that the former is only a means to the latter, since they both amount to the same thing differently described. We are acquainted with egoism, *égoïsme à deux, trois, quatres,* with familial and tribal egoism. But here is an *égoïsme à la système,* as the very etymology of "ecology" witnesses: the Earth is one's household. In this planetary confraternity, there is a confluence of egoism and altruism. Or should we say that egoism is transformed into ecoism? To advocate the interests of the system as a means of promoting the interests of humans (in an appeal to industry and to congressmen) is to operate with a limited understanding. If we wish, for rhetorical or pragmatic reasons, we may begin with maximizing human good. But when ecologically tutored, we see that this can be redescribed as maximizing the ecosystem. Our classical ought has been transformed, stretched, coextensively with an ecosystemic ought.

To illustrate, ponder the observation that biotic-environmental complexity is integrally related to the richness of human life. That the stability and integrity of an ecosystem is a function of its variety and diversity is a fairly well-established point and it is frequently observed that complex life forms evolve only in complex environments. The long evolution of humans, accordingly, has been possible only under the stimulation of many environments—marine, arboreal, savannah, tropical, temperate, even arctic. Even when humans live at a distance from some of these, they remain tributary to our life support. Without oceans, forests, and grasslands, human life would be imperiled. Thus the complex life of humans is a product of and is underlain by environmental complexity.

This complexity is not simply biological but also mental and cultural. For maximum noetic development, humans require an environmental exuberance. So Shepard eloquently introduces the "universal wisdom" of *The Subversive Science:*

Internal complexity, as the mind of a primate, is an extension of natural complexity, measured by the variety of plants and animals and the variety of nerve cells—organic extensions of each other. The exuberance of kinds as the setting in which a good mind could evolve (to deal with a complex world) was not only a past condition. Man did not arrive in the world as though disembarking from a train in the city. He continues to arrive. . . . This idea of natural complexity as a counterpart to human intricacy is central to an ecology of man. The creation of order, of which man is an example, is realized also in the number of species and habitats, an abundance of landscapes lush and poor. Even deserts and tundras increase the planetary opulence. . . . Reduction of this variegation would, by extension then, be an amputation of man. To convert all "wastes"—all deserts, estuaries, tundras, ice-fields, marshes, steppes and moors—into cultivated fields and cities would impoverish rather than enrich life esthetically as well as ecologically.[14]

Mountains have both physical and psychic impact. Remove eagles from the sky and we will suffer a spiritual loss. For every landscape, there is an inscape; mental and environmental horizons reciprocate.

This supports, but only by curiously transforming, the preservation of the ecosystem in human self-interest, for the "self" has been so extended as to be ecosystemically redefined. The human welfare which we find in the enriched ecosystem is no longer recognizable as that of anthropocentrism. Humans judge the ecosystem as "good" or "bad" not in short anthropocentric focus, but with enlarged perspective where the integrity of other species enriches humans. The moral posture here recalls more familiar (if frequently unsettled) ethical themes; that self-interest and benevolence are not necessarily incompatible, especially where one derives personal fulfillment from the welfare of others; that treating the object of ethical concern as an end in itself is uplifting; that one's own integrity is enhanced by recognition of other integrities.

3. This environmental ethic is subject both to limits and to development, and a fair appraisal ought to recognize both. As a partial ethical source, it does not displace functioning social-personal codes, but brings into the scope of ethical transaction a realm once regarded as intrinsically valueless and governed largely by expediency. The new ethical parameter is not absolute but relative to classical criteria. Such extension will amplify conflicts of value, for human goods must now coexist with environmental goods. In operational detail this will require a new casuistry. Mutually supportive though the human and the ecosystemic interests may be, conflicts between individuals and parties, the rights of the component members of the ecosystem, the gap between the real and the ideal, will provide abundant quandaries.

Further, interpreting charitably, we are not asked to idolize the whole except as it is understood as a cosmos in which the corporate vision surrounds and limits, but does not suppress the individual. The focus does not only enlarge from humans to other ecosystemic members, but from individuals of whatever kind to the system. Values are sometimes personalized; here the community holds values. This is not, of course, without precedent, for we now grant values to states, nations, churches, trusts, corporations, and communities. And they hold these values because of their structure in which individuals are beneficiaries. It is similar with the ecosystem, only more so; for when we recall its diffusion of the boundary between the individual and the ecosystem, we cannot say whether value in the system or in the individual is logically prior.

Leopold and Shepard do not mean to deep freeze the present ecosystem. Despite their preservationist vocabulary, their care for the biosystemic welfare allows for "alteration, management, and use."[15] We are not committed to this as the best possible ecosystem; it may well be that the role of man—at once "citizen" and "king"—is to govern what has hitherto been the partial success of the evolutionary process. Though we revere the Earth, we may yet "humanize" it, a point made forcefully by René Dubos.[16] This permits interference with and rearrangement of nature's spontaneous course. It enjoins domestication, for part of the natural richness is its potential in human life support. We recognize man's creativity, development, openness, and dynamism.

Species regularly enter and exit nature's theater; perhaps natural selection currently tests species for their capacity to coexist with humans. Orogenic and erosional forces have produced perpetual environmental flux; humans may well transform their environment. But this should complement the beauty, integrity, and stability of the planetary biosystem, not do violence to it. There ought to be some rational showing that the alteration is enriching; that values are sacrificed for greater ones. For this reason the right is not that which maintains the ecosystemic status quo, but that which preserves its beauty, stability, and integrity.

What ought to be does not invariably coincide with what is; nevertheless, here is a mood that, recalling etymology again, we can best describe as humans being "at home" in their world. Humans accept, cherish their good Earth. Purely scientific descriptions of an ecosystem may warrant the term "stability," neutrally used; they facilitate the estimate of its beauty and integrity. Added, though, is a response of the ecologist to his discoveries, an evocation of altering consciousness. We see integrity and beauty we missed before, partly through new realization of fact—interdependence, environmental fitness, hydrologic cycles, population rhythms, and feedback loops—and partly through transformed concepts of what counts as beauty and integrity, for world and concept mutually transform each other.

Though the full range of that shifting concept of nature and the ecological description that underlies it are beyond our scope, we can suggest their central axis. After Darwin (through misunderstanding him, perhaps), the world of design collapsed, and nature, for all its law, seemed random, accidental, chaotic, blind, crude, an "odious scene of violence."[17] Environmental science has been resurveying the post-Darwinian natural jungle and has increasingly set its conflicts within a dynamic web of life. Nature's savagery is much less wanton and clumsy than formerly supposed, and we are invited to see the ecosystem not merely in awe, but in "love, respect, and admiration."[18] Ecological thinking "moves us to silent wonder and glad affirmation."[19] Oppositions remain in ecological models, but in counterpoint. The system resists the very life it supports; indeed it is by resistance not less than environmental conductivity that life is stimulated. The integrity of species and individual is a function of a field where fullness lies in interlocking predation and symbiosis, construction and destruction, aggradation and degradation. The planet that Darrow characterized, in the post-Darwinian heyday, as a miserable little "wart"[20] in the universe, eminently unsuited to life, especially human life, is now a sheltered oasis in space. Its harmony is often strange, and it is not surprising that in our immaturity we mistook it, yet it is an intricate and delicate harmony nevertheless.

Humans, insiders, are not spared environmental pressures, yet, in the full ecosystemic context, human integrity is supported by and rises from transaction with the world and therefore requires a corresponding dignity in the world partner. Of late, the world has ceased to threaten, save as we violate it. How starkly this gainsays the alienation that characterizes modern literature, seeing nature as basically rudderless, antipathetical, in need of monitoring and repair. More typically modern man, for all his technological prowess, has found himself distanced from nature, increasingly competent and decreasingly confident, at once distinguished and aggrandized, yet afloat on and adrift in an indifferent, if not a hostile universe. His world is at best a huge filling station; at worst a prison, or "nothingness." Not so for ecological humans; confronting their world with deference to a community of value in which they share, they are at home again. The new mood is epitomized, somewhat surprisingly, in reaction to space exploration, prompted by vivid photography of Earth and by astronaut's nostalgia, generating both a new love for Spaceship Earth and a resolution to focus on reconciliation with it.

We shall surely not vindicate the natural sequence in every detail as being productive of ecosystemic health, and therefore we cannot simplify our ethic to an unreflective acceptance of what naturally is the case. We do not live in Eden, yet the trend is there, as ecological advance increasingly finds in the natural given stability, beauty, and integrity, and we are henceforth as willing to open our concepts to reformation by the world as to prejudge the natural order. The question of evolution as it governs our concept of nature is technically a separate one. We must judge the worth of the extant ecosystem independently of its origins. To do otherwise would be to slip into the genetic fallacy. A person has rights for what he is, regardless of his ancestry; and it may well be that an ignoble evolutionary process has issued in a present ecosystem in which we rightly rejoice. No one familiar with paleontology is likely to claim that the evolutionary sequence moves unfailingly and without loss toward an optimally beautiful and stable ecosystem. Yet many ecological mechanisms are also evolutionary, and the ecological reappraisal suggests as a next stage an evolutionary redescription, in which we think again whether evolutionary history, for all its groping, struggle, mutation, natural selection, randomness, and statistical movement, does not yield direction enough to ponder that nature has been enriching the ecosystem. The fossil record is all of ruins. We survey it first with a certain horror; but then out of the ruins emerges this integral ecosystem. Any who can be persuaded of this latter truth will have an even more powerful ecological ethic, for the injunction to maximize the ecosystemic excellences will be an invitation to get in gear with the way the universe is operating. Linking the right to nature's processes, we will have, at length, an authentic naturalistic ethic.

The perils of transposing from a new science to a world view, patent in the history of scientific thought, are surpassed only by the perils of omitting to do so. Granted that we yet lack a clear account of the logic by which we get our values, it seems undeniable that we shape them in significant measure in accord with our notion of the kind of universe that we live in. Science has in centuries before us upset those values by reappraising the character of the universe. One has but to name Copernicus and Newton, in addition to our observation that we have lately lived in the shadow of Darwin. The ecological revolution may be of a similar order; it is undeniably at work reilluminating the world.

Darwin, though, often proves more fertile than his interpreters. When, in *The Descent of Man,* he traces the natural history of man's noblest attribute, the moral sense, he observes that "the standard of his morality rises higher and higher." Initially each attended his self-interest. The growth of conscience has been a continual expansion of the objects of his "social instincts and sympathies," first to family and tribe; then he "regarded more and more, not only the welfare, but the happiness of all his fellow-men"; then "his sympathies became more tender and widely diffused, extending to men of all races, to the imbecile, maimed, and other useless members of society; and finally to the lower animals. . . . "[21] After the fauna, can we add the flora, the landscape, the seascape, the ecosystem? There would be something magnificent about an evolution of conscience that circumscribed the whole. If so, Leopold lies in the horizon of Darwin's vision. Much of the search for an ecological morality will, perhaps in necessary pragmatism, remain secondary, "conservative," where the ground is better charted, and where we mix ethics, science, and human interests under our logical control. But we judge the ethical frontier to be beyond, a primary revaluing where, in ethical creativity, conscience must evolve. The topography is largely uncharted; to cross it will require the daring, and caution, of a community of scientists and ethicists who can together map both the ecosystem and the ethical grammar appropriate for it.

Perhaps the cash value is the same whether our ethic is ecological in secondary or primary senses; yet in the latter I find appeal enough that it has my vote to be so if it can. To the one, humans may be driven while they still fear the world that surrounds them. To the other, they can only be drawn in love.

NOTES

Also published in Donald Scherer and Thomas Attig, eds., *Ethics and the Environment* (Englewood Cliffs, N.J.: Prentice-Hall, 1983) and in Martin Wachs, ed., *Ethics in Planning* (New Brunswick, N.J.: Center for Urban Policy Research, Rutgers University, 1985). For critical discussion see: William K. Frankena, "Ethics and the Environment," and K. E. Goodpaster, "From Egoism to Environmentalism," both in K. E. Goodpaster and K. M. Sayre, eds., *Ethics and Problems of the 21st Century* (Notre Dame, Ind.: University of Notre Dame Press, 1979), pp. 3-20 and 21-35; Don E. Marietta, Jr., "The Interrelationship of Ecological Science and Environmental Ethics," *Environmental Ethics* 1(1979):195-207; William T. Blackstone, "The Search for an Environmental Ethic," in Tom Regan, ed., *Matters of Life and Death, New Introductory Essays in Moral Philosophy* (New York: Random House, 1980), pp. 299-335; Robin Attfield, *The Ethics of Environmental Concern* (New York: Columbia University Press, 1983), chapters 8-10; J. Baird Callicott, "Non-Anthropocentric Value Theory and Environmental Ethics," *American Philosophical Quarterly* 21(1984):299-309.

1. Robert Disch, ed., *The Ecological Conscience: Values for Survival* (Englewood Cliffs, N.J.: Prentice-Hall, Inc., 1970).

2. Paul Shepard and Daniel McKinley, eds., *The Subversive Science* (Boston: Houghton Mifflin Co., 1969).

3. Ian L. McHarg, "Values, Process, and Form," in Disch, *Ecological Conscience*, p. 21.

4. Roger Revelle and Hans H. Landsberg, eds., *America's Changing Environment* (Boston: Beacon Press, 1970), p. xxii.

5. Shepard and McKinley, *Subversive Science*, p. 401.

6. Garrett Hardin, "The Tragedy of the Commons," *Science* 162 (1968):1243-48, citation on p. 1243.

7. Thomas B. Colwell, Jr., "The Balance of Nature: A Ground for Human Values," *Main Currents in Modern Thought* 26, no. 2 (Nov.-Dec. 1969):46-52, citation on p. 50.

8. Aldo Leopold, "The Land Ethic," in *A Sand County Almanac* (New York: Oxford University Press, 1949), pp. 201-26, citation on pp. 224-25.

9. Ludwig Wittgenstein, *Tractatus Logico-Philosophicus*, trans. D. F. Pears and B. F. McGuiness (London: Routledge & Kegan Paul, 1969), 6:421, 522.

10. Leopold, "Land Ethic," p. 211.

11. Réné Dubos, *A God Within* (New York: Charles Scribner's Sons, 1972), pp. 166-67.

12. Ibid., pp. 40-41, 45.

13. Shepard, in Shepard and McKinley, *Subversive Science*, p. 2.

14. Ibid., pp. 4-5.

15. Leopold, "Land Ethic," p. 204.

16. Dubos, *God Within*, chap. 8.

17. John Stuart Mill, "Nature," in *Collected Works* (Toronto: University of Toronto Press, 1969), 10:398. The phrase characterizes Mill's estimate of nature.

18. Leopold, "Land Ethic," p. 223.

19. Shepard, in Shepard and McKinley, *Subversive Science,* p. 10.

20. Clarence Darrow, *The Story of My Life* (New York: Charles Scribner's Sons, 1932), p. 417.

21. Charles Darwin, *The Descent of Man,* new ed. (New York: D. Appleton & Co., 1895), pp. 124-25.

2

Can and Ought We to Follow Nature?

"Nature knows best" is the third law of ecology according to Barry Commoner and the gravity of his claim is underlined by its ranking with the first two, that everything is interconnected and that nothing is ever destroyed, only recycled.[1] But this third law is curiously normative, not merely describing what nature does, but evaluating it, and implying that we ought to follow nature. Such following may ordinarily be more prudential than moral for Commoner, but for others, if not for him too, the deepest commands of nature reach the ethical level. Radcliffe Squires writes of Robinson Jeffers, "To direct man toward a moral self by means of the wise, the solemn lessons of Nature: that has been Jeffers' life work."[2]

But there are dissenting voices. We have for too long thought of "Mother Nature" as "sensitive, efficient, purposeful, and powerful," laments Frederick E. Smith, a Harvard professor of resources and ecology. She does not exist; nature is adrift. "This absence of 'goal' in the world systems is what makes the concept of Mother Nature dangerous. In the final analysis nothing is guiding the ship."[3] This, of course, exempts us from following nature—to the contrary, we must take control of our aimless ecosystem. And, again, if this is for Smith more a matter of prudence than of morality, another, earlier Harvard professor noted with intensity the moral indifference of nature. Coining a memorable phrase, William James called us to "the moral equivalent of war" in our human resistance to amoral nature:

> Visible nature is all plasticity and indifference,—a moral multiverse. . . and not a moral universe. To such a harlot we owe no allegiance; with her as a whole we can establish no moral communion; and we are free in our dealing with her several parts to obey or to destroy, and to follow no law but that of prudence in coming to terms with such of her particular features as will help us to our private ends.[4]

Those with a philosophical memory will see that the environmental debate

Reprinted by permission from *Environmental Ethics* 1(1979):7-30.

reconnects with a longstanding problem in the ethics of nature, and recognize the two camps into which those before us have so often divided, the one setting human conduct morally and valuationally in essential discontinuity with our environment, the other finding continuity there. John Stuart Mill stands within one paradigm: "Conformity to nature has no connection whatever with right and wrong."[5] Ralph Waldo Emerson represents the other: "Right is conformity to the laws of nature so far as they are known to the human mind."[6] Sometimes old debates can be thrown into fresh perspective by more recent insights and discoveries. Of late, having become ecologically aware, can we say anything more about the question, "Can and ought we to follow nature?"

Much of the puzzle is in the way we use that grand word *nature* and here an analysis of our language is necessary. Still, it is not a sufficient answer to the question. The issue will finally turn on one's sensitivities to value, and to what degree this can be found in the environment we address. We shall try here to disentangle the phrase "follow nature," reaching in conclusion limited but crucial senses in which we both can and ought to follow nature. *Nature* is an absolutely indispensable English word, but there are few others with such a tapestry of meanings. In this respect it is like other monumental words round which life turns to such a high degree that we often capitalize them—*Freedom, the Good, the Right, Beauty, Truth, God, my Country, Democracy, the Church*—words that demand an ethical response, words that we cannot altogether and at once keep in logical perspective, but can only attack piecemeal, always reasoning out of the personal backing of our responsive perceptual experience. Earlier and in the foreground, we will put "following nature" into logical focus. But, later on and in the background, we can only invite the reader to share our moral intuitions. In ethics, Aristotle remarked, "The decision rests with perception."[7]

Nature is whatever is, all in sum, and in that universal sense the word is quite unmanageable. Even the sense of the physical universe, going back to the Greek *physis*, is both too broad and too simple. We reach the meaning we need (which also recalls the sense of *physis*) if we refer to our complex earthen ecosphere—a biosphere resting on physical planetary circulations. Nature is most broadly whatever obeys natural laws, and that also includes astronomical nature. Used in this way the word has a contrast only in the supernatural realm, if such there is. But nevertheless we restrict the word to a global, not a cosmic sense, as our typical use of the word *nature* still retains the notion, coming from the Latin root *natus* and also present in *physis*, of a system giving birth to life. No one urges that we follow physicochemical nature—dead nature. What is invariably meant features that vital evolutionary or ecological movement we often capitalize as *Nature* and sometimes personify as *Mother Nature*.

In the present state of human knowledge we are not in any position to estimate the cosmic rarity or frequency of this motherhood on our planet. Perhaps it has regularly appeared wherever nature has been given proper opportunity to organize itself; if so, that would tell us a great deal about the tendency of nature. But it may be that all this vitality is but an eddy in the all-consuming stream of entropy. Although it seems that the stars serve as the necessary furnaces in which all the chemical elements except the very lightest are forged—elements foundational to any biosystem—we nevertheless know little about the contributions of astronomical nature to our local ecosystem. We draw many conclusions about universal nature based on our knowledge of physics and chemistry, but we are reluctant to do so with biology, for we do not like to project from only one known case. Furthermore, profound and mysterious though it is, astronomical nature is too simple. We know nature in its most sophisticated organization on Earth; so, we speak now only of that face of nature which has yielded our own flourishing organic community—eco-nature.

In what follows we distinguish seven senses in which we may follow nature—first, in general terms, an *absolute* sense, an *artifactual* sense, and a *relative* sense, and then, in more detail, four specific relative senses, a *homeostatic* sense, an *imitative ethical* sense, an *axiological* sense, and finally a *tutorial* sense. We answer our basic question, whether we can and ought to follow nature, in terms of each.

FOLLOWING NATURE IN AN ABSOLUTE SENSE

Everything that conducts itself or is conducted in accordance with the laws of nature "follows nature" in a broad, elemental sense, and here it is sometimes asked whether human conduct does or ought to follow these laws. The human species has come into evolutionary nature lately and yet dramatically and with such upset that we are driven to ask whether persons are some sort of anomaly, literally apart from the laws that have hitherto regulated and otherwise still regulate natural events. No doubt our bodies have very largely the same biochemistries as the higher animals. But in our deliberative and rational powers, in our moral and spiritual sensitivities, we do not seem to run with the same mechanisms with which the coyotes and the chimpanzees so naturally run. These faculties seem to "free" us from natural determinisms; we transcend nature and escape her clutches.

Perhaps it is true that in their cultural life humans are not altogether subject to the laws of evolutionary nature. But we may immediately observe that humans are, in a still more basic sense, subject to the operation of these natural laws which we sometimes seem to exceed. If nature is defined as the aggregate of all physical, chemical, and biological processes, there is no reason why it should not *include* human agency. The human animal, as much as all the others, seems to be subject to all the natural laws that we have so far formulated. Although we live at a higher level of natural organization than any other animal, and even though we act as intelligent agents as perhaps no other animal can, there does not seem to be any law of nature that we violate either in our biochemistry or in our psychology. It is, however, difficult to get clear on the logical connections, to say nothing of the psychosomatic connections, of agency with causation. In any case, insofar as we operate as agents on the world, we certainly do so by using rather than by exempting ourselves from laws of nature. No one has ever broken the laws of gravity, or those of electricity, nutrition, or psychology. All human conduct is natural inasmuch as the laws of nature operate in us and on us willy-nilly. We cannot help but follow nature, and advice to do so in this basic law-of-nature sense is idle and trivial even while some high-level questions about the role of human deliberation in nature remain open.

FOLLOWING NATURE IN ARTIFACTUAL SENSE

Still, within this necessary obedience to the laws of nature humans do have options through agentive capacities. Submit we must, but we may nevertheless sometimes choose our route of submission. Something remains "up to us." We alter the course of spontaneous nature. That forces us to a second extreme—asking whether, in what we may call an *artifactual* sense, we can follow nature. The feeling that deliberation exempts us from the way that nature otherwise runs suggests the possibility that all agentive conduct is unnatural. Here nature is defined as the aggregate of all physical, chemical, and biological processes *excluding* those of human agency. What we most commonly mean by a natural course of events lies not so much in a scientific claim about our submission to natural laws as it does in a contrast of the natural with the artificial, the artifactual. Nature runs automatically and, within her more active creatures, instinctively; but persons do things by design, which is different, and we for the most part have no trouble distinguishing the two kinds of events. A cabin that we encounter hiking through the woods is not natural, but the rocks, trees, and the stream that form its setting are. A warbler's nest or a beaver's skull is natural while a sign marking the way to a lake or an abandoned hiking boot is not. These things differ in their architecture. The one kind is merely caused. The other kind is there for reasons.

By this account no human has ever acted deliberately except to interfere in the spontaneous course of nature. All human *actions* are in this sense unnatural because they are artifactual, and the advice to follow nature is impossible. We could not do so if we tried, for in deliberately trying to do so we act unnaturally.[8]

Each extreme—the absolute and the artifactual—so strongly appeals to part of our usage of the word *nature* that some inquirers are stalled here and can go no further. Yet even Mill, whose celebrated essay on "Nature" begins with these as the only two options, continues to ask at length about following nature as though it is possible and optional, an inquiry that cannot arise in terms of either of the above senses of the phrase. Are there not some other intermediate and reasonably distinct senses in which we can follow nature?

FOLLOWING NATURE IN A RELATIVE SENSE

There is a relative sense in which we may follow nature. Although always acting deliberately, we may conduct ourselves more or less continuously or receptively with nature as it is proceeding upon our entrance. Man is the animal with options who, when he acts, chooses just how natural or artificial his actions will be. All human agency proceeds in rough analogy with the sailing of a ship, which, if it had no skipper, would be driven with the natural wind. But the skipper may set the sails to move crosswind or even tack against the wind using the natural wind all the while. There are no unnatural energies. Our deliberative agency only manages to shift the direction of these natural forces, and it is that intervention which we call unnatural. But our interventions are variously disruptive, and, having admitted these senses in which they are all both natural and unnatural, we recognize further a range across which some are more and some are less natural.

Any parents who "plan" their children act unnaturally in the artifactual sense. Yet marriage, mating, and the rearing of children proceed with the laws of nature. In between, we debate just how natural or artificial birth control methods really are. Some moralists and some medical persons dislike methods that greatly tamper with natural cycles. In contrast to the natural love of man and woman, homosexual conduct is unnatural, "queer," which is one of the strongest reasons why many condemn it. All childbirth is natural, all medically attended childbirth is unnatural, and in between we speak of natural childbirth as opposed to a more medically manipulative childbirth.

All landscaping is artificial. On the other hand, no landscaping violates the laws of nature. Some landscaping, which blends with natural contours and uses natural flora or introduced plants compatible with it, is considered natural; however, landscaping that involves bulldozing out half a hill and setting a building and artificial shrubbery against a scarred landscape is unnatural. All farming is unnatural, against spontaneous nature, but some farming practices fit in with the character of the soil and climate while others do not. Bluegrass does well in Kentucky and in the Midwest, but the Southern farmer is foolish to plant it; and who would plant cotton in New England? On millions of acres found on every continent our unnatural agricultural practices strain fragile semi-desert ecosystems with the fate of millions of persons at stake. Highly manipulative industrial agriculture seems increasingly unnatural with its hybrid "strains," herbicides and pesticides, monocultures, factory farming of chickens, and hormone lacing of beef cattle on feedlots. Some lakes are natural while others are man-made, but among the latter, a pond with a relatively fixed shoreline that permits natural flora to flourish there seems more natural than a drawdown reservoir with barren edges.

All clothing is unnatural; only nudists go *au naturel.* We are usually oblivious to whether style and color have any connection with our environment, but still, when the issue arises, we may prefer "the natural look." The traditional Scots plaids come almost literally from the landscape; "earth tones" are in. The iridiscent, gaudy colors of modern chemistry are unnatural. Some prefer furniture with a "natural finish" to having the wooden grain hidden beneath Du Pont's latest exotic colors. We hardly object to trails for hikers in our natural areas, but if humans go there with motors and highways the wildness is spoiled. Even along interstate highways we prohibit billboards lest they pollute the countryside.

It is sometimes thought that with increasing amendation and repair of spontaneous nature the degree of unnaturalness is roughly the same as the degree of progress—the successful shift from nature to culture. But our ecological perspective has forced us to wonder whether modern life has become increasingly out of kilter with its environment, lost to natural values that we ought to conserve. Big city life in a high rise apartment—to say nothing of the slum—as well as a day's work in a windowless, air-conditioned factory represent synthetic life filled with plastic, everything from teeth to trees. They are foreign to the earthen element from which we were reared. We have lost touch with natural reality; life is, alas, artificial.

This relative sense of following nature has to do with the degree of alteration of our environment, with our appreciative incorporation of this environment into our life styles, and with our nearness to nature. But is it not natural for us to be cultured? Consider our hands, each composed of four dexterous fingers and an opposable thumb. Their natural homologues run back through the primates and even to the birds and reptiles. Consider our brain evolving for speech with the jaw released from prehensile functions, and our eyes moving round to frontal focus on hands that enable us to be agents in the world. What are we to say when we deliberately use this natural equipment? That we act unnaturally? Surely not more so than when we use our eyes and ears. Yet with the brain and hand what are we to do? To follow nature? To build a culture that opposes it? Or is there room for the pursuit of both?

With these questions in mind we now examine four specific relative senses of following nature.

FOLLOWING NATURE IN A HOMEOSTATIC SENSE

The ecological crisis has introduced us to what we may call the homeostatic sense of following nature: "You ought not to upset the stability of the ecosystem." Here human welfare and survival depend upon our following nature, but in a sense so basic and rudimentary that we wonder whether it is moral. Human conduct may run through a spectrum from what is minimally to what is maximally disruptive of natural cycles. In its primitive state the human race had only local and relatively inconsequential environmental impact, but technological humanity has at its option powers capable of massive environmental alteration. We use these clumsily and wrongly, partly out of ignorance, partly because of the erratic, unplanned growth of society, but significantly too because of our defiant refusal to participate in our environment, to accept it, and to fit into it. Environmental rebels, we seek to exploit nature and become misfits. Our modern conduct is thus unnatural.

Ecology awakens us to these unnatural actions. Natural systems fluctuate dynamically and sometimes dramatically, but there is also a resilience and recuperative capacity built into them. Still, they may be pushed to the point of collapse. Ordinarily, if a species becomes too much of a misfit, it perishes while the system continues. But humankind may push the system to collapse, perish taking nearly everything else down with it, and thus wreck all. This danger is especially clear in the case of hundreds of soil/water/air interactions. What will supersonic jets or aerosol cans do to the ozone layer? Where does all the DDT go, or the strontium 90? What becomes of the pollutants from coal-fired generators, or from nuclear plants? Where we use natural chemicals, we sling them around in unnatural volumes allowing lead from gasoline, arsenic from pesticides, mercury from batteries, and nitrogen from fertilizers to find their way into places where they are more disruptive than most people imagine. Worse, so much of our chemistry is exotic, not biodegradable, unnatural in the sense that nature cannot break it down and recycle it, or does so very slowly. Every rock made underground can be eroded at the surface; every compound organically synthesized has some enzyme that will digest it, and so on. But our artificial products choke up the system. Alas, not only our technology, but our whole profiteering, capitalistic, industrial system may be "unnatural" in that it cheats by incurring an environmental debt that moves us ever onward toward reduced homeostasis.

Should we then behave naturally? Humans are the only animals with deliberate options and these options do enable us to command nature, the more so with the advance of science. This capacity to command nature is indeed a sort of escape from obeying nature, but of the sort that must remain in intimate contact with nature if the capacity is to continue. We can no more escape from nature than we can from human nature, than the mind can from the body, but we can bring all these increasingly under our deliberative control. Technology does not release us from natural dependencies; it only shifts the location and character of these, releasing us from some dependencies while immediately establishing new ones. A tree escapes above the soil, pushing ever higher only by rooting ever more deeply. On the one hand, we are driven back to our original observation that we can never escape the laws of nature, but must obey them willy-nilly. The only sense in which we can ever break natural laws is to neglect to consider their implication for our welfare. We might even say that any creature acts unnaturally whose behavior is such that the laws of nature run to the detriment of that organism, and when that happens such an unnatural creature soon becomes extinct.

On the other hand, we must not forget our second observation, that all our human actions are unnatural. According to this viewpoint, our successful actions relieve us from the need of following nature—in the sense of submitting to narrow natural constraints—by enlarging our sphere of deliberate options. Room for the homeostatic sense of following nature must be found somewhere between these extremes. The key point we need to consider seems to be that among our deliberate options some will help retain stability in the ecosystem and in our relationship to it while others will not. In this sense it seems perfectly straightforward to say that we may or may not follow nature, and that we both can and ought to do so. To follow nature means to choose a route of submission to nature that utilizes natural laws for our well-being.

It may be objected that the advice to *follow* nature has been subtly converted into the injunction to *study* nature—conduct with which no rational person will quarrel. According to this objection, *studying* nature has nothing to do with *following* nature. To the contrary, its purpose is to repair nature, to free us from conforming to its spontaneous course, by examining just how much alteration we can get by with. This objection has force, but its scope is too narrow, for we study nature to manipulate only parts of it, always within the larger picture of discovering our organic, earthen roots, the natural givens to which we have to submit and with which we have to work. We study cancer in order to eradicate it; we study diabetes in order to repair a natural breakdown in insulin production; but we study the laws of health in order to follow them. We study the causes of floods in order to prevent them, but we study the laws of ecosystemic health in order to follow them. Those who study nature find items they may alter, but they also discover that the larger courses of nature are always to be obeyed. This applies not only in the strong sense in which we have no option, but also in the weak, optional sense of intelligently fitting ourselves into their pattern of operation; and in that sense we do study nature, in the end, in order to follow nature.

But is any of this moral? There are a great many ways in which morality readily combines with the injunction to find a life style compatible with our planetary ecosystemic health. The jet set who have insisted on flying in SSTs, should these planes prove to deplete the protective ozone in the atmosphere, would be acting immorally against their fellow humans, as would farmers who continue long-term poisoning of the soil with nonbiodegradable pesticides in order to achieve short-term gains. But it is relatively easy to isolate out the *moral* ends here—respect for the welfare of others—and to see the natural means—conformity to the limitations of our ecosystem—as *nonmoral.*[9] So we are forced to conclude that there is nothing moral about following nature in and of itself; our relations with nature are always technical or instrumental; and the moral element emerges only when our traffic with nature turns out to involve our interhuman relations. We establish no moral communion with nature, but only with other persons. It is not moral to repair a ship nor immoral to sink it except if it happens to be one that we and our fellow travelers are sailing in. We have reached, then, a homeostatic sense in which we both can and ought to follow nature only to find it submoral or premoral because the morality surrounding such following can be separated from it and referred elsewhere.

FOLLOWING NATURE IN AN IMITATIVE ETHICAL SENSE

It is difficult to propose that we ought to follow nature in an imitative ethical sense because our usual estimate—and here we vacillate—is that nature is either amoral or immoral. We call nature amoral because morality appears in humans alone and is not, and has never been, present on the natural scene. Human conduct may be moral or immoral, but the "conduct" of nature, if indeed it can be called that, is simply amoral. The moral dimension in human nature has no counterpart in mother nature. No being can be moral unless he is free deliberatively; something must be "up to him"; and nothing else in nature has sufficient mental competence to be moral. Mother nature simply unfolds in creatures their genetic programming, like the developing seed, and they respond to their environments driven like the leaf before the wind. Even if there are erratic, indeterminate elements in nature, these provide no moral options; they just happen. Biological and evolutionary processes are no more moral than the laws of gravity or electricity. Whether something does or must happen has nothing to do with whether it ought to happen. Out of this estimate arises the basic cleavage that runs through the middle of the modern mind dividing every study into the realm of the *is* and the realm of the *ought*. No study of nature, whether physical, biological, or even social, can tell us what ought to happen, and following nature where it is possible and optional is something that is never in itself moral. Nature is blind to this dimension of reality. It is a moral nullity.

We immediately grant that there are no other moral agents in nature, whether orangutans, butterflies, wind, or rain; nor is nature as a whole a moral agent even when personified as "Mother Nature." We have no evidence that any natural species or forces do things deliberately, choosing the most moral route from less moral options. If anyone proposes that we "follow nature" in something like the ethical sense in which Christians "follow Jesus," or the Buddhists, Buddha, he or she has very much gone astray, and the blind does indeed lead the blind. Such a person ignores the emergent sphere of deliberative morality in humans for which there is no precedent in birds or field mice. In this sense, Mill is undoubtedly right when he protests that conformity to nature has no connection with right and wrong. There is no way to derive any of the familiar moral maxims from nature: *"One ought to keep promises." "Tell the truth." "Do to others as you would have them do to you." "Do not cause needless suffering."* There is no natural decalogue to endorse the Ten Commandments; nature tells us nothing about how we should be moral in this way, *even* if it should turn out that this is approximately the morality ingrained by natural selection in human nature.

But this does not end the matter, for there may nevertheless be some good or goods in nature with which we morally ought to conform even if these goods have not been produced by the process of deliberate options necessary to us if we are to be moral. The resolution of this form of our question will prove more difficult. Because nature has no moral agency, and because interhuman relations are clearly moral, it has been easy to suppose that there is nothing moral in our relations with nature. It has also been easy to conclude that morality is not "natural," but rather belongs to our "super-natural" nature. But to grant that morality appears with the emergence of human beings out of non-moral nature does not settle the question whether we, who are moral, should follow nature.

When the issue of good in nature is raised, we are at once confronted with the counterclaim that the course of nature is bad—one which, if we were to follow it, would be immoral. Nature proceeds with an absolute recklessness that is not only indifferent to life, but results in senseless cruelty that is repugnant to our moral sensibilities. Life is wrested from her creatures by continual struggle, usually soon lost, those "lucky" few who survive to maturity only face more extended suffering and eventually collapse in disease and death. With what indifference nature casts forth to slaughter ten thousand acorns, a thousand grasshoppers, a hundred minnows, and a dozen rabbits, so that one of each might survive! Things are no sooner sprouted, hatched, or born than they are attacked; life is unrelieved stress, until sooner or later, swiftly or by inches, fickle nature crushes out the life she gave, and the misery is finally over. All we can be sure of from the hands of nature is calamity. We are condemned to live by attacking other life. Nature is a gory blood bath; she permits life only in agony. The world's last word is what the Buddhists call *duhkha,* suffering. Few persons can read Mill's essay on "Nature" without being chastened in their zeal for following nature:

> In sober truth, nearly all the things which men are hanged or imprisoned for doing to one another, are nature's everyday performances. . . . Nature impales men, breaks them as if on the wheel, casts them to be devoured by wild beasts, burns them to death, crushes them with stones like the first Christian martyr, starves them with hunger, freezes them with cold, poisons them by the quick or slow venom of her exhalations, and has hundreds of other hideous deaths in reserve, such as the ingenious cruelty of a Nabis or a Domitian never surpassed. . . . A single hurricane destroys the hopes of a season: a flight of locusts, or an inundation, desolates a district. . . . Everything, in short, which the worst men commit either against life or property is perpetrated on a larger scale by natural agents.[10]

The Darwinian paradigm of nature in the nineteenth century strongly reinforced that of Mill. Nature became a kind of hellish jungle where only the fittest
survive, and these but barely. The discovery of the genetic basis of Darwin's
random variations only added to the sense of nature's rudderless proceedings,
law-like to be sure in the sense that natural selection conserves beneficial mutations, but still aimless, since natural selection operates blindly over mutations,
which are mostly worthless, irrelevant, or detrimental. There seemed a kind of
futility to it all, certainly nothing worthy of our moral imitation. This portrait
of nature affected several generations of ethicists who frequently concluded that
ethics had nothing to do with the laws of nature unless it was to alter and
overcome our natural instincts and drives, lest we too behave "like beasts." The
is/ought cleavage became entrenched in earlier twentiety-century philosophy in
large part because of this nineteenth-century portrait of nature. G. L. Dickinson
expresses with great force the protest of this period:

> I'm not much impressed by the argument you attribute to Nature, that if we don't
> agree with her we shall be knocked on the head. I, for instance, happen to object
> strongly to her whole procedure: I don't much believe in the harmony of the final
> consummation . . . and I am sensibly aware of the horrible discomfort of the
> intermediate stages, the pushing, kicking, trampling of the host, and the wounded
> and dead left behind on the march. Of all this I venture to disapprove; then
> comes Nature and says, "but you ought to approve!" I ask why, and she says,
> "Because the procedure is mine." I still demur, and she comes down on me with a
> threat—"Very good, approve or no, as you like; but if you don't approve you will
> be eliminated!" "By all means," I say, and cling to my old opinion with the more
> affection that I feel myself invested with something of the glory of a martyr. . . .
> In my humble opinion it's nature, not I, that cuts a poor figure![11]

Here we have undoubtedly reached a moral sense of following nature, but
one we cannot recommend. Virtually none of us, except perhaps ethical mav-
ericks like Nietzsche, will recommend that this pushing, kicking, and trampling
be taken as a moral model for interhuman conduct. So, offered this imitative
ethical sense of following nature, we observe that nature is not a moral agent
and therefore really cannot be followed, and secondly that there are elements in
nature which, if we were to transfer them to interhuman conduct, would be
immoral, and therefore ought not to be imitated. But does it follow that nature
is therefore bad, a savage realm without natural goods? Is this ferocity and
recklessness all that is to be said, or even the principal thing to be said, or can
this be set in some different light?

FOLLOWING NATURE IN AN AXIOLOGICAL SENSE

In order to develop an axiological sense in which human conduct may be natural, let us make a fresh start and postpone answering the question we have just posed until we can come at it from another side. Three environments—the urban, the rural, and the wild—provide three human pursuits—culture, agriculture, and nature. All three are vocations that ought to be followed and environments that are needed for our well-being. We are concerned for the moment with human activity collectively and will examine individual responsibility later. When Aristotle observed that "Man is by nature a political animal,"[12] he was speaking in terms of the Greek word *polis,* city-state, of which Athens is such a memorable example. Here *city* refers indiscriminately to village, town, and city. We are social animals and story of civilization is largely the growth of our capacity for building a cultured state. We are both *Homo sapiens* and *Homo faber;* the brain and the hand combine in wisdom and in craft to construct the enormous world of artifacts that is our urban environment. All these products are unnatural in the sense that they are independent of nature's spontaneous production. It cannot, on the other hand, be unnatural for us to build cities, for, after all, nature has supplied us with the brain and the hand as well as the social propensities for community. Humans are the creatures whom nature did not specialize, but rather equipped with marvelous faculties for culture and craft. We ought to use them, both prudentially and morally, for is not wasted talent a sin? In this sense, it is not unnatural for man to be urban even though, as soon as we do anything deliberately, we alter spontaneous nature. We reach the paradox that "Man is the animal for whom it is natural to be artificial."[13]

In culture we allow a discontinuity between human life and nature, but this discontinuity is still an extension of the ultimate natural environment. Nature releases us to develop our culture; here she offers no model. We are on our own; the mores of the human city are up to us, albeit judged by a culturing of these native endowments we call reason and conscience. The city is in some sense our *niche;* we belong there, and no one can achieve full humanity without it. Cultured human life is not possible in the unaltered wilderness; it is primitive and illiterate if it remains at a merely rural level. The city mentality provides us with literacy and advancement, whether through the market with its trade and industry, or through the library and laboratory, out of which so much of our knowledge of nature has come.

By the term *rural environment* we mean nature as domesticated for the life support of the human population, primarily the cultivated landscape, the field, the woodlot, the pasture, the groved road, the orchard, the ranch. The farm feeds the city, of course, and that may be taken as a metaphor for the whole support of society in soil, water, and air—for the organic circulations of the city in nature. The rural environment is the one in which humans meet nature in productive encounter, where we command nature by obeying her. Here there is a judiciously mixed sense of discontinuity and continuity: by human agency we adapt the natural sense—yet we adopt it too; we alter nature—yet accept its climates and capacities. We both get into nature's orbit and bring nature into our orbit. We direct nature round to our goals; yet, if we are intelligent, we use only those disruptions that nature can absorb, those appropriate to the resilience of the ecosystem under cultivation. In the urban environment, no burden of proof rests on a person proposing an alteration whether or not the change is natural (so long as it does not spill over to disrupt rural or wild areas). But in the rural environment, a burden of proof does rest upon the proposer to show that the alteration will not deteriorate the ecosystem. Within our agricultural goals our preference is for those that can be construed as "natural," those most congenial to the natural environment; and we prohibit those that disfigure it.

The rural environment is an end in itself as well as an instrument for the support of the city. It has beauty surpassing its utility. If we ask why there are gardens, we answer "for food," only to recall that there are also flower gardens. The English garden combines both the rose and the berry bush. Both the farm and the park belong in the pastures of the Shenandoah Valley, the bluegrass farms of Kentucky, and the cornfields of Iowa, where there is a form of beauty not possible either in the city or in the wilderness. We love the green, green grass of home, the trees in the meadow, the forested knobs behind the church, and the walk down by the pond. We are deeply satisfied by the rural environment. Although we appreciate our modern freedom from the drudgery of the farm, many still cherish, within limits, experiences that can only be had in the country—sawing down an oak tree, shelling peas, drawing a bucket of water from a well.

The rural environment is, or ought to be, a place of *symbiosis* between humankind and nature, for we may sometimes improve a biosystem. The climax forest of an ecosystemic succession is usually not suited for the maximum number and kinds of fauna and flora, and this succession can be interrupted by agriculture with benefit to those natural species that prefer fields and edging. There are more deer in Virginia now than when the Indians inhabited its virtually unbroken forests, and that is probably true of cottontails, bobwhites, and meadowlarks. Suitable habitat for all but a few of the wildest creatures can be made consistent with the rural use of land. With pleasant results, humans have added the elm and the oak to the British landscape, the Russian olive to the high plains, the eucalyptus to California, the floribunda rose to interstate highway roadsides, and the ring-necked pheasant to the prairies. In his idyllic love of nature, Emerson did not write of the wilderness so much as of the domestic New England countryside. When we sing "America the Beautiful," we sing largely of this gardened nature.

We may even speak of a microrural environment—an urban garden, a city park, an avenue of trees with squirrels and rabbits, a suburban fence row with cardinals and mockingbirds, a creekside path to a school. Anyone who flies over all but the worst of our Eastern cities will be impressed by how much nature is still there. We love something growing about us if only trees and lawns, and everyone would consider a city improved if it had more green space, more landscape left within it. We prefer our homes, bridges, streets, offices, and factories to be "in a natural setting." We want our cities graced with nature, and that alone suffices to undermine Mill's claim that "All praise of Civilization, or Art, or Contrivance, is so much dispraise of Nature."[14] The wood fire on the stone hearth or the gentle night rain on a tin roof recall for us this natural element; even our plastic trees vicariously return us to nature.

Our requirements for wild nature are more difficult to specify than those for tamed nature, but nonetheless real. The scarcest environment we now have is wilderness, and, when we are threatened with its possible extinction, we are forced to think through our relationships to it. Do we preserve wild nature only as a potential resource for activity that humans may someday wish to undertake in terms of urban or rural nature? Or are there richer reasons, both moral and prudential, why we ought to maintain some of our environment in a primitive state?

It is beyond dispute that we enjoy wild places, that they fill a *recreational* need, but that word by which we typically designate this fulfillment seems a poor one until we notice a deeper etymology. Something about a herd of elk grazing beneath the vista of wind and sky, or an eroded sandstone mesa silhouetted against the evening horizon, *re-creates* us. We have loved our national parks almost to death, the more so because they are kept as close to spontaneous nature as is consistent with their being extensively visited. Worried about park overuse, we are now struggling to preserve as much wilderness area as possible, resolving to keep the human presence there in lower profile. We set aside the best first—Yellowstone, the Grand Canyon, the High Sierra, the Great Smokies, the Everglades—but later found that there was really no kind of landscape for which we did not wish some preservation—the desert, the pine barrens, the grasslands, the wild rivers, the swamps, the oak-hickory forests. We began by preserving the buffaloes and lady-slippers, and soon became concerned for the toads and mosses. But why is it that sometimes we would rather look for a pasqueflower than see the latest Broadway hit?

Wild nature is a place of encounter where we go not to act on it, but to contemplate it, drawing ourselves into its order of being, not drawing it into our order of being. This accounts for our tendency to think of our relationship to wild nature as recreational, and therefore perhaps idle, since we do not do any work while there. We are at leisure there, often, of course, an active leisure, but not one that is economically productive. In this respect our attitude toward wilderness will inevitably be different from that of our grandfathers, who, for the most part, went into it to reduce the wild to the rural and urban. Their success forces us to the question of the worth of the wild. But, when the answer has to be given in nonresource terms, it is not the kind or level of answer to which we are accustomed in questions about nature. For in important senses wild nature is not for us a commodity at all. Even when the answer is given in terms of some higher, noneconomic value, our philosophical apparatus for the analysis and appraisal of wild value is, frankly, very poorly developed, for we have too much fallen into the opinion that the only values that there are, moral or artistic or whatever, are human values, values which we have selected or constructed, over which we have labored. Modern philosophical ethics has left us insensitive to the reception of nonhuman values.

We need wild nature in much the same way that we need the other things in life that we appreciate for their intrinsic rather than their instrumental worth, somewhat like we need music or art, philosophy or religion, literature or drama. But these are human activities, and our encounter with nature has the additional feature of being our sole contact with worth and beauty independent of human activity. We need friends not merely as our instruments, but for what they are in themselves, and, moving one order beyond this, we need wild nature precisely because it is a realm of values that are independent of us. Wild nature has a kind of integrity, and we are the poorer if we do not recognize it and enjoy it. That is why seeing an eagle or warbler, a climbing fern or a blue spruce is a stirring experience. The Matterhorn leaves us in awe, but so does the fall foliage on any New England hillside, or the rhododendron on Roan Mountain. Those who linger with nature find this integrity where it is not at first suspected, in the copperhead and the alligator, in the tarantula and the morel, in the wind-stunted banner spruce and the straggly box elder, in the stormy sea and the wintry tundra. Such genuine nature precedes and exceeds us despite all our dominion over it or our uniqueness within it, and its spontaneous value is the reason why contact with nature can be re-creating.

We are so indisposed to admit the possibility of wild value that cautious naturalists, finding themselves undeniably stimulated by their outings, will still be inclined to locate these values within themselves—values which they believe they have somehow constructed or unfolded out of the raw materials of natural encounter. These encounters provide an account of why only some of nature has value. If humans have successfully used it, it has value. The rest of nature, left unused, has no value, not yet at least. Wild nature, then, according to this account, serves only as an occasion of value; it triggers dormant human potential. Even such naturalists, however, need wild nature for the triggering of these values, and they will have to reckon with why nature has this capacity to occasion value, being necessary if insufficient for it. But what makes this account peculiarly unsatisfying is its persistent anthropocentrism and its artificiality in actual natural encounter. It takes considerable straining, even after studying philosophy, to accept the idea that the beauty of the sunset is only in the eye of the beholder. The sensitive naturalist is again and again surprised by nature, being converted to its values and delighted by it just because he or she has gone beyond previous, narrowly human values. It is the autonomous otherness of the natural expressions of value that we learn to love, and that integrity becomes vain when this value secretly requires our composing.

This value is often artistic or aesthetic, and is invariably so if we examine a natural entity at the proper level of observation or in terms of its ecological setting. An ordinary rock in microsection is an extraordinary crystal mosaic. The humus from a rotting log supports an exquisite hemlock. But this value also has to do with the intelligibility of each of the natural members; here natural science, especially ecology, has greatly helped us. This intelligibility often leads to a blending of the autonomy of each of the natural kinds, creating a harmony in the earthen whole. A world in which there are many kinds of things, the simple related to the complex, is a valuable world, and especially so if all of them are intelligibly related. Everything has its *place,* and that justifies it. Natural value is further resident in the vitality of things, in their struggle and zest, and it is in this sense that we often speak of a reverence for life, lovely or not. Or should we say that we find all life beautiful, even when we sometimes must sacrifice it? We love the natural mixture of consistency and freedom; there is something about the word *wild* that goes well with the word *free,* whether it is the determined freedom of the wild river or the more spontaneous freedom of the hawk in the sky. In this splendor, sublimity, and mystery the very word *wild* is one of our value words. Simply put, we find *meanings* in wild things.

In this context we may offer yet another answer to our question. We may be said to follow that which is the object of our orienting interest, as when we follow sports, medicine, or law, or the latest news developments. Many scientists, perhaps all the "pure" ones, "follow nature" in that they find its study to be of consuming interest—intrinsically worthwhile—and those who are also naturalists go on in varying senses to say that they appreciate nature, find great satisfaction in it, and even love it. We follow what we "participate in," especially goals we take to be of value. This sense of "follow" is less than "ethical imitation," but it is significantly more than the notion that our conduct toward nature is not moral. For we look to nature as a realm of natural value beyond mere natural facts, which, maintained in its integrity, we may and ought to encounter. The notion of "following" nature, in addition, is deeper than following art, music, or sports, in that, when encountering nature, we are led by it through sensitive study to the importation of nonhuman kinds of meaning. When I delight in the wild hawk in the wind-swept sky, that is not a value that I invent, but one that I discover. Nature has an autonomy that art does not have. We must follow nature to gain this meaning—in the sense of leaving it alone, letting it go its way. We take ourselves to it and listen for and to its natural forms of expression, drawn by a range and realm of values that are not of our own construction. We ought not to destroy this integrity, but rather preserve it and contemplate it, and in this sense our relations with nature are moral.

Even G. E. Moore, who so much lamented the "naturalistic fallacy," by which we mistakenly move from a natural *is* to an ethical *ought,* still finds that appreciation of the existence of natural beauty is a good.[15] But morality is the science of the good; so, as soon as we move from a natural *is* to a natural is *good*, our relations with that natural good are moral. We follow what we love, and the love of the intrinsic good is always a moral relationship. We thus find it possible to establish that moral communion with nature that James thought impossible. In this axiological sense, we ought to follow nature, to make its value one among our goals; and, in so doing, our conduct is here guided by nature.

How far is this value so distributed that each individual is obligated to moral conduct toward nature? There is no person who ought not to be concerned with the preservation of natural goodness, if only because others undeniably do find values there. Nevertheless, we allow individuals to weight their preferences, and there may be differing vocations, some seeking the social goods more than the natural ones. But a purely urban person is a one-dimensional person; only those who add the rural and the wild are three-dimensional persons. As for myself, I consider life morally atrophied when respect for and appreciation of the naturally wild is absent. No one has learned the full scope of what it means to be moral until he has learned to respect the integrity and worth of those things we call wild.

FOLLOWING NATURE IN A TUTORIAL SENSE

In positing a tutorial sense in which human conduct may follow nature, I admit that I can only give witness and invite the sharing of a gestalt, rather than provide a reasoned conceptual argument. I find I can increasingly "draw a moral" from reflecting over nature—that is, gain a lesson in living. Nature has a "leading capacity"; it prods thoughts that educate us, that lead us out (*educo*) to know who and where we are, and what our vocation is. Take what we call natural symbols—*light and fire, water or rock, morning and evening, life and death, waking and sleeping, the warmth of summer and the cold of winter, the flowers of spring and the fruits of fall, rain and rivers, seeds and growth, earth and sky*. How readily we put these material phenomena to "metaphorical" or "spiritual" use, as when we speak of life's "stormy weather," of strength of character "like a rock," of insecurity "like shifting sand," of the "dark cloud with the silver lining," or of our "roots" in a homeland. Like a river, life flows on with persistence in change. How marvelously Lanier could sing of the watery marshes of Glynn—and the darky, of Old Man River! How profound are the psychological forces upon us of the gray and misty sky, the balmy spring day, the colors we call bright or somber, the quiet of a snowfall, the honking of a skein of wild geese, or the times of natural passage—birth, puberty, marriage, death! How the height of the mountains "elevates" us, and the depths of the sea stimulates "deep" thoughts within!

Folk wisdom is routinely cast in this natural idiom. The sage in Proverbs admonishes the sluggard to consider the ways of the ant and be wise. The farmer urges, "Work, for the night comes, when man's work is done." "Make hay while the sun shines." The Psalmist notices how much we are like grass which flourishes but is soon gone, and those who understand the "seasonal" character of life are the better able to rejoice in the turning of the seasons and to do everything well in its time. Jesus asks us in our search for the goods of life, to note the natural beauty of the lilies of the field, which the affected glory of Solomon could not surpass, and he points out birds to us, who, although hardly lazy, are not anxious or worried about tomorrow. *"What you sow, you reap." "Into each life some rain must fall." "All sunshine makes a desert." "By their fruits shall you know them." "The early bird gets the worm." "Time and tide wait for no man." "The loveliest rose has yet its thorns." "The north wind made the Vikings." "The tree stands that bends with the wind." "White ants pick a carcass cleaner than a lion." "Every mile is two in winter." "If winter comes, can spring be far behind?"* It is no accident that our major religious seasons are naturally scheduled: Christmas comes at the winter solstice, Easter with the bursting forth of spring, and Thanksgiving with the harvest. Encounter with nature integrates me, protects me from pride, gives a sense of proportion and place, teaches me what to expect, and what to be content with, establishes other value than my own, and releases feelings in my spirit that I cherish and do not find elsewhere.

Living well is the catching of certain natural rhythms. Those so inclined can reduce a great deal of this to prudence, to the natural conditions of value; we may be particularly prone to do this because nature gives us no ethical guidance in our interhuman affairs. But human conduct must also be an appropriate form of life toward our environment, toward what the world offers us. Some will call this mere efficiency, but for some of us it is a kind of wisdom for which prudence and efficiency are words that are too weak. For we do not merely accept the limits that nature thrusts upon us, but endorse an essential goodness, a sufficiency in the natural fabric of life which encompasses both our natural talents and the constitution of the world in which, with our natural equipment, we must conduct ourselves. What I call a larger moral virtue, excellence of character, comes in large part, although by no means in the whole, from this natural attunement; and here I find a natural ethic in the somewhat old-fashioned sense of a way of life—a life style that should "follow nature," that is, be properly sensitive to its flow through us and its bearing on our habits of life. A very significant portion of the *meaning* of life consists in our finding, expressing, and endorsing its naturalness. Otherwise, life lacks propriety.

We have enormous amounts of nature programmed into us. The protoplasm that flows within us has flowed naturally for over a billion years. Our internal human nature has evolved in response to external nature for a million years. Our genetic programming—which largely determines what we are, making each of us so alike and yet so different—is entirely natural. It is difficult to think that we do not possess a good natural fit in the wellsprings of our behavior. Our cultural and our agentive life must be, and, so far as it is optional, ought to be consistent with that fit—freeing us no doubt for the cities we build, permitting our rural adaptations, and yet in the end further fitting us for life within our overarching natural environment. We are not, in the language of geographers, environmentally determined, for we have exciting options, and these increase with the advance of culture. But we are inescapably environmentally grounded as surely as we are mortal. This *is* the case, and hence our optional conduct *ought* to be commensurately natural; and, if we can transpose that from a grudging prudential *ought* to a glad moral *ought,* we shall be the happier and the wiser for finding "our place under the sun." Life moves, we are saying, not so much against nature as with it, and that remains true even of cultured human life which never really escapes its organic origins and surroundings. Our ethical life *ought* to maintain for us a good natural fit in both an efficient and a moral sense. This is what Emerson means when he commends moral conduct as conformity to the laws of nature. There is in this communion with nature an ethic for life, and that is why exposure to natural wilderness is as necessary for a true education as is the university.

Someone may complain, and perhaps fiercely, that in this ethic nature only serves as an occasion for the construction of human virtues; that the natural wisdom we have cited shows only the virtues that develop *in us* when we confront nature; and that thus there is no following of nature, but rather a resistance to it, a studied surmounting in which we succeed despite nature. But this anthropocentric account is too one-sided. Evolution and ecology have taught us that every kind of life is what is not autonomously but because of a natural fit. We are what I call *environmental reciprocals* indebted to our environment for what we have become in ways that are as complementary as they are oppositional. Nature is, I think, not sufficient to produce all these virtues in us, and that allows for our own integrity and creativity—but nature is necessary for them. Admittedly, we must attain these virtues before we find and establish natural symbols for them—we must undergo the natural course in order to understand it—but I do not think that this ethical strength is merely and simply inside us. It is surely relational, at a minimum, arising out of the encounter between humans and nature. At the maximum, we are realizing and expressing in this strong and good life which we live something of the strength and goodness which nature has bequeathed us.

Nature is often enigmatic. Human life is complex. Each contains many times and seasons. The danger here is that any secretly desired conduct can somehow be construed as natural and found virtuous. Nature gives us little help concerning how we are to behave toward one another. In these matters we are free to do as we please, although nature has endowed us with reason and conscience out of which ethics may be constructed. Especially suspicious are arguments that assign human roles to nature, as is sometimes done with women or blacks, for we easily confuse the natural with the culturally conventional.

There may also be cases where we learn what is bad from nature. In rare cases, we may unwisely elect to follow some process in nature that in itself is indefensible—as some say the bloodthirsty conduct of the weasel is. I do not wish to defend the course of nature in every particular, but most of these cases involve learning something bad—an ethic of selfishness, a dog-eat-dog attitude, or a might-makes-right life style—by inappropriately projecting into moral inter-human conduct, and thereby making bad, what is quite appropriate at some lower, nonmoral level—for example, the principle of the survival of the fittest or the self-interest programmed into the lower life forms. We cannot assume that the way things work at lower, nonmoral levels is the way that they ought to work at human, moral levels, for the appearance of the capacity for moral deliberation makes a difference. This is what is correct about the *is-ought* distinction. Our moral conduct exceeds nature, and we must deliberate with an ethic based on reason and conscience which supplants instinct. It is our conduct or mores insofar as it fits us to our environment—our ethic of bearing toward the natural world, not toward other persons—that I refer to in the tutorial sense, and which I here defend. Moreover, I call this conduct moral too in the sense that it contributes to our wisdom and our excellence of character.

In catching these natural rhythms, we must judiciously blend what I call *natural resistance* and *natural conductance*. Part of nature opposes life, increases entropy, kills, rots, destroys. Human life, like all other life, must struggle against its environment, and I much admire the human conquest of nature. However, I take this dominion to be something to which we are naturally impelled and for which we are naturally well-equipped. Furthermore, this struggle can be resorbed into a natural conductance, for nature has both generated us and provided us with life support—and she has stimulated us into culture by her resistance. Nature is not all ferocity and indifference. She is also the bosom out of which we have come, and she remains our life partner, a realm of otherness for which we have the deepest need. I resist nature, and readily for my purposes amend and repair it. I fight disease and death, cold and hunger— and yet somehow come to feel that wildness is not only, not finally, the pressing night. Rather, wildness with me and in me kindles fires against the night.

I am forced, of course, to concede that there are gaps in this account of nature. I do not find nature meaningful everywhere, or beautiful, or valuable, or educational; and I am moved to horror by malaria, intestinal parasites, and genetic deformities. My concept of the good is not coextensive with the natural, but it does greatly overlap it; and I find my estimates steadily enlarging that overlap. I even find myself stimulated positively in wrestling with nature's deceits. They stir me with a creative discontent, and, when I go nature one better, I often look back and reflect that nature wasn't half bad. I notice that my advanced life depends on nature's capacity to kill and to rot, and to make a recycling and pyramidal use of resources. Nature is not first and foremost the bringer of disease and death, but of life, and with that we touch the Latin root, *natus*. When nature slays, she takes only the life she gave, as no murderer can; and she gathers even that life back to herself by reproduction and by re-enfolding organic resources and genetic materials, and produces new life out of it.

Environmental life, including human life, is nursed in struggle; and to me it is increasingly inconceivable that it could, or should, be otherwise. If nature is good, it must be both an assisting and a resisting reality. We cannot succeed unless it can defeat us. My reply, then, to G. L. Dickinson's lament over the kicking and pushing in nature is that, although I do not imitate it, certainly not in human ethics, I would not eliminate it if I could, not at least until I have come to see how life could be better stimulated, and nobler human character produced without it. Nature is a vast scene of birth and death, springtime and harvest, permanence and change, of budding, flowering, fruiting, and withering away, of processive unfolding, of pain and pleasure, of success and failure, of ugliness giving way to beauty and beauty to ugliness. From the contemplation of it we get a feeling for life's transient beauty sustained over chaos. There is as it were a music to it all, and not the least when in a minor key. Even the religious urges within us, though they may promise a hereafter, are likely to advise us that we must for now rest content with the world we have been given. Though we are required to spend our life in struggle, yet we are able to cherish the good Earth and to accept the kind of universe in which we find ourselves. It is no coincidence that the ecological perspective often approaches a religious dimension in trying to help us see the beauty, integrity, and stability of nature within and behind its seeming indifference, ferocity, and evils.

Dickinson's portrait can give an account of only half of nature, natural resistance, and even that is an enigmatic account of human life set oddly, set for martyrdom, in a hostile world. He can give no account of natural conductance; indeed, he cannot even see it, and thus he has mistakenly taken the half for the whole. But the account that I am seeking contains both elements, and not merely as a nonsensical mixture of goods and evils—each a surd in relation to the other. A world in which there is an absurd mixture of helps and hurts is little better than a world of steady hostility. Neither could tutor us. What one needs is a nature where the evils are tributary to the goods, or, in my language of philosophical ecology, where natural resistance is embraced within and made intelligible by natural conductance. It is not death, but life, including human life as it fits this planetary environment, which is the principal mystery that has come out of nature. For several billion years, the ongoing development and persistence of that life, culminating in human life, have been the principal features of eco-nature behind which the element of struggle must be contained as a subtheme. Our conduct morally ought to fit this natural conductance. Life follows nature because nature follows life.

I do endorse in principle, though not without reservations, the constitution of the ecosystem. I do not make any long-range claims about the invariable, absolute law of evolution, about who is guiding the ship, or about the overall record of cosmic nature. There is beauty, stability, and integrity in the evolutionary ecosystem that we happen to have. There is a natural, an earthen, trend to life, although we cannot know it as a universal law. We ought to preserve and to value this nature, if only because it is the only nature that we know in any complexity and detail. If and when we find ourselves in some other nature, of a sort in which we earthlings can still maintain our sanity, we can then revise our ethic appropriately. In the meantime, however, we can at least sometimes "seek nature's guidance" in a tutorial sense almost as one might seek guidance from the Bible, or Socrates, or Shakespeare, even though nature, of course, does not "write" or "speak." None of us lives to the fullest who does not study the natural order, and, more than that, none of us is wise who does not ultimately make his or her peace with it.

When Mill faces the prospect of an unending expansion of the urban and rural environments, his attitude toward nature shifts, and, rather surprisingly, we find him among the defenders of nature. Suppose, God forbid, he writes, that we were brought by our industry to some future "world with nothing left to the spontaneous activity of nature; with every rood of land brought into cultivation, which is capable of growing food for human beings; every flowery waste or natural pasture ploughed up, all quadrapeds or birds which are not domesticated for man's use exterminated as his rivals for food, every hedgerow or superfluous tree rooted out, and scarcely a place left where a wild shrub or flower could grow without being eradicated as a weed in the name of improved agriculture." Such a world without "natural beauty and grandeur," Mill asserts, "is not good for man." Wild nature "is the cradle of thoughts and aspirations which are not only good for the individual but which society could ill do without."[16] Thus, in the end, we must enlist even this celebrated opponent of our morally following nature among those who wish to follow nature in our axiological sense.

For a closing statement on the tutorial sense of following nature, however, we do better to consult a poet rather than an ecologist or an ethicist. "I came from the wilderness," remembers Carl Sandburg as he invites us to reflect on the wilderness—how it tries to hold on to us and how, in our tutorial sense, we ought not to be separated from it:

> There is an eagle in me and a mockingbird . . . and the eagle flies among the Rocky Mountains of my dreams and fights among the Sierra crags of what I want . . . and the mockingbird warbles in the early forenoon before the dew is gone, warbles in the underbrush of my Chattanoogas of hope, gushes over the blue Ozark foothills of my wishes—And I got the eagle and the mockingbird from the wilderness.[17]

NOTES

For critical discussion, see Allen Carlson, "Nature and Positive Aesthetics," *Environmental Ethics* 6(1984):5-34.

1. Barry Commoner, *The Closing Circle: Nature, Man & Technology* (New York: Alfred A. Knopf, 1972), p. 41.
2. Radcliffe Squires, *The Loyalties of Robinson Jeffers* (Ann Arbor: University of Michigan Press, 1956), p. 134.
3. Frederick E. Smith, "Scientific Problems and Progress in Solving the Environmental Crisis" (Address delivered at conference on "Environment, the Quest for Quality," Washington, D.C., February 19, 1970), pp. 3, 5.
4. William James, "The Moral Equivalent of War," in *Memories and Studies* (New York: Longmans, Green, and Co., 1911), pp. 267-96; "Is Life Worth Living?" in *The Will to Believe* (New York: Longmans, Green, and Co., 1896), pp. 43-44.
5. John Stuart Mill, "Nature," in *Collected Works* (Toronto: University of Toronto Press, 1963-77), 10:400.
6. Ralph Waldo Emerson, *Journals* (Cambridge, Mass.: Riverside Press, 1910), 3:208.
7. Aristotle, *Nicomachean Ethics* 2, 8, 1109^b 23.
8. We take notice here of a common usage of *natural* in order to set it aside. The word is sometimes used in the sense of "not affected, spontaneous" and applied to conduct that is not studied or strained. Such conduct is not deliberated, not a result of intentional effort, and, hence, natural like the spontaneous course of nondeliberative nature. Notice that our senses of "follow" shift, although they all unfold from the basic sense of "going in the track of." The senses of "follow" that mean to replace or to succeed in a chronological or causal sequence are not used here.
9. See "Is There an Ecological Ethic?" pp. 12-29.
10. Mill, "Nature," 10:385-86.
11. Goldsworthy Lowes Dickinson, *The Meaning of Good* (New York: McClure, Phillips and Co., 1907), p. 46.
12. Aristotle, *Politics* 1, 2, 1253^a 2.
13. Lucius Garvin, *A Modern Introduction to Ethics* (Cambridge, Mass.: Houghton Mifflin, 1953), p. 378.
14. Mill, "Nature," *Collected Works*, 10:381.
15. George Edward Moore, *Principia Ethica* (Cambridge: Cambridge University Press, 1903), pp. 36-58, 188, 193, 195-98, 200, 206.
16. John Stuart Mill, *Principles of Political Economy*, in *Collected Works*, 3:756. Mill also records that reading Wordsworth's poetry reawoke in him a love of nature after his analytic bent of mind had caused a crisis in his mental history. See John Stuart Mill, *Autobiography* (Boston: Houghton Mifflin, 1969), pp. 88-90.
17. Carl Sandburg, "Wilderness," in *Complete Poems* (New York: Harcourt, Brace, Jovanovich, 1970), p. 100. Ellipsis in original.

3

Philosophical Aspects of the Environment

"Philosophy bakes no bread," runs an old lament. Yet the hand is joined to the mind; action rises from belief. Ecology, when it becomes human ecology, thrusts humans into a logic of their *oikos,* their home; ultimately it turns on a state of mind. The activist will soon become impatient with just "thinking." We concede that we often must act with unclear heads and, sometimes, understanding comes after action. But "Act now, think later" is a slogan the inadequacy of which has been amply demonstrated in environmental transactions. Granted that, untranslated into pragmatic proposals, even the soundest eco-logic is useless; ponder, on the other hand, the mischief done by a faulty one. *Environ mental* competence presupposes a mindset.

Nature is perhaps the most ancient philosophic category, yet the genius of many centuries has, ultimately, hardly left nature less enigmatic. We begin in one discipline, whether philosophy or physics, or biology or geology, only to find interfaces with many, whether geography, or economics, or politics, or art, or religion. We know, only to find the unknown vaster. We search, to find that the search returns upon ourselves, for the measure of nature requires the measure of man. Of late, this perennial quest has been thrown into fresh ferment. What is the temper of this ecological reevaluation?

ECOLOGY, THE ULTIMATE SCIENCE

Ecosystem science is being often offered as an ultimate science that synthesizes even the arts and the humanities. "Although ecology may be treated as a science, its greater and overriding wisdom is universal," claims Paul Shepard, introducing an influential anthology, *The Subversive Science.*[1] Its first law and commandment is the dynamic steady state requisite between organism and environment, homeostasis. Popularly, this yields needed recycling. Pragmatically, few

Reprinted by permission from Phillip O. Foss, ed., *Environment and Colorado: A Handbook* (Fort Collins, Colorado: Environmental Resources Center, Colorado State University, 1974).

will quarrel with insistence on a balanced budget. Philosophically, though, if proposed as an ultimate principle relating humans to nature, there arise some crucial questions.

How far are humans so continuous with nature that they must accept environmental limits? Is the steady state, for instance, compatible with unending progress? Does it compel a no-growth economy, or even a reduction of our standard of living? To answer, we need an inventory of potential resources in materials and energy, but also we employ axioms about an ever-advancing technology, limitless scientific development, what counts as betterment, and the wits of man in bypassing nature's limits. The presumptions of ecological spokesmen are strikingly reminiscent of the debate about geographical determinism—the belief that the physical environment significantly limits and fixes the character of a society. Humans must submit to and operate with certain natural, ecological givens.

Doubtless we must. Yet much of the Western genius lies in its sense of the human discontinuity with nature, a vision awakened in us by the Hebrews and Greeks, and climaxing somewhat paradoxically in modern science as it uses our knowledge of our natural connections to achieve an omnipotence through technology. This mindset regards as a tragic, oppressive mistake human immersion in cyclic natural rhythms, human submission to the web of nature. Precisely this led to the stagnation of preliterate societies. A requisite of modern society is that humans discover their uniqueness—their linear history, creativity, progress—by which increasingly they master nature, turn it to their advantage, and remold their environment to their liking. Against this, the ecological mood recalls us to a wisdom of relatedness, of our necessary linkage to biological communities, to an affirmation of our organic essence. Can we reaffirm this without compromising our enormous adaptive capacities in our relationships with nature?

Nature approximates but never long maintains a steady state; evolution is superimposed on equilibrium, rather as a melody develops against a rhythm. Disequilibrium generates the novelty of process. Evolution too has profoundly influenced our outlook, and must we not blend the vector with the circle to get the spiral? In human history, might not homeostasis, however necessary, be but a half truth, true only when complemented by the advancing human environmental competence as humans civilize their planet—a transformation that may well involve continual disequilibriums, studied replacements, and alterations of the natural ecosystems?

ECOLOGY AS AN ETHICAL SCIENCE

Anyone who would be a philosopher of nature must soon learn the naturalistic fallacy. The disciplined logic of modern philosophy has found itself unable to move from an *is* to an *ought,* from a *scientific description* to a *moral pre-*

scription. Alternately stated, science is value-free; nature is amoral. In a classic inquiry, John Stuart Mill asks whether one ought "follow nature?" If nature means the sum of all phenomena including human agency, then man trivially follows nature; he cannot do otherwise. Natural laws are unexceptionable. If nature excludes human agency, then all human actions consist in altering nature and all useful ones in improving nature, and the advice to follow nature is by definition irrational; human agency is inevitably nonnatural. Moreover, much or perhaps most of what nature does, if regarded as morally prescriptive, is immoral. Mill recounts at length nature's ferocity, brutality, and indifference. Study nature though he may, and allowing all prudence, Mill can find nothing there which is right at all. "Conformity to nature has no connection whatever with right and wrong."[2]

But the ecologist has recalled another philosophical heritage. Western thought has been ambivalent; other sages, with different logic, have confronted nature to discover a larger wisdom. Lest we listen with short memories, let us recollect this other legacy, illustrated for instance in the Romantics, whose love of nature infected so many of the pioneers of the conservation movement. Emerson, for instance, in an equally classic appraisal, argues that nature yields commodity, beauty, wisdom, and discipline. When poetry and mysticism complement science, nature educates the character and serves as the touchstone of values. Though the vision proves complex and demanding, it is in environmental encounter that Emerson discerns the essence of morality. "Right is a conformity to the laws of nature so far as they are known to the human mind."[3]

Although the minority paradigm in recent philosophy, how remarkably has this claim been reappearing with the ecological turn! Ian L. McHarg, for instance, insists: "We must learn that nature includes an intrinsic value system."[4] In an article significantly entitled "The Steady State: Physical Law and Moral Choice," Paul B. Sears writes, "But morality today involves a responsible relationship toward the laws of the natural world of which we are inescapably a part."[5] Roger Revelle and Hans H.Landsberg introduce a prestigious study: "Science has another, deeper significance for our environmental concerns . . . This is the building of the structure of concepts and natural laws that will enable man to understand his place in nature. Such understanding must be one basis of the moral values that should guide each human generation in exercising its stewardship over the earth. For this purpose, ecology . . . is central."[6] In deservedly a seminal essay, Aldo Leopold's "Land Ethic," we are urged, "A thing is right when it tends to preserve the integrity, stability, and beauty of the biotic community. It is wrong when it tends otherwise."[7] Exceeding prudence and pragmatism, human alignment with ecological law has become the great commandment. Ecology is an ethical science.

ECOLOGY AND EVOLUTION

However prophetic these insights, correcting as they do the contemporary de-valuation of nature, their confidence and exuberance do well to be chastened by the fires of a related query. After Darwin, it first seemed to the tough-minded that the new science endorsed a kind of ruthless egoism, a gladiatorial "tooth and claw" ethic; then, oppositely, repulsion from this prompted others to search for an ethic which abated evolutionary evils. Still others selected ethically significant trends. Evolution promotes life—survival and increase, or harmony, or integration, interdependence, and so on. But the selection was problematic, for did not evolution equally extinguish life, destroy and decrease species, disin-tegrate countless communities? Ethicists invariably suppressed premises that guided their selection. A century of search for naturalistic ethics has been inconclusive.

The search for an ecological ethics must resurvey this ground, and that remapping has largely yet to be done. Whether or not it succeeds will rest largely on its reappraisal of nature.

The post-Darwinian world was, for all its law, yet an odious chaos and jungle. The previous debate did not yet know the interdependent ecosystem, though it partially anticipated it. Only in recent decades have we been able adequately to set these conflicts within a dynamic web of life. Even predation, we now see, is beneficial to a species. Nature's savagery is much less wanton and clumsy than formerly supposed, and many are inclined to see in the ecosystem a certain wisdom not merely calling for awe but more nearly for reverence. So conceived, following nature is not merely a prudential means to independent moral ends, but is an end in itself, or, more accurately, it is within the human environmental relatedness that all our values are constructed. Humans doubtless exceed any environmental prescription, but this is not antagonistic to, but rather complementary to their world.

The ecological vision invites philosophical critique. But the problems are, hopefully, and alternately put, opportunities for deeper understanding. Take Leopold's intuition of the right as the preservation of the biotic community in which man is at once a citizen and a gentle king. How starkly this gainsays the alienation that characterizes modern literature, if not science, seeing nature as basically rudderless, antipathetical, in need of monitoring and repair! More typically modern man, for all his technological prowess, has found himself distanced from nature, increasingly competent and decreasingly confident, at once distinguished and aggrandized, yet afloat on and adrift in an indifferent if not hostile universe. His world is at best a huge filling station, at worst a prison, or "nothingness." Not so for ecological humans; they are "at home" in their world, they confront it with deference to a community in which they share; their planetary home is seen as a thing of beauty to be cherished. The new mood is epitomized, somewhat surprisingly, in reaction to space exploration prompted by vivid photography of Earth and the astronauts' nostalgia generating both a new love for spaceship Earth and a resolution next to focus on reconciliation to it.

As we reengage our landscape, we must develop a calculus for an ecosystemic utilitarianism—the greatest good for the greatest number in a planetary community—a program that is likely to occupy ethicists for a generation but that is already urgently needed. How do we balance the need for electric power against the worth, for us and for our children, of wild rivers? How do we set the right to life of endangered species against the right to life of humans who wish living and leisure space or resources? How in a hungry world do we justify a preservationist mentality with its dislike of pesticides and herbicides? In the most pressing and unanswered of the specific issues, how do we calculate the expense of environmental protection against its social costs, especially to the underprivileged? We do not know, and we flounder.

Humans unexceptionally obey natural laws, whether of gravity, of health, or of ecosystemic homeostasis. But because, virtually alone among the creatures, humans can deliberate and foresee, there are options in their necessary obedience. Given the premise of the survival, if not the excellence and beauty, of the ecosystem and the worth of human life within it, natural law provides us with a norm that humans flaunt to their detriment. Humans choose their route of submission, or should we say nature permits and frees them to be prudent—or moral? Like the laws of personal health, the laws of ecosystemic health may be obeyed or broken, only to be reckoned with at length. Is this ecological circumscription irrelevant, even alien, to our value systems, neatly articulated from it? Or do we prefer to say that humans, construct values though they may, must set these values in ecosystemic obedience? Some will swiftly reduce this to prudence, a matter of intelligent but not of moral action. But to the ecologically tutored, the current reappraisal suggests more.

GOD, MAN, NATURE

How thin the line between virtue and vice! Consider Western man's virile conquest of nature and its ecological transvaluation. His religion urged him with Genesis injunctions to subdue his earth. Reversing the faiths around them, the Hebrews put man over nature, not under it; they forbade astrology and the placatory fertility sacrifices to the baals of earth, sun, moon, and stars. Nor did they suppose nature to be evil, but rather God's good creation, neither to be hated, feared, nor worshipped, but rather "kept" and used as a bounteous gift. Man is the dominant creature, at once in nature and yet, under God, over it. The hierarchy is *God — man — nature*. This vision blended with and transformed the Greek rationalistic bent and sustained the medieval centuries.

In the secularizing of the modern age, though the monotheism lapsed, the axioms about man's dominion persisted. Comte's scientific positivism taught that "Civilization consists, strictly speaking, on the one hand, in the development of the human mind, on the other, in the result of this, namely, the increasing power of Man over Nature."[8] Emmanuel Mesthene, among the most persuasive of the apologists for technology, can ably rejoice that in our era man has broken his bondage to "the bruteness and recalcitrance of nature," no longer submissive to its hostility and indifference. "Nature is coming increasingly under control as a result of restored human confidence and power . . . We are therefore the first age which can aspire to be free of the tyranny of physical nature that has plagued man since his beginnings."[9]

But there is an inverse account which worries that this long entrenched legacy is obsolete, if not pernicious. In a celebrated address to scientists, Lynn White charged: "Modern science is an extrapolation of natural theology and . . . modern technology is at least partly to be explained as an Occidental, voluntarist realization of the Christian dogma of man's transcendence of, and rightful mastery over, nature . . . Over a century ago science and technology joined to give mankind powers which, to judge by many of the ecologic effects, are out of control. If so, Christianity bears a huge burden of guilt."[10] Or, take C. J. Glacken's forceful claim that our posture is aberrant. "The concept of man against nature as a philosophy has lost whatever creative force it had in the past. . . . Man's technological, innovative, conservative, conserving, humane role can be understood much better in an ecological setting than in one of contrast and antithesis."[11]

The ambivalence has long been there. Nature is wilderness yet paradise, demonic yet divine, asset yet enemy, jungle yet garden, harsh yet healing, means for man yet end in itself, commodity yet community, the land provoking man's virility yet evoking his sentimentality. The American's commonwealth violates yet rests on his continent, all his arts improve yet incorporate his surroundings, and in ultimate irony the pioneer slays what most he loves. There is oscillation: aggressiveness/submission, exploitation/respect, struggle/harmony, insular man/man grafted to his landscape, independence/relatedness, man the conquering engineer/man the biotic citizen. What is new in the current debate is that the ecosciences are underscoring the continuities so as to humble the pride of the muscular West.

Can we sort out the truth? It is axiomatic in ecological models that there is not only mutuality but opposition in counterpoint. The system resists the very life it supports; indeed, it is by resistance not less than environmental conductivity that life is stimulated. The integrity of the species and the individual is a function of a field where fullness lies in interlocking predation and symbiosis, construction and destruction, aggradation and degradation. The inclusion of humans generates a philosophy, an *ought,* an intentionality, a transcendence. Yet for all their options, humans remain insiders. They are not spared environmental pressures; these precipitate the human uniqueness and define human integrity. But if we do not inhibit this truth with its complement, we fall into an anthropocentrism. Man is most optimistically the sole locus of values in a world merely tributary to him, or most pessimistically, orphaned, autonomous, lost in a hostile cosmos.

A CREATIVE STRUGGLE

Kept in its environmental context, our humanity is not absolutely "in" us, but is rather "in" our world dialogue. Our integrity rises from transaction with our opponent-partner and therefore requires a corresponding integrity. If we cannot derive values even from ecological facts, neither ought we so to locate values in humans as to deny them to the nature that encompasses us. Thus the technological antagonism of humans and nature is an ecological half-truth and, when taken for the whole, inverts the true constitution of experience, which is that human nature is deeply rooted in, indebted to, and conditioned by nature, and that human valuation of nature, like our perceptions, is drawn from environmental intercourse, not merely brought to it. Can we achieve a synthesis that preserves the dichotomy as a creative struggle exhibiting the excellence both of humans and the world within which we are set?

Could it be that the human presence is most noble when reciprocal to planetary community, when our mastery over nature interpenetrates our submission? Humans may and must moderate or mind their world, yet the more competently and effectively we manipulate, the more urgently we must respect the worth of our empire. If we profane nature, we profane ourselves. Surely it is cardinal that our dominion be a commonwealth that provides for the integrity of all its component members, and that we govern in love.

NOTES

1. Paul Shepard and Daniel McKinley, eds., *The Subversive Science* (Boston: Houghton Mifflin, 1969), p. 4f.

2. John Stuart Mill, "Nature" in *Collected Works* (Toronto: University of Toronto Press, 1963-77), 10:400.

3. Ralph Waldo Emerson, *Nature* (San Francisco: Chandler Publishing Co., 1836, 1968), p. 68; *Journals* (Cambridge, Mass.: Riverside Press, 1910), 3:208.

4. Ian L. McHarg, "Values, Process, and Form," in Robert Disch, ed., *The Ecological Conscience: Values for Survival* (Englewood Cliffs, N.J.: Prentice-Hall, 1970), p. 21.

5. Paul B. Sears in Shepard and McKinley, *The Subversive Science*, p. 396.

6. Roger Revelle and Hans H. Landsberg, eds., *America's Changing Environment* (Boston: Beacon Press, 1970), p. xxii.

7. Aldo Leopold, "The Land Ethic," *A Sand County Almanac* (New York: Oxford University Press, 1968), p. 224f.

8. Auguste Comte, *Early Essays on Social Philosophy* (London: Routledge, 1911), p. 144.

9. Emmanuel G. Mesthene, "Technology and Religion," *Theology Today* 23 (1967):481-495, citations on pp. 482, 492.

10. Lynn White, Jr., "The Historical Roots of Our Ecologic Crisis," *Science* 155 (1967):1203-1207, citation on p. 1206.

11. C. H. Glacken, "Man Against Nature: An Outmoded Concept," in Harold W. Helfrich, Jr., ed., *The Environmental Crisis* (New Haven: Yale University Press, 1970), pp. 127-142, citation on p. 140.

4

The River of Life:
Past, Present, and Future

To speak of a river of life is more poetry than philosophy, but images have an evocative power that may launch critical reflection. Life is organic, and much too complex to be illuminated by many of the features of a simple, inorganic river. Our purpose here is only to abstract out the notion of a current, a naturally impelled flow that is energetically maintained over time. Life is often said to be a countercurrent to entropy, its negatively entropic flow in that respect the reverse of a merely physical current; still the notion of a current is generic enough to provide considerable insight into the life process. It provides the thought of continuity and ceaseless flow in a life-stream that transcends the individual, and here we gain a model fertile in its capacity to channel together ideas that under other gestalts become differentiated into troublesome opposites. In this processive on-rolling we can find a confluence of the actual and the potential, the self and the other, the human and the natural, the present and the historical, and the *is* and the *ought*.

Most of us attach life to the immediate present, to encapsulated individuals, and we locate the ethical life in the interrelations of subjective human selves. We often find life to be a notion that belongs incongruously to biology and to ethics, to nature and to culture. We do not here mean to deny that the individual human life is a subjective matter, of moral concern, when we notice that it is also an adjectival property of a collective, still more substantive flow, which also is of moral concern. This concept of a current in which the individual is buoyed up and on is at once biologically viable, culturally informed, and satisfying to many of our deepest ethical intuitions. Its corporate nature perhaps does not give due place to that individual integrity that is so well served by the more atomistic paradigms, but our experiment here is to discover an ethical vision of more scope, one with a more open run than any single life can provide. The thesis here is that an individualistic ethic is short-sighted and needs

Reprinted by permission from Ernest Partridge, ed., *Responsibilities to Future Generations* (Buffalo, N.Y.: Prometheus Books, 1981).

to be corrected by a collective vision, as a result of which we have clearer insight in five areas especially problematic under traditional ethical analysis.

THE ACTUAL AND THE POTENTIAL

Our notions of justice have been finely honed around the concept of individual rights as these can be defended against the interests of others, and the casuistry that has here developed has some cross-generational usefulness. Still, when we move beyond our grandchildren, we falter; for future persons are indeterminate and remote, and one wonders how present persons have duties to such faceless nonentities. Our ethical skills deploy ahead uncertainly, owing to the lack of concrete, identifiable rights-carriers. We who are actually present do not know how to adjudicate our interests against such a potential "they," claimants all too nebulous and "iffy." These anomalies dissipate in part when life is observed as a corporate current, for then there is a present carrier of this possibility. This future belongs not to some abstract, hypothetical others; it is our future, which we who exist now do bear and transmit. It does not appear *ex nihilo,* but flows through us, it is the future of our generation, the future we generate, the downstream of our life. We are dealing with a potentiality of and in the actual.

The river has a geographical extension, which, though we typically view the stream at one point, we easily keep in mind. As an analogy it helps us to realize that, though we now see life locally, it has chronologically extended reality. We may then say that this present life, which we now compose, ought to have this tensed potential. Humans have, so to speak, a class right to the future; this race ought to run on, collectively, statistically, although we cannot individuate our posterity or prejudge entirely now "their" needs, "our" needs then. The mature self is able to envision itself in any present moment as enjoying but one slice in a temporally extended life. To be a self is to endure over time, in the processive stages from birth to death. But those endpoints of articulation, so vital in an egoistic ethic, are submerged in this life-pulse, which overflows those very individuals that it flows through. We pass away, but we pass life on. We share a common life with posterity, not in that they are now available for reciprocal obligations, but in that a common life is transported from here to there. This corporate passage also treats as concurrent what are usually separated out as deontological and teleological concerns. It would be a present, intrinsic wrong to deprive ourselves of a future, as it would also be wrong for us not to be instrumental to future good.

For a living thing to be actual is to be generative. If we think electrically, no current actually flows except as maintained by a potential. Life is another sort of current, more autonomously propelled, in which being actual and having potential are much the same thing; being is always becoming. Biologically, life must be procreative; the life-stream is one of parenting and growing, sowing and reaping, a dynamism that turns acorns into oaks into acorns into oaks. Further, this natural, seminal adventure has its human, educational extensions. We are so built as to be both reproductively and culturally *projective*. That is the notion of *con/sequences,* that there are "sequences" that follow "together with" past and present acts, and these consequences overleap the death of the individual. When there appear any living things, any life ways, whose consequences are not sufficiently projective, those forms may enjoy local successes and values, but they soon vanish. That is so, and, we shall later add, it ought to be so.

The river flows under the force of gravity, and the life-stream moves under an inner conative urge. The philosopher may have trouble supplying rational arguments why this life, now instantiated in me, should want to flow on, but he is unlikely to eradicate this natural passion. If any do fall into an entire disconcern to project themselves, careless about the future, they will soon be eliminated as unfit, the stream of life by-passing them. Such failure of nerve will be swept aside by other currents in which more fight remains. Most of us are going to find that the will to life that we have inherited from past generations floods through us, and thence to the future. Thus, fortunately, to a certain point, our class right, and our duty, and our compelling natural urge are discharged in the production of a surviving, future generation.

Unfortunately, this is not entirely so, else we should not have the problem of the *ought* and the *is,* to which we will come. More unfortunately still, we appear to have reached troubled waters, where these productive urges to reproduce and build will, without ethical control, become pathogenic and misfit us for survival. Our actual lifestyle might now be reducing our potential, which would be lamentable both biologically and ethically.

THE SELF AND THE OTHER

A person's ethical capacity can be roughly measured by the span of his "we." Egoism marks off an isolated "I," and beyond this boundary discovers only "he" and "she," finding ethical contests in the clashes of these irreducible cores, the one against the many, each unit pursuing its own enlightened interest. Altruism finds "others" and is also pluralistic, but there now appear sympathetic capacities. Beyond both egoism and altruism, the "I" is sometimes so moved to identify with a "you" that the capacity to say "we" emerges. My self is stretched over to the other, and ethical concern does not stop with my skin but overflows to my kin. Ethical maturity comes with a widening of that sense of kinship, and, with broad enough recognition of this togetherness, the self is immersed in a communal life.

Most of us can dissociate our identity beyond our own memory traces and reassociate it with parents and children, even with our ethnic and national kind.

We could not be biologically or culturally successful without the capacity to do this, for we could not, as we have said, be sufficiently projective. There is a certain biological and psychological soundness to egoism's focus on the individual organism, but we also have to recognize the provision for regeneration. Thus we have a natural beginning for the development of the moral sense in the defense not merely of the self but of the in-group. The two senses of *kind*, "considerate" and "related," have a single etymological origin. The evolution of conscience proceeds with a widening out of both senses of *kind* so that they become less familial, less tribal, more ecumenical, reaching in the end a universal moral intent, and this extended sweep is not only a global but a chronological one.

We may notice here that far-off descendants and distant races do not have much "biological hold" on us. Across the era of human evolution, little in our behavior affected those remote from us in time or in space, and natural selection shaped only our conduct toward those closer. Now that our actions have such lengthened impact, we may indeed need ethics to survive, since this is required to enlarge the scope of concern for which we are biologically programmed. If our ethical concern can evolve to equal our awesome modern capacities to help and to hurt, around the globe and across generations to come, in such moral development, we would no doubt find new truth in the old moral paradox that a concern for others benefits one's own character.

In this life-current, distinctions that earlier were so clear begin to dissolve. Even the egoist knows that a person can have a duty to his future self, and hence he sacrifices for his retirement. All his stages are eventually present, and "now" has no favored status. But what of parents who bequeath possessions to their children and grandchildren, what of the farmer who for them conserves his soil, what of donors who endow the communities and institutions they have cherished? If we narrowly define the self, we shall say that prudence has become charity. But if we recognize the larger, more enduring group from which the self takes its identity, we will redescribe as a sort of corporate egoism what first seemed private charity; for the enlarging self extends into and continues in the course of the things that it loves. What then happens as this sense of kinship widens further under influences less ethological, less ethnological, more ethical? We may wonder whether egoism has vanished and altruism remains, or vice versa, as we wonder whether the drop of water remains or dissolves in the river. There are those who insist that every corporation is a fiction and that any goods and interests it may have are analyzable into those of individuals, and they will have here somehow to assign fractions to egoism and to altruism. But this is a type of ethical nominalism, not well served by recent biological and sociological theory where the goods and interests of the individual are constituted interdependently with the larger genetic and social movements out of which that person is composed.

When one pauses to consider the life that one "has," only an ignorant person would think of oneself as really "self-made" or "self-sufficient"; it is rather the lonesome self that is closer to fiction. The natural and cultural truth is in this otherness of the self, that we are participants in a shared flow, of which the self is an integral but momentary instantiation, rightly to be cherished in what autonomy it is given but responsibly and responsively to be emplaced in its supporting matrix. The old Jewish fathers put this aphoristically: "If I am not for myself who will be for me? And if I am only for myself, what am I?" (Hillel). The train of thought and of life we are following here lets us apply this to a generation; if there are those who find this application difficult, we recommend that they go and stand at their great-grandparents' graves.

Love cares what happens after we are gone. The biological roots of this lie in parenting, but this concern matures and bears fruit in culture and in ethics. All authentic love is causally transitive, propagative, projecting that level of life that one most enjoys, but in this it goes out to invest itself in the other. Where this is not so, where one is careless about what happens after the demise of the local self, then there is only pretended, inauthentic love, stagnant self-love, unworthy of survival. Where this is so, we gain a much richer notion of the "commons" than has lately been current, for we no longer have self-aggrandizing egos, each wresting out its share of the commons, kept in check from stupidly overloading it only by finding some keener, more calculating self-interest to which we can appeal.[1] The self can live in love on this commons that we commend, but on the fought-over one it can live only in careful fear. Those who join this collective current find new meaning in the Earth's carrying capacity.

THE HUMAN AND THE NATURAL

It is no coincidence that environmental ethics and intergenerational ethics are often a single issue, for our survival requires a habitat. It is typically, though not invariably, the case that what is good now for the environment is good for the human future, and we next find that the flow of this living river erodes and rounds off the sharp edges of the human/natural distinction. Soil, air, water, forests, grasslands, seas, the fauna, the flora are confluent with what, seen too narrowly, too artificially, some call the course of human events. Ecology has taught us vastly to expand our notions of circulation; human life moves afloat on a photosynthetic, nutritional biocurrent, with organic life in turn dependent on hydrologic, meteorologic, and geologic cycles. Life does not stop at the skin here either; it is an affair of natural resources. All that we are and have was grown or collected. If the word *resources* by its prefix "re" introduces the thought of a source that has been "turned into" human channels, away from its spontaneous course, it recalls more prominently the substantive earthen "source" out of which all springs.

No life form, the human included, can be projective enough to survive if it is not also, at a minimum, environmentally homeostatic. "Homeostasis" is not so much a static word as it is a hydraulic word, portraying in its biological use the steady state of a life-current maintaining itself over time in exchange with supporting movements in the physical environment. Consumption is always at odds with conservation; life endures in a delicate tension of the two. In prehuman life this balance is nondeliberate; with human life the challenge emerges to make this deliberate—and ethical. Homeostasis need not preclude evolution or historical development, but it does specify that any future human course shall include the carrying on of these natural processes with which collectively we move. We can "regenerate" only if our sources are "renewable." In both these words the prefix "re" no longer has to do with the making over of something natural into something human but, rather, with a human continuance by fitting into an uninterrupted flow of earthen sources. It was those concerned with natural conservation who early became concerned about future generations.

Life is a current in organismic as well as in environmental biology. Being water-based, life nowhere proceeds without its fluids, whether it be the sap in the trees or the blood in our veins. These support the protoplasmic process, and when we consider its future we speak still further of a genetic flow. Though individuals are the necessary carriers of genes, this notion again is not so individualistic as it is populational. No one of us carries all the human genetic reservoir, each one draws an integral humanity from a pool that enormously transcends what any one person owns. It is to the regeneration of that communal reservoir that I contribute. Biologically, I am perhaps urged to preserve my germ line in that pool, as this may be edited by natural selection for the most viable genetic reservoir; ethically, the self can also enlarge its concern to care more broadly for the entire genealogical stream. If this seems to reduce our human life too much to the microscopic, genetic level, then we can readily return to the macroscopic, personal life, where the phenotype expresses a genotype, but always remembering how the subjective self manifests this genetic current.

It is fruitful to view the evolution of life as a kind of information flow. Against a basic physical flow, the disordering tendency to increase entropy, a biocurrent emerges with the capacity to build up and reproduce ordered, organic structures, passing this constructive information along genetically. In this nondeliberate sense all life is intelligent, logical, communicative, and the linguistic models employed in genetics give evidence of this. This flow diversifies, becomes more sophisticated and creative, more sentient and intelligent, until at length there emerges the capacity in humans for culture; and then a radically new sort of information flow appears, surpassed in significance only by the initial appearance of the negatively entropic life process itself. Acquired information can be transmitted, linguistically stored, and evaluated, and intelligence becomes deliberate. But the cultural process is still a part of, if the apex of, a natural life process. Life is always a cybernetic question, one of information transfer, as life is steered along over time, with both biological and civilized currents. The projecting of ourselves biologically and culturally, different though these may be, are inseparably integrated facets in the survival process.

Life is one of nature's projects, but it has flowed on so as to become one of our projects. We are the tip of an iceberg. We do dramatically emerge out of nature, but beneath the surface life remains nine-tenths natural. What is often wrong with the model of a "contract," in terms of which ethics is argued out, is that it is anti-natural, finding individualistic humans reluctantly banded together against threatening nature. There, rights-talk understandably appreciates individuals and depreciates nature. This countercurrent of the human before the natural is not wrong, as the notion of a countercurrent of the organic before the inorganic is not wrong, but both become fragmentary truths when placed in a still larger picture that sees an interflowing of the human and the natural, the biological with the physical. Nature gives us *objective* life, of which the *subjective* life of the individual is but a partial, inner face. Upon this given ecosystem we are what biologists call obligate parasites, and at this point we become interestingly confused—are we morally obligated to conserve and value merely the human or also the natural, since these have fused? Those who are ethically conservative will prefer to insist that ethics applies only to the human race, with all other processes auxiliary to this; those who are ethically liberal may find that their moral concern ranges over this catholic river of life and even includes the landscapes over which it flows.

THE PRESENT AND THE HISTORICAL

The river is a billion years long and persons have traveled a million years on it, recording their passage for several thousand years. If the river were to stretch round the globe, the human journey would be halfway across a county and we would have kept a journal for only a few hundred feet. The individual's reach would be a couple of steps. Such a linear scale admits the natural length of the river, yet it does not record an increasing turbulence in the human epoch, owing to the augmented information-flow. What is upstream flows down so as progressively, logarithmically to become tributary to more depth and stir. This past distance traveled is only partially forgotten and gone; it is rather largely here. It survives in us, for the present is what endures out of the past.

We are, as it were, the "*is*-ness of the was," not only in an evolutionary sense but also in an educational sense. Socrates and Moses, Jesus and Buddha, Newton and Copernicus, are not merely prior to us; their effects have been carried here by thousands now nameless who cherished and taught them, so transmitting them across time that something of them is recomposed in our composition. We sometimes think of the past as a kind of corpse; the dead are nothing but memories and phantoms. But if life is an on-rushing current, this is not so; for it is the past that germinates us. Our present life is just that past life in a cumulative, contemporary incarnation. In a legal phrase, we are both the executors and beneficiaries of the "wills" of our forebears, which outlast them. We do well to "will" that this providence lasts on, to ensure the *"will-be-ness* of the *is."* In a natural idiom, we have roots, and we ought to have fruits.

Life is a splendid sort of "project," the ultimate drama. Some of its meanings are, and ought to be, transient. But the deepest meaning is found not merely in the present but, as in all narrative, when leading features of the past survive, deepen, and cohere to govern across repeated chapters in a whole plot. Incidentals may be delighted in for the present, but they pass away, peculiar to an era. Discontinuities and emergents surprise us; still each generation's noblest adventures are tributary to a meaning flow that is intergenerational. In the flow of a symphony, the present melody is enjoyed in itself, but not only so; it often recapitulates and leads. Else there is less beauty and no real movement. That we cannot entirely foresee the outcome is a positively dramatic feature, and so we do not and cannot know the future course of this life tide, whether of success or of catastrophe. But that does not diminish in present actors a duty to thrust forward what they most cherish. Nor does this duty diminish their own immediate integrity; it rather establishes it.

Every scientist, every humanist, every educator, and every parent knows how the single life needs these dimensions of retrospect and prospect. We are set in motion with what was delivered to us; we carry it on a bit, but not to its conclusion; we pass from the scene, and our students, disciples, and children carry on. This age has seen the remarkable revelations of Watson and Crick, but only as they follow those of Darwin, Mendel, and Linnaeus; others will continue the succession. Democracy has been a long time building, and most of us would die to pass it on. The musician, the artist, the novelist, the philosopher—all flourish in the heritage of their predecessors, and they themselves create works to be appreciated now but also to pass into the objective public domain. Particular lives and labors are most often forgotten, but that does not mean that they were not part of the cybernetic circuits over which a culture was transmitted.

No one should deny important asymmetries between past, present, and future; they are well recognized in what McTaggart called the temporal A-series, where a knife-edged present moves inexorably across time to convert the future into the past. But it is likewise possible, more scientific, and just as moral, to view time as what he called a B-series, having only an earlier-than/later-than in a serial whole.[2] If we couple these series, past, present, and future are not three things, with only one convincingly real. But there is one life-stream that bears the predicates of the past into the future by conveying them through the present. Past, present, and future are not strung together like beads on a string, each a detachable existent *simpliciter.* They flow together like the upstream and downstream of a river, only more organically. The myopic, arrogant "now" generation thinks of the past as dead, the future as nonbeing, with only the present alive. The far-sighted see that to be alive in the present is to carry the past on to the future; and, if so, it is rather the ephemeral "now" generation that is as good as dead, for they do not know what survival means. We are constituted in memory and hope, and it is indeed a prophetic truth that where there is no vision, the people perish.

THE *IS* AND THE *OUGHT*

Life flows on. Life ought to flow on. Few can specify how we make that descriptive-prescriptive jump, but here, where biology and history draw so close to ethics, it is made easier than anywhere else. Fact and fact-to-be-desired join in "the *ought*-ness is the *is*," which is not to endorse all, nor to deny that some life-forms are passing, but to cheer for this fabulous life project. Not only in our genes but also in our consciences we are constructed for a sort of keeping faith with those upstream and down. Here are joined the twin meanings of "conduct" that constrain the present; we ought each and all to *conduct* ourselves (to behave responsibly) so as to *conduct* ourselves (to lead the race safely on) from past to future. Life protects life; such survival is "becoming," again in biological and ethical senses. Should we fail, that would abuse our resources and abort our destiny.

This judgment is not entirely shared by those who find life's currents to be all in tragedy. The older, Indian Buddhists called the world a maelstrom of dependent origination, one misery causing another, but they hoped to find a deliverance by putting out these urges in a quiescent *nirvana*. We may agree with them that an unrelieved, individualistic plurality is bad, an illusory gestalt that intensifies suffering, but we disagree in our wish to conserve and corporately to integrate the world of birth and death, preserving just that blessed life-stream that survives these agonies. The recent nihilists screamed that life was absurd and, in despair, said they cared nothing about its going on. Both rightly perceived life's suffering, but underwent it so intensely that they misperceived its meaning. This suffering, however, can become a sacrament of life; it takes on significance as, and only as, in these tears, we insist on the projection in this world of this life-stream. And, whatever their theories, in practice both still found life heroic—the compassionate Buddhists in their reverence for life, and the adamant nihilists in their protest that we manufacture meaning despite our nothingness.

These extremes aside, most of us find our earthen life to be more a gift than a meaningless given, a gift that obligates us as trustees to the task of carrying it on. Against all the arguments, sometimes forceful ones, about nature's heartlessness and culture's mindlessness, here we are, alive and even well, products at once of nature and of culture, glad of it, and rather persuaded that the real tragedy, the ultimate in absurdity, lies not in our being here but in the possibility of our failing to pass life forward.

We do not suppose that there is no discontinuity when the moral *ought* emerges where hitherto there was only an *is*. In the wild, each fends for itself competitively. The cooperative flow is an unintended consequence of this self-interest, which is edited by natural selection to shape the survival of the most vigorous species. Life is advanced by a kind of libido, and, while we must be careful not to judge this to be bad, neither is it moral. Looking out after oneself has its necessary place in this ensuring of life, although this is not sufficient for its continuance; it must be kept in check by the interests of others, by eco-systemic balances and evolutionary pressures. What *is* the case in the prehuman world, and often even in the premoral human world, can and henceforth *ought* at deliberative levels to be accomplished morally.

One's self-interest, which is still required, can now be kept in its desirable place, sufficiently checked by capacities for sympathy, by judgments finding rightness in the corporate currents of life, to which one belongs. What before was externally and genetically controlled can by this advance be internalized and freely acted upon. The moral sense then becomes a new form of cybernetic control. But the effect of that switch can be, and ought to be, to ensure the continuity of a life process that has long been under way. Indeed, such are our recently maturing powers for the exercise of self-interest that, unless these ethical capacities also unfold, the earlier natural checks may no longer be effective and we may plunge into that terminal tragedy which we most fear.

In front of Eiheiji, Dogen's mountain temple in Japan, there stands the Half-Dipper Bridge, so named because the Zen sage was accustomed to drink there; but he would take only half a dipperful and pour the rest back into the river, rejoicing in its onward flow. We may puzzle about whether this denies or fulfills that earlier, Indian Buddhist estimate of the *samsara* world, to which we just referred, but we must surely admire so simple a gesture with such a rich ethical concern. There is much scientific analysis now of the "energy through-put" in the biosystem and in the economy. A moral concern for a "life through-put" would help even more. A fair criticism of what we have proposed is that it is impressionistic and difficult to make "operational," so accordingly we do also need the logic that unfolds under other models of life and responsibility. Their arguments may help us, in the conflict of life against life, to protect individual integrity, to compute maximums in quantity and quality, and to balance each against the other. But we operate as impressed by our metaphors too, as well as by our calculations, whether those images are of the survival of the fittest, or the social contract, or lifeboat ethics, or the way of the cross. If seen as a symbol, this river of life is no longer merely a metaphor, it is a truth that bears moral insight, because it helps us see more deeply how the life process is and how it ought to be.

NOTES

1. Garrett Hardin, "The Tragedy of the Commons," *Science* 169 (1968):1243-1248.
2. J. M. E. McTaggart, *The Nature of Existence,* vol. 2 (Cambridge: University Press, 1921), chap. 33.

II. VALUES IN NATURE

When the question about human conduct toward nature arises, some ask about *rights*, others about *duties*, others about *respect*, others about *resources*. But there is no more profitable line of inquiry than to press at this point the question of *value*. We turn now from environmental ethics to what we might call environmental axiology. How should we value nature? That question has proved surprisingly urgent in the last half of the twentieth century, and it has been most insistent in those civilizations that thought themselves the most advanced, those that have moved farthest from nature. How we should value nature logically precedes a later question, how should we act toward nature?

But here again, when philosophy goes wild, it must swim against the stream of a longstanding paradigm that conceives of value as a product of human interest satisfaction. Values may be associated with natural things, which carry assigned human values. But strictly speaking, there are no values in the wild. An undue anthropocentrism in values is what we will be contesting in the essays to follow. But this requires first a careful account of just what values humans do find in their encounters with nature. Only afterward can we probe these encounters further to see whether and how far they imply instrumental and intrinsic value in wild nature itself.

The problem of instrumental versus intrinsic values in nature, even when its anthropocentric bias is shed, proves more complex than first appears. In an ecological perspective, values no longer attach merely to individuals, at least not in absolute or unqualified ways. An organism defends and enjoys its own values, local and intrinsic to the individual. But at the same time, it plays roles instrumental to other organisms and to the systemic whole. Values, both instrumental and intrinsic, are storied achievements in a projective nature.

5

Values in Nature

"The world's largest monument to the world's smallest fish!" With that hyperbole, a Tennessee governor once lamented the apparent fate of the $116 million Tellico dam, stopped first by the Supreme Court and later by the Endangered Species Committee in order to save the three-inch snail darter, *Percina tanasi*. Congress afterward voted to finish the dam. The gates have been closed, the lake is filled, and the critical habitat is destroyed. It may be that the darter has been successfully transplanted, though the director of that project is doubtful.[1] If not, the dam will indeed be the world's largest gravestone—for which the tiny perch was sacrificed, the first deliberate extinction of one species by another—and we must then decide whether to view the dam as a monument of pride or of shame. The Dickey and Lincoln dams on the St. John River in Maine are being planned with the careful protection of the rediscovered Furbish lousewort, *Pedicularis furbishiae,* once thought extinct in the United States. A technologist may consider concern for these "lousy louseworts" to be "total stupidity."[2] A naturalist may be glad for test cases that force us to ask whether rare life forms are not worth more than those dam(n) machines. These dramatize an increasingly insistent question about what values we meet in nature, and scientists find themselves hardly better able than anyone else to answer it.

Value is the generic noun for any positive predicate, and it is commonplace to notice that in a strict sense science works only with neutral, descriptive predicates. This means, however, that science cannot teach us what we need most to know about nature, that is, how to value it. A partial response, relieving the embarrassment of scientists at the incompetence of their discipline here, is to point out that values are mental and ideal, not actual or material, so that objective value is no part of nature as such, and thus forms no part of science. Values appear only in the human response to the world. To ask about values in nature is, then, to form a misleading question, for values are only in people, created by their decisions.

Reprinted by permission from *Environmental Ethics* 3(1981):113-128.

But that seems to err on the subjective side, for some values appear in our relationships with nature. Natural things at least become *carriers* of value. We may not want to say that the valuing of nature is a descriptive registering of properties, but neither do we value nature altogether oblivious of its descriptions. We make something a target merely by aiming at it. But our interest in apples is not so arbitrary. It depends in part on something that is found there. Philosophers of science make a traditional, if also troublesome, distinction between primary and secondary qualities. We might say that values in nature are tertiary qualities, that is, contain a still additional level of subjective contribution by the beholder. The recipient of value is more active than is the viewer of color, far more so than is the observer of motion. Nevertheless even the participant in natural values does not compose them *ex nihilo,* for there are actual facts which are the crucial supports of these values. Such qualities in any case are properties of the natural object in the sense that, whatever the contributions made by humans in constituting worth, there are prevaluational antecedents necessary for value, if not sufficient for it. I propose here to examine the kinds of value that arise *in association with* nature, being founded on physical and biological properties there, especially as these have been unfolded by the sciences.

Notice that if we are going to talk about any natural values, we must be "in on" them, that is, "share" those values in personal experiences adequate to judge them. Indeed, careful scientists now realize that they always bear some relationship beyond that of passive observers to whatever they seek to know, but the ownership features loom larger here. We are rather more "turned on" in doing evaluative judgments than in doing straightforward empirical ones, but that can mean that we are rather more "tuned in" with what is so. That does add a dimension of biography to every report about nature, but it would be valuational solipsism to conclude that in those values that natural things seem to carry I am getting back absolutely nothing but my projections. Values are actualized in real things, often natural things, which seems to warrant the view that valuing is sometimes in part a form of knowing where we register properties—aesthetic properties of the Grand Canyon, for instance, in the appreciating mind—notwithstanding what we may add in the appreciating process. Otherwise we commit the fallacy of misplaced location, and ascribe to the viewer what is really in the scene, or at least what comes relationally. Scientists, more than others here, ought to be alert for the objective properties involved. We should also be warned that the myriad items of the natural panorama need not all be expected to carry value alike, qualitatively or quantitatively. Some may carry none at all, and some may carry disvalue. Being valuable, like being colored, takes many forms and shades.

ECONOMIC VALUE

The price of petroleum proves that nature has economic value, but the sense in which it does can be contested, for human labor so dramatically adds to its raw value that an economist may here see valuing as a kind of adding on of labor to what is initially valueless. "Crude" oil" has no value, but a petroleum engineer may "refine" it. The sense of the prefix re- in resource is that nature can be re-fitted, turned to use by human labor, and only the latter gives it value. Valuing is a kind of laboring, more than a kind of knowing. If this were entirely so, we should not say, strictly speaking, that nature has economic value any more than we say that an empty glass has water in it. It only carries the value of labor. Marxists often argue that natural resources should be unpriced, for in fact resources as such have no economic value.[3] But research scientists, mindful of the remarkable natural properties on which technology depends, may immediately add that human art has no independent powers of its own, and they may give a different valuation of this natural base.

There is a foundational sense in which human craft can never produce any unnatural chemical substances or energies. All we can do is shift natural things around, taking their properties as givens. There is nothing unnatural about the properties of a computer or a rocket; as much as a warbling vireo or a wild strawberry, both are assemblages of completely natural things operating under natural laws. This sets aside essential differences between artifacts and spontaneous nature, but it does so to regain the insight that nature has economic value because it has an instrumental capacity—and this is to say something about the material on which the craftsmanship is expended. Nature has a rich utilitarian pliability, due both to the plurality of natural sorts and to their splendid multifaceted powers. This is its economic value in a basic and etymological sense of something we can arrange so as to make a home out of it. Nature is, as it were, a fertile field for human labor, but that agricultural metaphor (which applies as well to industry) praises not only laborers but their surrounding environment. Nature is sometimes recalcitrant, but often agreeable and useful, frequently enough to build our entire culture on it.

Despite the prefix, resource preserves the word source, and recalls these generative qualities so profuse in their applications. It is sometimes thought that the more civilized we become the further we get away from nature, released from dependency on the spontaneous natural course. This is true, but science and technology also take us further into nature. A pocket calculator is, in this perspective, not so much an exploitation of nature as it is a sophisticated appreciation of the intriguing electronic and mathematical structure of matter-energy, properties enjoying an even more sophisticated natural use in the brain of the fabricator of the calculator.

To be sure, such economic value is a function of the state of science, but it is also a function of valuable natural properties, which often quite unpredictably mix with human ingenuity to assume value. *Penicillium* was a useless mold until 1928, when Flemming found (and much amplified) the natural antibacterial agency. The bread wheat, on which civilization is based, arose from the hybridization (probably accidental) of a mediocre natural wheat with a weed, goat grass. Who is to say where the miracle foods and medicines of the future will come from? Given the striking advances of technology, an endangered ecosystem is likely to contain some members of potential use. If we accordingly conserve nature, we hope in the genius of the human mind; but we also reveal our expectations regarding the as yet undiscovered wealth of natural properties, which we may someday convert into economic value.

LIFE SUPPORT VALUE

The ecological movement has made it clear that culture remains tethered to the biosystem and that the options of our arts, however expanded, provide no release from nature. Evolutionary theory adds that culture, despite its novelties, is but the latest chapter in an epic of development. Our economic wealth may be labored, but our ecologic welfare has deeper, natural roots. The ordinary currencies of economic value are much distorted when one tries to count ecological values with them, for they are poorly equipped to preserve these noncommercial values—those tied to the atmosphere, the oceans, polar ice caps, and ozone layer—which are essential to the health of the ecosystem and thus to human welfare. Such prophets as Rachel Carson or Aldo Leopold launched what has proved to be a difficult quest for better modes of "caring for" the land, forests, grasslands, soil, and rivers. This caring is for natural communities but also must be distributed into a valuing of individual members—honeybees, blacksnakes, earthworms, fungi, or alders and the nitrogen-fixing bacteria in their root nodules—all of which contribute to enviromental quality and, thus, to human life support. At this point, the economist's sense of a labored value has been entirely left behind, and geological and biological qualities are in immediate focus.

Still the humanistic principle seems dominant. None of these processes has any value except in its support of cultural values. Value is not always an economic predicate, but it arrives only with human interest. From one perspective that is so, but, as before, the natural scientist is entranced by the objective features of this life support, found in profusion by recent science, as with the electromagnetic light window in the atmosphere that screens harmful radiation but admits the energy to drive the ecosystem. The intricate analyses made by the ecologists sum up into an overview of the Earth suggested by photographs taken by the astronauts; we increasingly see it as a blue, white, and green jewel, a home set lonesomely in the abysses of space. In many respects, though by no means all, the earthen setup is a "happy place." Those who find value to be entirely subjective will smile and say that in that kind of remark we are only getting back our reflected emotions, as when others say that it is a "lonely place." Evolutionists may also charge that humans have necessarily been selected to fit and even to like this world, for the misfits were eliminated. But those who prefer a more objective gestalt will wonder why we find ourselves alive and well in a life support system that can, by means of natural selection, evolve such a flourishing of life. Do we not value Earth because it is valuable, and not the other way round? Is it really just a matter of our late-coming interests, or is not Earth in some puzzling way an interesting, lively place even antecedently to the human arrival?

The astronomical reaches of space can be taken as a consummate example of worthless nature. But the heavens seem to have provided the space-time place for the genesis of all the heavier elements on which everything else is built, and so the stars are the furnaces in which once was constructed the stardust now in the hand, the brain, and the pocket calculator. A pragmatic scientist may dismiss this celestial prologue as so remote from local issues as to set Earth in a value vacuum quite as nearly as it is set in a spatial one. But a philosophical scientist can reply that such a prologue is not so much "nebulous" as it is rather foundational. A tough-minded analyst can insist that nothing has value until humans arrive. One moment that may seem right, but then again is he not a provincial who supposes that his part alone in the drama in which he participates establishes all its worth?

RECREATIONAL VALUE

It may seem frivolous to move from labor to play, from creation to recreation, but the question is a quite serious one: why we enjoy nature even when we no longer need it for economic or life supportive reasons, when the sense of "enjoy" alters from beneficial use to pleasurable appreciation. For some, nature here is instrumental to some active human performance; they want only terrain tough enough to test a jeep, or a granite cliff sound enough for pitons. Even so, it serves as a field for skill and joy. For others, the natural qualities are crucial in contemplating an autonomous performance. They watch the fleecy cumulus building over the Great White Throne in Zion, listen for the bull elk to bugle, laud the aerial skills of the hummingbird at the bergamot, or laugh at the comic ostrich with his head in the sand. For the first group, nature's recreational value is as a place to *show what they can do;* for the other, values are reached as they are *let in on nature's show*—a difference surprisingly close to that between applied and pure science. Even for the latter persons, nature is in a way an instrument of pleasure, but only special sorts of instruments can be enjoyed by contemplation. Music and art are like this, but we also speak of their intrinsic worth, and, even more oddly here, although appreciative skills are required, no human performance is required upon this instrument. These two sorts of recreational value can often be combined, as when a botanist enjoys the exertion of a hike up a peak and also pauses at the Parry's primrose by the waterfall enroute. But they often need to be compromised and are sometimes irreconcilable. It will strike a sportsman as ridiculous to say that snail darters and Furbish louseworts have more recreational value than will the reservoirs behind those dams, stocked with game fish, while it will seem obscene to the naturalist to exterminate a rare life form in exchange for one more place to water-ski. These natural history values seem lately to be counting more, for every state wildlife magazine devotes more space to the nongame species than it did a decade ago, and every national park and wilderness area is under increasing visitor pressure. And what if these count still more in the next generation? We can always build a dam, but extinction is forever.

Recreational values can be in sports and popular pastimes, and thus can be humanistic, but they are not always so. They can be in sober sensitivity to objective natural characters, and here we regain our main track toward natural values in a scientific perspective. Is being a naturalist a matter of recreation or of science? Does one do it for play or for pay? Some ornithologists and mineralogists hardly ask; rather, whether avocationally or vocationally, they unite in valuing nature as an object worthwhile to be known apart from economic concerns, always caring for the fascinating natural characteristics we now attempt to unfold.

SCIENTIFIC VALUE

Science was in its origins the leisurely pursuit of intellectuals, and a good test still for unalloyed scientists is to ask whether they would continue their researches if they were independently wealthy and if these had no economic or life supporting consequences. The alliance of pure science with naturalistic recreation is seldom noticed, but this only reveals how far recent science has sold its soul to the economists. Like music and the fine arts, natural science is an intrinsically worthwhile activity, but scientists find this dfficult to say and, sometimes with much ingenuity, sell their study short by retreating to some utilitarian subterfuge. But natural science *per se* cannot be worthwhile unless its primary object, nature, is interesting enough to justify being known. To praise cognitive science here is also to praise its object, for no study of a worthless thing can be intrinsically valuable, and, filtering out all applied values, one reaches a residual scientific value in nature, an interest in both the natural stuff and the study of it that has enlisted the greatest human genius.

Natural science is our latest and perhaps most sophisticated cultural achievement, but we should not forget that its focus is primitive nature. Valuing science does not devalue nature, for it tells us something about the absorbing complexity of the natural environment that it can serve as the object of such noble studies. There is an intellectual adventure in discerning how the tunicates and the vertebrates are so structured as to include both among the chordates, which are related to the echinoderms more closely than to the cephalopods, an accomplishment possible only because nature is a rich developmental system. Some say that we first understand things and afterward evaluate them, but if there is anyone for whom pure science has value, then nature contains at least the raw precursors of value, and bears these in concrete particulars, in benzene molecules and ptarmigans, however one may seek universals in these particulars.

The Jurassic fossil *Archaeopteryx,* linking the reptiles with the birds, has great scientific value but no economic or life supporting value. The steaming pools of Yellowstone preserve an optimal thermal habitat for primitive anaerobic bacteria that, recent studies suggest, survive little changed from the time when life evolved under an oxygen-free atmosphere.[4] It is typically odd, useless, and often rare things that have high scientific values, like the finches on the Galapagos, for the clues they furnish to life's development and survival. If there had lain below the threatening flood waters of the Tellico dam an archaeological site suspected to contain hints of human origins in the West, we would not have closed those gates. And yet there does lie flooded now the ancient Indian site, *Tanasi,* from which the state of Tennessee and the little *Percina tanasi* both take their names, as well as the Icehouse Bottom (c. 7,500 B.C.), an excavation representing the oldest documented textile use in eastern North America, two sites among hundreds of unexcavated sites spoiled by the flooding. The flooded valley, in the testimony of one expert, is "undoubtedly the most interesting archaeological section in the entire Appalachian district, with some 280 sites, only a few more than 5% excavated, most wholly unexcavated."[5] Who is to say, worrying over the elimination of a snail darter or a wild stretch of an ancient river, where tomorrow's scientific values may lie? A scientist might have been pardoned a generation back for thinking the Yellowstone microhabitats and methanogens unimportant.

Science tells the natural tales—how things are, how they came to be. That story cannot be worthless, not only because our roots lie in it, but because we find it a delightful intellectual pursuit. The older sciences, and many abstract ones still, fastened on morphology, structure, and homeostatic processes. That itself was engaging, but now no natural science, whether astrophysics or ecology, escapes the evolutionary paradigm, and mankind is only beginning to understand what, in a sometimes despised term, *natural history* is all about. That history has an epic quality—a considerable wandering notwithstanding—and it is surely a story worth telling. But the scientist can be beguiled into severing values from nature at the same time that she finds her principal intellectual entertainment in unraveling an account of the physical and biological saga. Those who are humanistically inclined can still claim that nature is valueless and that all the cleverness of science is an artifact, for science too is an art. But there is this difference between the cleverness of a scientist and that of an artisan: the latter mostly creates, while the former partly creates but also largely discovers the satisfactions in his subject matter.

AESTHETIC VALUE

We value the Landscape Arch of the Canyonlands for the same reason that we value the Winged Victory of Samothrace; both have grace. Every admirer of the Tetons or of a columbine admits aesthetic value in nature, and the photographs in *Audubon* or *National Wildlife* bring out well this natural aesthetic value. Yet justifying such value verbally is as difficult as is justifying the experience of pure science. The intrinsically valuable intellectual stimulation that the scientist defends is, in fact, a parallel to the aesthetic encounter that the aesthetician defends, for both demand a distance from everyday personal needs and yet a participatory experience that is nontransferable to the uninitiated. Sensitivity in both pure science and in natural art helps us see much further than required by our pragmatic necessities. In both, one gets purity of vision.

In discovering such aesthetic value, it is critical to separate it from both utility and life support, and only those who recognize this difference can value the desert or the tundra. The mist that floats about an alpine cliff, spitting out lacy snowflakes, tiny exquisite crystals, will increase the climber's aesthetic experience there, although the gathering storm may be dangerous to him. The glossy chestnut, half covered by the spined husk, is pretty as well as edible, and we lament its vanishing; but the head of a much too common weed, *Tragopogon*, is just as shapely. The distance that a scientist cultivates, as well as the habit of looking closely, fits him to see the beauty that the coldblooded scientist is supposed to overlook. But it keeps turning up, and in unsuspected places, as in the stellate pubescence on the underside of a *Shepherdia* leaf or in a kaleidoscopic slide of diatoms. No one who knows the thrill of pure science can really be a philistine.

A prosaic scientist will complain that the admirer overlooks as much as he or she sees, chestnuts aborted by the fungal blight, fractured snowflakes, imperfections everywhere. Contingencies sometimes add beauty, for a skein of geese is not less moving if one is out of line, nor is the cottonwood silhouetted against the wintry sky any less dramatic for the asymmetries within its symmetrical sweep. Still, every natural thing is marred by accidents and eventually destroyed by them. Doesn't the aesthetician repair nature before appreciating it? He sometimes does, but in so doing, if we consider the case of organic beauty, he may see that ideal toward which a living thing is striving, and which is rarely reached in nature. So, the artist paints a perfect lady-slipper orchid. Perhaps we could say, in the language of the geneticists, that the artist portrays the phenotype producable by the normal genotype in a congenial environment. Or, borrowing from the computer scientists, the artist executes the program built into a thing, although that has not been executed in nature, owing to environmental constraints. Such an ideal is, in a way, still nature's project. In a distinction going back to Aristotle, it is true to the poetry of a thing, though not true to its history, and yet the poetry directs its history.[6] The form, though not wholly executed, is as natural as is the matter. Some will simply insist that all this is not true to the plain facts of nature; others will realize that this is not so much fiction as a way of getting at what one might call a natural essence only partly expressed in any individual existence.

It is sometimes said that science tells the story like it actually is, art like it ideally ought to be. But that is not entirely so. Art can enjoy the conflict and resolution in the concrete particular expression of a natural thing. On the other hand, science typically seeks a universal law to which no particular ever quite conforms. The physicist who rounds out his slightly erratic lab data into a symmetrical sine wave and the botanist who describes a generic type in his herbarium specimens, ignoring anomalies, both think they are truer to nature by overlooking some data. Again, art may abstract from nature in order to help us see it better. Impressionistic painters, such as Cézanne and Monet, have often said that by exaggeration they reeducate our perceptions to help us capture qualities *in nature,* as with the flair in an elm, chromatic qualities in a sandstone mesa, or the intricacy of a fern leaf. They may even abstract out lines, edges, solidity, or luminous qualities. But the scientist need not say that this is unrealistic, for theoretical science also abstracts in order to appreciate generic qualities illustrated in particular things. Both science and art have the capacity to help us see much further than our everyday economy requires.

LIFE VALUE

Reverence for life is commended by every great religion, and even moralists who shy from religion accord life ethical value. John Muir would not let Gifford Pinchot kill a tarantula at the Grand Canyon in 1896, remarking that "it had as much right there as we did."[7] A thoroughgoing humanist may say that only personal life has value, making every other life form tributary to our interests, but a sensitive naturalist will suspect that this is a callous rationalization, anthropocentric selfishness calling itself objective hard science. The first lesson learned in evolution was perhaps one of conflict, but a subsequent one is of kinship, for the life we value in persons is advanced from, but allied with, the life in monkeys, perch, and louseworts. Mixed with other values, this Noah principle of preserving a breeding population is powerfully present in the Endangered Species Act. But if life generically is of value, then every specific individual in some degree instances this value, and this is why, without due cause, it is a sin to kill a mockingbird.

This organic value has various components. We have already noticed how life is an artist; indeed, it is always a tribute to a work of art to say that it has organic unity. A further component that recent science is unfolding is what we may call life's intelligibility. Inorganic things have a passive intelligibility, as when minerals crystallize into thirty-two mathematically deducible classes or the elements form an atomic table, so that rational legibility, like aesthetic value, is broader than life. Beyond this, living things are active information systems, as is proved by genetic and biochemical "linguistics." The purines and pyrimidines of the DNA and RNA helixes serve as an "alphabet," organized by codons, word units, into chains rather like sentences and paragraphs. The double helix can be unzipped and "read"; one stereospecific molecule can "recognize" another and by this "coded messages" are "communicated." Life continues by a steady "problem solving," and evolution accumulates a sophisticated "memory," as organisms are better programmed by natural selection to "deal with" their environment. The bio-*logical* chemistries have such a cybernetic power that, though it is precognitive, the information content routinely in a single human cell is more than that in any human book.

A book can be read, but so too can a chambered nautilus. The microscopic ribs, typically thirty in a chamber, seem to be secreted daily in relation to the lunar-tidal cycle, forming a logarithmic spiral known as the Fibonacci series. With its complex physiology and ecology, *Nautilus pompilius* is an intelligible organic system quite as impressive as the atomic submarine named for it, and the beauty of its pearly orange and white spiral vault is greater. Under X-ray photography exquisite subsurface symmetries appear. We congratulate Leonardo Fibonacci for discovering the series, but why not value the *Nautilus* for so exquisitely graphing it? Intelligible things do not have to be produced intentionally, any more than aesthetic ones do. The *Nautilus'* history is interwoven with the whole, and here lie unsuspected scientific values. Across half a billion years and numerous species in a stable genus, the number of ribs in a *Nautilus* chamber gradually decreases to eight or nine, which, if anciently keyed to the lunar cycle, suggests that the moon circled the Earth more rapidly.[8] Its evolution may hide clues to the story of our planet and to ecological stability. There is even romance here; Oliver Wendell Holmes could find much poetry in this "ship of pearl."

Those who cannot find these organic, aesthetic, or intelligible justifications for valuing life cannot deny to it an interest value. Mind is the most interesting and, presumably, the rarest thing in the universe but life is the second most rare phenomenon, which ought alone to prove it of interest. And all life is natural. We can bring ourselves to say that the culture which unfolds from mind is artificial, but we can never say that life is anything but natural, which makes it an unequivocal natural value. If a space probe were to find on Mars life of the complexity of the Yellowstone thermophiles, to say nothing of those "lousy louseworts," this would be the most epochal discovery in the history of science, and we would value there what is daily despised on Earth. Lower life may be sacrificed for higher forms, of course; still, a principal task in ethics is for humans to find a suitable place for the integrity of other life forms.

DIVERSITY AND UNITY VALUES

We may next harness a pair of complementary values. The sciences describe much natural *diversity* and also much *unity,* terms that are descriptive and yet contain dimensions of value. The physical sciences have revealed the astronomical extent of matter coupled with its reduction into a few kinds of elements and particles, which dissolve into interradiating wave fields. The taxonomist has enlarged the array of natural kinds, while the biochemist has found only the materials of physics organized everywhere in parallel chemistries, such as glycolysis and the citric acid cycle or the DNA and RNA at the core of life. Evolution has traced every life form back to monophyletic or a few polyphyletic origins, while ecology has interwoven these myriad forms to connect them at present as fully as they have been related by paleontology. This macroscopic web is matched by the unity revealed by the electron microscope or the X-ray spectrometer. The natural pageant is a kind of symphony of motifs, each interesting, often orchestrated, sometimes chaotic, and all spun from a few simple notes.

The story of science is the discovery of a bigger universe with more things in it, and the finding of laws and structures to explain their common composition and kinship. One need not defend every species or reduction to prize the natural collectivity as always absorbing and often agreeable. A few centuries ago we supposed this universe to have far less spatiotemporal and biological diversity, and its structural unity was unknown or denied. Everywhere there was dualism and opposition—in heaven and earth, mind and matter, life and nonlife, man and nature, gods and demons. No scientist would return to that universe, if he could, for it was oppressively small, less diverse, and yet also superstitious and lacking in the natural unity that we now know it to possess.

Nature is sometimes locally poor, as in a lodgepole forest with its sparse *Vaccinium* undercover, but in the ensemble the natural sorts are lush and many splendored. This greatly entertains the naturalist, widened as his/her acquaintance with it is by lenses, voyages, and books, and it will be perceptibly sacrificed if we trade snail darters or louseworts for a few more generating machines. This diversity will be substantially threatened if the present rate of extinction, accelerated by human intervention perhaps a thousand times over natural rates, continues unabated. The same naturalist will enjoy realizing how these natural kinds have an ecosystemic connectedness, with their autonomous integrities balanced by interdependencies, but with this immediately comes a concern how often these are upset by ill-considered human interventions.

If this is too metaphysical, then perhaps one need only notice how both this diversity and unity feed the human mind. Mind cannot be formed under the homogeneity of a blank wall nor before the heterogeneity of a bewildering jungle. A complex mind evolves in order to deal with a diverse world, yet one through which unifying relationships run. That was true in Pleistocene times in the Olduvai Gorge, and it is true now, for our minds are still developing. Emerging out of nature, we have become geniuses by confronting nature's plurality-in-unity, both historically and scientifically. But do we then say that these features are of no value until thickened by the addition of human interest? Or do we wonder that just this system, evolving so, did thicken human interest to form the mind prehistorically and that it continues to do so now? The mind is a mirror of these properties in nature, and there is even a sense in which the mind, founded on the cerebral complexity and integrating capacities, is a product of nature's inclination both to diversify and to unify. When this mind reflects, in turn, on the natural world, it can assign value at once to diverse particulars and to the universal and global regularities that underlie and permeate these particulars.

STABILITY AND SPONTANEITY VALUES

A pair of complementary natural values rests on a mixture of ordered stability with what, rather evasively, we must call the appearance of spontaneity, counterparts that are not only descriptive but also valuational. That the natural processes are regular—that gravity holds, rains come, and oaks breed in kind—yields laws and trends rooted in the causal principle, and means that nature is dependable, as well as being unified and intelligible. Every order is not a value; but some order supports value, and why is not this natural dependability a quite basic value? A requisite of any universe is that it be ordered, but we need not despise a necessary good, nor does such minimum essential order account for the ecological and biochemical constancy that supports life and mind, and upon which all our knowledge and security depend.

The polar value, really a sort of freedom, is hardly known to science by any such name; indeed, it is with some risk of offense and oversimplification that we here touch the long-debated issues surrounding determinism. Still, nature sometimes provides an "appearance" of contingency. Neither landscapes nor aspen leaves are ever twice the same. In the laboratory, science abstracts out the regularly recurring components in nature to attain predictive control, while in the field nature always remains in part unique and particular, nonrepetitive. What happens there is always something of an adventure, as the way the cottontail evades the coyote, or just when the last leaf is tossed from this maple and where the gusting wind lands it. We hardly know how to give a complete account of this. Rigorous determinists insist that nothing in nature (or in culture) can be either of chance or of choice, believing that to say otherwise is to destroy the fundamental axiom of all science. But others require a less rigidly closed system, finding that science still prospers when positing statistical laws that need not specify every particular. Physics and chemistry contain more highly probable, if not absolute, causal laws, while the life and historical sciences are likely to use generalizations intermixed with more unexceptionable laws, and even to recognize that nature is at some points contingent.

If there are real natural possibilities in excess of what actually comes to pass, the possible event that does happen can be selected by chance or by choice or by some intermediate autonomy for which we hardly yet have an adequate model. Genetic experimentation seems to rest partly on microscopic contingencies, as in crossing-over or mutation affected by random radioactivity, and these effects are sometimes amplified into phenotypic expressions. The macroscopic level to a large degree suppresses any microscopic contingencies, and yields in consequence those stabilities that we also value, but the scene of natural history is on occasion a place of emergent surprises.

We are not sure whether *Australopithecus* had to develop in Africa, or whether giraffes had to mutate so as to develop long necks, although both events may have been probable. Did the first ancestral birds storm-blown to the Galapagos Islands absolutely have to be finches? For the conservatives, it is safest to say theoretically that here we only reveal our ignorance of nature's detailed determinism, that nature's surprises are only apparent, though perhaps we cannot now or ever escape this appearance. For the liberals, it is bolder and more satisfying, as well as true to practical experience, to say that nature sometimes allows the real appearance of spontaneous novelty. What the Darwinian revolution did to the Newtonian view was to find nature sometimes a jungle and not always a clock, and many have disliked this. Contingencies do put a bit of chaos into the cosmos. But you can have a sort of adventure in Darwin's jungle that you cannot have in Newton's clock. This openness brings risk and often misfortune, but it sometimes adds excitement. Here nature's intelligibility, aesthetic beauty, dependability and unity are checked by the presence of spontaneity and contest, and this can sometimes be valued too.

Eventually, as a product of chance mixed with natural stabilities and with evolutionary trends that we dimly understand, living things gain a partial integrity to go on their own. Causality is not here altogether denied, but it is put to a pliable organic, rather than a mechanistic use, as a self-caused, functional organism seeks helps and avoids hurts in a mixedly stable and contingent environment. Psychical, deliberate freedom seems largely to be reserved for persons, but this capacity evolved out of choice-like precedents in the proto-psychologies of animal behavior. A nearsighted person will value only the climaxing, epiphenomenal human freedom, but a farsighted person may cherish these lesser precedents, if only as a glowing of what is fully ignited in humans. That a lioness is "born free" is part of the romance of nature, not of science, but this does not make her freedom any less real. Such poetry, again, helps us to get at the facts. Indeed, as even scientists better observe such animals, and trace their kinships with us, it becomes increasingly difficult to say why we should value human freedom so much, and animal freedom so little.

Nor are these features of constancy and contingency in nature beyond our capacity to affect them. One of our fears is that technology with its manipulations and pollutants, including radioactive ones, will destabilize long-enduring ecosystems; another is that unabated human growth will transgress virtually the whole domain of natural, spontaneous wildness; another is lest we should make the Earth a bit less autonomous by losing snail darters. Alas, we sometimes hate to stem even inanimate wildness, and the Little Tennessee River was among the last really wild rivers in the East. A river is, of course, free only in the sense that it is unconstrained, for it is without chance or options in its flow. It has none of those organic features of animate freedom that preface our own. Still, the thoughts that come when pondering a really ancient river flowing on forever unhindered are thoughts deep enough to make us wonder whether we humans have abused our freedom in deciding to dam one of the last of such streams.

DIALECTICAL VALUE

We are not really bounded by our skin, but life proceeds within an environmental theater across a surface of dialectic. The leg muscles are the largest in the body, and we need room to roam down by the river or along the seashore. The hands have evolved for grasping natural things, but so has the brain, and sentient experience underruns mental life. The crafting of an arrow point, a rifle, or a rocket is an environmental exchange. Society and artifacts are also requisite for mind, as is abstract thought, but nature is the most fundamental foil and foundation for mind, and this diffuses the human/natural and the value/fact line. Culture is carved out *against* nature but carved out *of* nature, and this is not simple to handle valuationally. Superficially, as far as nature is antagonistic and discomforting, it has disvalue. Even here a subjectivist must take care lest nature gain objective value first on the negative side of the field, only later to require it positively. We cannot count the hurts in nature as objectively bad unless we are willing to count its helps as objectively good.

With deeper insight, we do not always count environmental conductance as good and environmental resistance as bad, but the currents of life flow in their interplay. An environment that was entirely hostile would slay us; life could never have appeared within it. An environment that was entirely irenic would stagnate us; human life could never have appeared there either. All our culture, in which our classical humanity consists, and all our science, in which our modern humanity consists, has originated in the face of oppositional nature. Nature insists that we work, and this laboring and even suffering is its fundamental economic pressure. The pioneer, pilgrim, explorer, and settler loved the frontier for the challenge and discipline that put fiber into the American soul. One reason we lament the passing of wilderness is that we do not want entirely to tame this aboriginal element in which our genius was forged.

But this is of a piece with the larger natural process of conflict and resolution. Half the beauty of life comes out of it, as do the yellow flowers of those nearly extinct louseworts or the exquisite nautilus shell secreted against its environment. The cougar's fang sharpens the deer's sight, the deer's fleet-footedness shapes a more supple lioness. We admire this element of fight even in the maimed and blasted, even in the inanimate as with the gnarled timberline fir. The coming of Darwin is often thought to have ruined nature's harmonious architectures, but the struggles he posits, if sometimes overwhelming, are not always valueless. None of life's heroic quality is possible without this dialectical stress. Take away the friction, and would the structures stand? Would they move? And when we recognize how we humans are emplaced within such stress, do we then say that we only wrest values from valueless nature, or has this necessary dialectical context of life and of mind no value? That we should struggle against storm and winter is not here denied, nor that we may need to oppose wolves and thistles, rattlesnakes and the malaria mosquito. But we add that we can respect the alien not only in its autonomous otherness, but even in its stimulus, provocation, and opposition. The hardest lesson in all ethics is to learn to love one's enemies.

SACRAMENTAL VALUE

Nature generates poetry, philosophy, and religion, not less than science, and at its deepest educational capacity we are awed and humbled by staring into the stormy surf or the midnight sky, by peering down at the reversing protoplasmic stream in a creeping myxomycete plasmodium. Like the theories of science, these values do not lie on the empirical surfaces of nature, though prompted there, but are found more deeply in asking for the realities to which the phenomena point, for the universals that the particulars instantiate, but now taking things as signs, or sacraments, of meaning. The *significance* of nature is one of the richest assignments of mind, and this requires detection, imagination, participation, and decision. It forces us at length to ask about the significance of the observing mind itself, the most complex of nature's projects. Those thoughts struck in contemplation of nature are just thoughts about who and where we are, about the life and death that nature hands us, and our appropriate conduct in this environment. This exceeds not only applied but even strict science; yet the purer a naturalist's inquiry is into the constitution of the universe, the more likely he is to enjoy this further search for philosophical experiences generated as nature is met.

If we may put it so, nature is a philosophical resource, as well as a scientific, recreational, aesthetic, or economic one. We are programmed to ask why, and the natural dialectic is the cradle of our spirituality. Humans are symbolic beings, which might be thought to divorce rational thought from the natural world, but the mind has for millenia evolved in association with nature, and we always interact with nature to discover and to create those symbols by which we understand. In metaphysics, we puzzle over whether it is best to conceive of nature as an organism, a jungle, an egg, a machine, or a mind-informing matter, models drawn from our experiences of nature and of its dynamisms and products. In religion, the fundamental themes of life and death are both natural givens. For some, the natural history is most fundamentally in suffering, but even they must ask whether it is not of more value for life to be tragic than for it not to be, or to be nothing. But others hope in some blessed, sacred point; and bread, water, wine, paths, fatherhood, motherhood, mountains, rivers, light, and darkness are not incidentally among our richest sacramental elements.

We cannot escape confrontation with nature; still, modern life can be lived at such remove from this naturalness that our wisdom is artificially led astray. The wilderness is as necessary as the university for our valuational education, and we can sometimes value snail darters sacramentally rather than economically, just because in their wildness they have a different sort of generating power from those machines that would exterminate them. The struggling life essence emerging overlaid on physical existence, the arrival of intelligence and whether it has any evolutionary point, the intellectual adventure in beholding the natural scene, the complementarity of spirit and matter—these remain puzzles never completely worked out, for we are always entering deeper waters than we can fathom. We can count that a disvalue; nature outgoes and disappoints us. We can even count it a value that nature breeds a creative discontent, keeps a distance from us, supplies a further question with each answer, and is so rich and demanding as to be at length inaccessible in the whole, knowable only in part. We are kept pilgrims and pioneers on a frontier, and to travel hopefully is better than to arrive. Meanwhile, this much as least we do value: that nature is endlessly stimulating to the mind, and bores only the ignorant or the insensitive.

NOTES

For critical discussion see Ernest Partridge, "Nature as a Moral Resource," *Environmental Ethics* 6(1984):101-130.

1. See the *Endangered Species Technical Bulletin* (U.S. Fish and Wildlife Service), May, June, July 1978, January, October, November 1979, May and September 1980.

Harold J. O'Conner, Endangered Species Program Manager for the Fish and Wildlife Service, reports, "We are afraid that the chances of long-term survival for these transplanted populations are not good" (*Bulletin,* October 1979). Former governor Ray Blanton is quoted in *Time,* 26 June 1978, p. 14. Other populations of the darter, then unknown, were subsequently discovered.

2. Quoting R. W. Scott in *World Oil,* January 1977, p. 5. See the *Endangered Species Technical Bulletin,* July 1978.

3. See Karl Marx, *Grundrisse* (New York: Random House, 1973), p. 366.

4. T. D. Brock, "Life at High Temperatures," *Science* 158 (1967): 1012-19.

5. J. Chapman and J. M. Adovasio, "Textile and Basketry Impressions from Icehouse Bottom, Tennessee," *American Antiquity* 42 (1977): 620-25. The quotation is from the testimony to the House Subcommitee on Fisheries and Wildlife Conservation made by Jefferson Chapman, anthropologist at the University of Tennessee, on 20 June 1978.

6. Aristotle, *Poetics* 1451b.

7. Gifford Pinchot, *Breaking New Ground* (New York: Harcourt, Brace and Company, 1947), p. 103.

8. P. G. K. Kahn and S. M. Pompea, "Nautiloid Growth Rhythms and Dynamical Evolution of the Earth-Moon System," *Nature* 275 (1978): 606-11.

6

Are Values in Nature
Subjective or Objective?

HOW SHOULD WE VALUE NATURE?

"Conceive yourself, if possible, suddenly stripped of all the emotions with which your world now inspires you, and try to imagine it *as it exists,* purely by itself, without your favorable or unfavorable, hopeful or apprehensive comment. It will be almost impossible for you to realize such a condition of negativity and deadness. No one portion of the universe would then have importance beyond another; and the whole collection of its things and series of its events would be without significance, character, expression, or perspective. Whatever of value, interest, or meaning our respective worlds may appear embued with are thus pure gifts of the spectator's mind."[1] William James' stark portrayal of the utterly valueless world, suddenly transfigured as a gift of the human coming, has proved prophetic of a dominant twentieth-century attitude. Since he wrote, we have spent upward of a century trying to conceive of ourselves as the sole entities bringing value to an otherwise sterile environment. The effort has pervaded science and technology, humanism and existentialism, ethics and economics, metaphysics and analytic philosophy.

John Laird protested, "There is beauty . . . in sky and cloud and sea, in lilies and in sunsets, in the glow of bracken in autumn and in the enticing greenness of a leafy spring. Nature, indeed, is infinitely beautiful, and she seems to wear her beauty as she wears colour or sound. Why then should her beauty belong to us rather than to her?"[2] But Wilhelm Windelband agreed with James: value "is never found in the object itself as a property. It consists in a relation to an appreciating mind, which satisfies the desires of its will or reacts in feelings of pleasure upon the stimulation of the environment. Take away will and feeling and there is no such thing as value."[3] R. B. Perry continued with what became the prevailing opinion: "The silence of the desert is without value, until some wanderer finds it lonely and terrifying; the cataract, until some human sensibility

---

Reprinted by permission from *Environmental Ethics* 4(1982):125-151.

finds it sublime, or until it is harnessed to satisfy human needs. Natural substances . . . are without value until a use is found for them, whereupon their value may increase to any desired degree of preciousness according to the eagerness with which they are coveted." "Any object, whatever it be, acquires value when any interest, whatever it be, is taken in it."[4]

But with the environmental turn, so surprising and pressing in the final quarter of our century, this subjectivism in values needs review. Ecology has a way of pulling into alternative focus the exchange between the organic self and the surrounding world. This can lead us to re-view what we have been learning in evolutionary biology and developmental biochemistry. I argue here that in the orientation of these recent sciences the subjective account of valuing becomes grossly strained. Living, as we say, "far from nature," it is remarkable to find as one of the insistent questions of our advanced civilization: how should we value nature? An ecological crisis has forced the question upon us. Environmental and evolutionary science suggest some different answers; and yet no science is quite prepared to handle the question.

Our valuational quandary is not merely a muddle into which philosophers have gotten us, although it is perhaps the last legacy of Cartesianism. Valuational incompetence is the soft underbelly of hard science. Something gone sour at the fact/value distinction is one of the roots of the ecological crisis. Values, it is typically said, form no part of nature, but only come with the human response to the world. This seems at once objective about nature and humane toward persons, but it also yields a value structure in the scientific West more anthropocentric by several orders of magnitude than were any of the value systems of the classical, Oriental, and primitive world views that have succumbed before it. But this more sophisticated view is, I think, wise in its own conceits.

My strategy in what follows is to fight a way through how we know what we know (what philosophers call epistemological issues surrounding the terms *subjective* and *objective*) in order to reach the state of affairs in the real world and to be able to defend the existence of value there (what philosophers call ontological issues surrounding subjectivity and objectivity). In doing this, I keep the whole discussion as close to science as I can, while demanding a full-blooded, no-nonsense account of the phenomenon of value in, and valuing of, the natural world. Earlier on, I admit to some inescapable blending of the subjective and objective, but later on, after this admission, I defend all the objectivity I can for natural value.

PRIMARY, SECONDARY, AND TERTIARY QUALITIES

Galileo's astronomy forced us to convert from a literal to a perspectival understanding of the claim that the sun is setting. His physics gave us the distinction, elaborated by Locke, between *primary* and *secondary* qualities. A secondary quality is observer-dependent, manufactured out of the primary motions of matter. Color is an experiential conversion of photon radiation; taste and smell are molecular operations. This account was problematic philosophically (as Berkeley quickly saw), but it nevertheless became entrenched. The colors and sounds that Laird found nature to wear seemed rather to go with the beholding of it, reducible in the world stripped of a perceiver to matter in motion. Coached by these theories, what was then to be said of value? If the sunset is not literally a setting sun, not even red, then surely it is not literally beautiful. Samuel Alexander proposed that values were *tertiary* qualities.[5] Humans agree about redness, owing to their having the same organs (apart from color blindness, etc.), but value appraisals require an interpretive judgment twice removed from the qualities actually there.

By this account, we have no organs to taste, touch, see, or smell value. So it must originate at a deeper mental level. We have no options in judging length or redness (although there are aberrations). Such experiences happen to us without any liberty to refuse them. The primary and secondary qualities are always there in the scope of consciousness. They perhaps fall into the background, but they never turn off during perception. Value judgments, by contrast, have to be decided. Beauty or utility are things we must attend to. When our minds turn aside to other thoughts, though still perceiving the object, such values entirely disappear from consciousness. We can use instruments—meter sticks, spectroscopes, thermometers, mass spectrometers—on primary and secondary qualities. Something there leaves records during photography, electrophoresis, or chromatography, puzzle though we may about the experiential translation of 6800 angstroms into redness, or how the shape of the fructose molecule, interlocked with receptors on the tongue, is experienced as sweetness. Both primary and secondary qualities are in this sense empirical, or natural. But valuational qualities do not show up on any instruments or organs devised or conceivable. This leads some, who still look for properties in the object, to think of value as an objective, but *nonnatural,* that is, *nonempirical,* quality. But, finding nothing that produces consensus or proves researchable, most judges become convinced that these tertiary qualities are overlays, not really there in the natural world. Rainbow-like, only more so, they are gifts of the spectator's mind.

But next the puzzle deepens. Just as philosophers were reaching this consensus, a revolution in physics threw overboard the primary, supposedly objective, qualities as well. Einstein showed length, mass, time, and motion to be observer dependent. They too are matters of perspective, although not so much of decision as of bodily relations. At the microlevel, Heisenberg's uncertainty principle forbade any precise hold on momentum and location. Quantum mechanics left a nonsubstantial nonpicture of nature as a gauzy haze of interpenetrating wave fields, where none of the common-sense qualities made much sense, and where even space and time grew vague. It was alarming to learn how much our mental constructions enter into the descriptions of physical science, how much the observer influences the natural phenomenon by his instrumentation or sense modality. Objectivity vanishes more and more as phenomena get smaller and smaller.

Summing this up, Einstein remarked that he had taken "the last remainder of physical objectivity" from the concepts of space and time.[6] John Wheeler wrote, "A much more drastic conclusion emerges: . . . *there is no such thing as spacetime in the real world of quantum physics.* . . . It is an approximation idea, an extremely good approximation under most circumstances, but always only an approximation."[7] Werner Heisenberg wrote, "When we speak of a picture of nature provided us by contemporary exact science, we do not actually mean any longer a picture of nature, but rather a picture of our relation to nature. . . . Science no longer is in the position of observer of nature, but rather recognizes itself as part of the interplay between man and nature."[8] Before this heady sort of runaway relativism, lost in a great and unspeakable plasma, the question about values being objectively "out there" hardly seems discussable. The subjectivists have won all the chips. Even physics, that bedrock science that gave great promise of "telling it like it is," has withdrawn entirely from that kind of claim. What hope is there for value theory to do anything more than to record what appears and seems? Any bolder claim is primitive naiveté.

But when we regain our wits, such relativism can be kept under more logical control. Contrary to first appearances, it can even support certain objective aspects in value judgments. For all that we have yet said, there is just as little or as much reason to think that physics is objective as that value theory is. Judgments about what *is* (mass, space, color) have proved observer-dependent and indistinguishable from judgments about what *is good* (pleasure, beauty, grandeur). Subjectivity has eaten up everything, even the fact/value distinction. But as a matter of fact, unless we are insane, we all believe that we know some nonsubjective things about the physical world. Our judgments are not free of perceptual modification of the incoming signals, but neither, *pace* Einstein, do they lack a very large "remainder of physical objectivity." At this everyday level, we do stand in some picturing relation to nature. The key is provided in Wheeler's qualification of "no such thing" with "an extremely good approximation."

"There is a hawk in the spruce beside that granite boulder." This judgment fades out on subatomic scales, diffusing away if we migrate far enough from our native range. Through optical microscopy we take photographs yet in color of garnet crystals from the granite. But on the shrinking scale of electron microscopy we begin to remind ourselves that the color (despite the black and white micrograph!) is no longer relevant, while the length and shape in crystal lattices is still pictorial. Smaller still, we become aware that we have only models of the electrons and protons that compose the granite. Shape and location dissolve into cloudy wave fields. We allow too that the weight and shape of the boulder would appear differently to an observer passing at nearly the speed of light.

Even the data from the other physical levels shows up objectively, though. The space-time dilations affect clocks, cameras, meters, one's body, and everything that ages. The nonspecifiable fuzziness of electron momentum and location registers in the bands on paper recording charts. These things are not entirely inventions of the mind, although they reveal our perspectival and theoretical reach to the microscopic and astronomical levels.

But, if I restrict the scope of my claims, none of this affects the fact that we know something objectively, factually about hawks, spruce trees, and boulders. We do not know entirely all that there is at every level, nor with an objectivity that is free from subjective contribution. But agnosticism and relativism about the ultimate structure of matter does not prevent objective knowing in a middle-level sense. The breakdown of a concept, claim, or function when extrapolated does not prevent its being quite true in the restricted range that it well serves. Our partial knowing need not be illusory or false, although it is approximate and perspectival. Here value judgments too can be short-scope claims about what is the case in the mundane world. The clue provided by Alexander's word *tertiary* is not something about twice-compounded observer-dependence. It is about participation at the middle structural levels where we live. The ownership feature in value judgments is important, but we need to think of value judgments as genuine, involved, if limited, claims about the world. Afterward, we can inquire how far they can be pressed away from our native range. They do not attach to bare primary or secondary levels, but to high-level constructions of matter with which we are in exchange—initially in common experience and afterward in the sciences of natural history. Just as we are getting incoming commands from "out there" about length, color, hawks, and trees, so too we are getting some commands about value. We start with these as native range judgments, not as absolute ones. They are phenomenal claims, not noumenal ones. This much makes them locally objective, although it leaves unresolved how deep they run.

JUDGMENTS ABOUT TYPES, FUNCTIONS, AND VALUES

A dose of candor from the biological sciences can help cure us of the dizzying revelations of physics. Notice, for instance, that before the panorama of an ecosystem, the primary, secondary, tertiary distinction cannot do much explanatory work. If one asks whether a thing is alive, whether it is a seed, or edible, a moss, or a microbe, and tries to answer with the vocabulary of primary, secondary, and tertiary qualities, however much compounded, one can only stammer. In order to get at the richness of the natural world, we need to make many judgments for which we have directly no organs and can make no instruments, judgments to which we must attend by decision and interpretation. Here most of our scientific judgments are third and higher order, but we nevertheless believe that through them we are accurately corresponding with the natural world. When we pass to judgments of value, we do not need to consider them radically different in kind. This erodes the dogma that factual judgments are objective while value judgments are subjective.

The *Picea* (spruce) and *Buteo* (hawk) genetic sets, for instance, are full of information. The information is long-lived, reproducing itself by means of amino acid replacement across millions of years, a kind of fire which outlasts the sticks that feed it. But is this a compounded primary, secondary, or tertiary quality? The self-maintaining know-how is there independently of our observation, unmodified by our sense perception, primary in Locke's sense. It is nonsubjective and nonsecondary. It is quite as real as atoms, if also a bit nonsubstantial and fluid. To deny reality to this information on the basis of anything learned in physics is like denying that a newspaper picture contains information, because, under the lens, it turns out to be nothing but black dots. Objectively encapsulated in informational molecules, the spruce and hawk have a technique for making a way through the terrain they inhabit, pragmatic facts for their life projects. Yet these DNA-based facts are not aggregated primary, secondary, or even tertiary qualities, but involve advanced, emergent compositional levels.

Meanwhile, we humans who make these judgments begin with at-hand uncontested experience, and via science move from our native experiential level to elaborate, often unsettled theories about structural levels and their histories. We say that the genetic information has accumulated in stages. Some of the earliest information was the code for glycolysis, evolving 3.5 billion years ago, before there was atmospheric oxygen. The citric acid cycle came later, cashing in on eighteen times as much energy as did glycolysis. Somewhere photosynthesis evolved so that *Picea* can capture directly the energy of sunlight, with oxidative phosphorylation subsequently arising to use the atmosphere as an electron sink, improving the efficiency of the citric acid cycle. The spruce and the hawk evolved under the pro-life pressures of a selective system operating over genetic mutations, fitting them into an ecological community. In all this, we are making highly educated guesses describing the objective facts, estimates that will be partly revised, partly conserved as science advances. But most of us do not believe that we inevitably become less objective and more subjective, less primary and more secondary or tertiary as we do this. World building does go on in the mind of the beholder, as we shape up theories over experience. But world building also takes place out there. We find the information or energy flow only by attending with deliberate focus of mind. But the mind does not contribute these features because it must model them by careful attention and decision. To the contrary, we discover richer qualities in nature.

What happens now if we introduce some value judgments? We might speak of the value of nutrients, of food pyramids, of the information keying glycolysis and photosynthesis, of the exploratory value of mutations, with the "good" ones conserved because they have survival value. We might speak objectively of the value of the hawk's protective coloration (even admitting the secondary nature of color). The word *value* easily attaches to life functions as these are known at and theorized for the middle ranges of experience. We need not yet speak of *human* values, not even of experienced values, but some notion of presubjective value seems to belong to these "going concerns" called living organisms as they move through the environment. Value here attaches to a whole form of life and is not just resident in the detached parts as elementary units. It overleaps although it is instantiated in the individual. It appears in a holistic cross play where neutral, lesser valued, and even disvalued parts may assume transformed value in a larger matrix. Value emerges in pronounced forms at advanced structural levels and may not be visible as a Lockean primary or secondary quality.

But as a "tertiary" quality, value can be embedded with the facts, quite as real as the information organisms contain, sometimes just the same thing differently described. Some will object that biological "value" ought to be kept in scare quotes, since this is not what we mean by value as a quality in experienced life. One then has to trace descriptively each of the natural selections culminating in the central nervous system. One can rejoice that value emerges epiphenomenally at the very last in consciousness, but one must judge value to be absent from the incubating steps. In all the precedents we should speak more carefully, using the term *biofunction* instead.

The hemoglobin molecule is structurally evolved from and much advanced over the myoglobin molecule. It is very much "better" (equals: more functional) at oxygen transport, having allosteric properties that make it a sort of microcomputer in its capacities to respond to the oxygen exchange needs of the blooded organism, as with the hawk in flight. Lubert Stryer, a biochemist, says of it, emphatically, *"In the step from myoglobin to hemoglobin, we see the emergence of a macromolecule capable of perceiving information from its environment."* [9] But a cautious value theorist will warn this chemist not to attach any "importance" to this, not to say that this step is of any value. To be really hard-nosed here, this "information perceiving" is subjective poetry, only a readback from our own experience. One might allow that it was "interesting," but not that any "interests" of the life forms in which hemoglobin evolved were at stake.

But all this careful reservation of value as a gift of the spectator's mind now seems arbitrary and narrow. As soon as we have described hemoglobin evolution, we are ready to judge it a vital and valuable step upward in the advance of life. The phenomenon of things "being important" does not arise with our awareness; it is steadily there in quantized discoveries all along the way. Galileo and Locke first subverted value theory with their mechanistic reduction of secondary to primary qualities, leaving us only an objective matter in motion. It was then compoundly subverted by Einstein's relativity, by quantum mechanics, indeterminacy, and nonpicturability. These sciences probe toward ultimacy with genius and skeptical rigor. They work in the substrata with simplicity, and so leave out all but the thousandth part of a historical eventfulness which we daily experience and which other sciences do teach us to appreciate. Only by the sort of gestalt switch that can be provided by sciences at the other end of the spectrum, such as evolutionary biochemistry or ecology, dealing with the richness of natural history, can we begin to get value theory recovered from its failure of nerve.

All judgments mix theory with fact. Even the simple cases close at hand involve elements of linguistic and conceptual decision about what to call what, and where to draw the lines. An Iroquois might view the hawk as his totem, or the tree and boulder as the haunt of a spirit. Certainly the scientific judgments about natural kinds (granite, *Picea, Buteo*) are theory-laden. It is admittedly difficult, as philosophers of science know, to say why we prefer science to superstition, but it has to do, at least in part, with our persuasion that the one is a better window into the way things are. The interpreter imports something of himself into the interpreted. But the fact that we use theory-laden decisions about natural operations does not stand in the way of description; it rather makes it possible. To know things as they objectively are, without observer bias, is a celebrated but elusive goal of natural science, a goal impossible of full attainment, but toward which we make progress. A physicist estimates the mass of a boulder, a mineralogist knows its composition; a biologist distinguishes spruce from fir; an ecologist describes an ecosystem. All are aided, not confused by their theories. *Mass, granite, Picea,* and *homeostasis* are technical terms that serve as descriptive forms. The mind answers to its object of study; with progressive reformation we approximately understand what is there.

In this context, judgments of natural value hardly differ from judgments of natural fact. In one sense, the subjectivists are in full command again and can insist that none of our seemingly objective seeing is done without wearing cultural eyeglasses. But, as before, the objectivist can reassert the common world of experience and the impressive observational force of science. We all do believe that in our native ranges humans know something of the structural levels of nature. We believe that scientific progress gives further, if approximate, access into what these natural types and processes are like. We judge between science and folklore, between good and bad science. When we then pass to judge whether this natural kind is good, or that life process has value, we are merely continuing the effort to map reality. One has to decide whether this is a *Picea,* as one has to decide whether this is a *lovely Picea.* On occasion, the judgment about value may be easier than is the judgment about fact. One can need more theory to "see" the information and energy flow, or the phylogenetic relationships, than one does to "see" the utility or beauty. That such interpretive judgments are subject to revision does not mean that value, in distinction from other natural properties, lies only in the mental state and is not an event in the space-time track. The constructions we see always depend upon the instructions with which we look; yet the evolving mind is also controlled by the matter it seeks to investigate. This is true alike in science and in valuation.

We can be thrilled by a hawk in the wind-swept sky, by the rings of Saturn, the falls of Yosemite. We can admire the internal symmetry of a garnet crystal or appreciate the complexity of the forest humus. All these experiences come mediated by our cultural education; some are made possible by science. An Iroquois would have variant experiences, or none at all. But these experiences have high elements of givenness, of finding something thrown at us, of successful observation. The "work" of observation is in order to understand the better. In value theory too we have as much reason to think that our appreciative apparatus is sometimes facilitating, not preventing, getting to know what is really there.

Some natural values are of the common-sense kind and nearly universal to cultures, as with the taste of an apple, the pleasant warmth of the spring sun, the striking colors of the fall. Even though these experiences come culturally bound, some natural impact here is shared by Iroquois and Nobel prize winner. Experience is required, but something is there which one is fitted for and fitting into; some good is transmitted and is productive of the experience. The native enjoying, just because it is relational to nature, but so universal among humans, faithfully attests what is there. It is precisely our experiential position as humans-in-nature that gives us factual access to events. Other natural values are opened up to us by scientific culture, by lenses and experiments. It is precisely our advanced knowledge, setting us apart from nature in theoretical abstraction over it, which takes us deeper into nature. Sometimes the purest revelations of science put us in a better position to evaluate these things as they objectively are.

NATURAL VALUING AS ECOLOGICAL-RELATIONAL

I next present an explanation sketch of valuing consistent with natural history. Our inquiry is about the kind of natural value met with in unlabored contexts, as in pure rather than applied science, in contemplative outdoor recreation rather than in industry, in ecology rather than in economics. We are not considering, for instance, how molybdenum has value as an alloy of steel, a use that it does not have in spontaneous nature. Further, we should be cautioned against thinking that nature has some few kinds of value, or no disvalue. Nature is a plural system with values unevenly distributed and counterthrusting. Like the meanings in life, values too may come piecemeal and occasionally. Still, they come regularly enough for us to wonder whether we are coping with some value-tending in the system.

Consider a causal sequence (A, B, C, D) leading to the production of an event associated with natural value (E_{nv}) which produces an event of experienced value (E_{xv}), perhaps of the beauty in a waterfall or the wealth of life in a tidal zone (figure 1).

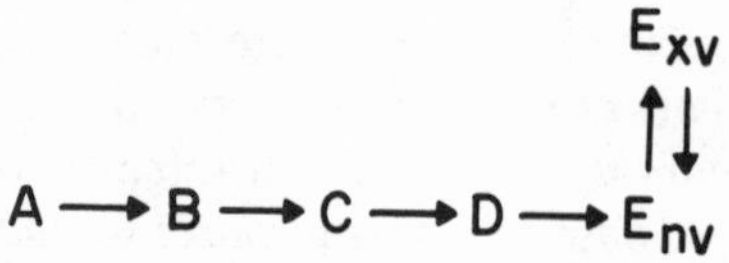

$$E_{xv}$$
$$\uparrow\downarrow$$
$$A \longrightarrow B \longrightarrow C \longrightarrow D \longrightarrow E_{nv}$$

Figure 1.

Our consciousness also responds to the waterfall or estuary, so that we need a reverse arrow (↓) making the affair relational. One is first tempted to say that value does not lie in either polar part, but is generated in their relations. Like science or recreation, valuing before nature is an interactive affair.

But with this, more has been reallocated to the natural world than may at first be recognized. The act of responding has been ecologically grounded. We pass from abstract, reductionist, analytic knowledge to a participant, holistic, synthetic account of humans in nature. The subjective self is not a polar opposite to objective nature, not in the dyadic relation suggested by the paired arrows. It is rather enclosed by its environment, so that the self values in environmental exchange, in the diagrammed case and in myriads of others (E'_{nv}, E''_{nv}) here only suggested (figure 2). The self has a semipermeable membrane.

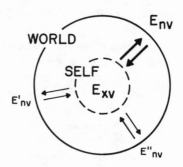

Figure 2.

The setting is a given, a datum of nature, even though the subject must respond in imaginatively resourceful ways. I see things out there in the "field" that I choose to value or disvalue. But on deeper examination I find myself, a valuing agent, located within the circumscribing field. I do not have the valued object in "my field," but find myself emplaced in a concentric field for valuing.

The whole possibility is among natural events, including the openness in my appraising. John Dewey remarked that "experience is *of* as well as *in* nature."[10] I say that valuing is *in* as well as *of* nature. What seems a dialectical relationship is an ecological one. We must now consider how the whole happening, subject and its valued object, occurs in a natural ambiance (figure 3).

When an ecologist remarks, "There goes a badger," he thinks not merely of morphology, as might a skin-in taxonomist. He has in mind a whole mosaic of functions, interconnections, food chains, a way of being embedded in a niche where the badger is what is environmentally. When a sociologist remarks, "There goes a vicar," he is not so much identifying a human as seeing a role in the

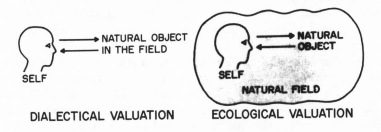

DIALECTICAL VALUATION   ECOLOGICAL VALUATION

Figure 3.

community. The being of a vicar, like that of badger, is a contextual affair. When a philosopher says, "There goes a valuer," he should not think of a happening inside the human in such a way as to forget how this is also an ecological event. The responsibility here is a response in our natural setting.

Add the fact that the valuing subject has itself evolved out of these surroundings. All the organs and feelings mediating value—body, senses, hands, brain, will, emotion—are natural products. Nature has thrown forward the subjective experiencer quite as much as the world that is objectively experienced. On the route behind us, at least, nature has been a personifying system. We are

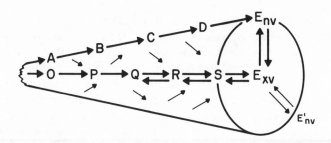

Figure 4.

where this track has been heading; we are perhaps its head, but we are in some sense tail. I next sketch a further productive sequence that generates the self *(S)* out of ancestral precedents *(O, P, Q, R)*, natural events in causal sequence, and here also place reverse, valuational arrows (←) indicating reactive elements that cultural and personal responses superadd to the natural basis of personality. I add an evolutionary time line to the holistic, ecological sketch (figure 4). Seen in broad historical scale, these lines go back to common beginnings, from which they become richer eventually to reach the experiencing self embraced by its environment. Diverse, simple, complex forms are all maintained in and by the ecosystemic pyramid, and there are many coordinating connections that we only suggest (↘). In such a picture, even though keeping the phenomenon of human valuing central, it is increasingly difficult to see valuing as isolated or even in dialectic. Values do not exist in a natural void, but rather in a natural womb.

The sudden switch in figure 1 from horizontal, merely causal arrows (   ), to a vertical, valuational arrow (↑) now seems too angular a contrast. How far experienced value is a novel emergent we need yet to inquire, but there has been the historical buildup toward value, and there is presently surrounding us the invitation to value. The first series would have been better sketched as it appears in figure 5.

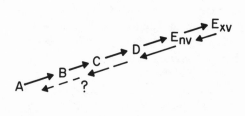

Figure 5.

The reason for the new sketch is that it is difficult to say why the arrows of valuational response should value only the immediately productive natural event and not include at least some of the precedents, with unshown coordinates as well. The last event is presently at hand, and we may have had no consciousness of value during former events. But in an evolutionary ecosystem nothing happens at all once and *per se;* everything is embedded in a developing process.

A critic might complain, and perhaps fiercely, that I have diagrammatically sketched out single sweep lines while the real world is a much more tumultuous affair, where the valuational and constructive lines are not vectors, but a near chaos of causes and happenstance, luck and struggle, serendipity and emergence, with much waste and little worth. The diagram screens off the heterogeneous and alien character of the ingredients of value. I have straightened out strands that do not lie straight in the actual world, as though I had never heard of Darwin and his jungle-like world.

There is truth in the complaint. We may wish conservatively to keep our judgments short-scope claims. Values immediately experienced might run back to some nonvaluable base out of which they have emerged. Analogously, living organisms once emerged out of lifeless nature. A present good might have come out of historically mixed values and disvalues, as when a little good comes from much evil. Natural values might be oddly occasional, though the causal sequence is continuous. Nature is not homogenized, but unevenly located, and so too with its values.

But meanwhile value is sometimes there before us, strikingly so, and we will sometimes be valuing contributors toward value, past or present, seen at whatever level. If we ever do extrapolate to try a systematic overview of what is going on, the likeliest account will find some programmatic evolution toward value, and this not because it ignores Darwin, but just because it heeds his principle of natural selection, and deploys this into a selection upslope toward higher values, at least along some trends within natural operations. How do we humans come to be charged up with values, if there was and is nothing in nature charging us up so? We prefer not to believe in the special creation of values, nor in their dumbfounding epigenesis. We let them evolve. Nor is our account merely a selection from the chaotic data of nature. Rather our interpretation notices how there is a world selection of events over evolutionary time (without denying other neutral or disvalued events) that builds toward the ecological valuing in which we now participate. Perhaps we will not want to say that this had to happen. But it did happen.

We can now view primary and secondary qualities holistically from above, drawn into an ecosystem at much higher structural levels, rather than viewing the ecosystem reductionistically from below as being merely aggregated lesser qualities. We have, so to speak, an ecology of atoms and molecules. These are not described as microparticles *per se,* but as events in their neighborhoods, valued in macroscopic waterfalls and tidal basins. Genetics and biochemistry are drawn into the drama of natural history.

Many evolutionary and ecological connections are shared between ourselves as experiencers and the natural events we appraise. These bring a new orientation toward the presence of photosynthesis, the appearance of hemoglobin, or the genetic keying of information. We discover that decomposers and predators have value objectively in the ecosystem, and then realize that our own standing as subjective valuers atop the biotic pyramid is impossible except in consequence of decomposition and predation. An interlocking kinship suggests that values are not merely in the mind but at hand in the world. We start out valuing nature like land appraisers figuring out what it is worth to us, only to discover that we are part and parcel of this nature we appraise. The earthen landscape has upraised this landscape appraiser. We do not simply bestow value on nature; nature also conveys value to us.

NATURAL VALUE AND CONSCIOUSNESS

If the experience of valuing is relational, what do we say of the product, value? We must clarify the connection between experience and its objective base, since, under prevailing theories, it is widely held that the phrase "unexperienced value" is a contradiction in terms, with "experienced value" a tautology. This assumption fits the existential notice that value is not received as the conclusion of an argument, or by the indifferent observation of a causal series. A value or disvalue is whatever has got some bite to it. In the case of bare knowing, the knower has an internal *representation* of what is there, perhaps calmly so. Valuing requires more, an internal *excitation.* That brings emoting, and perhaps this marriage of a subject to its object gives birth to value. It enters and exits with awareness.

Of course, if natural things have values, we cannot conceivably learn this without experiences by which we are let in on them. With every such sharing there comes a caring, and this may seem to proscribe objective neutrality. But it only prescribes circumspect inquiry. All natural science is built on the experience of nature, but this does not entail that its descriptions, its "facts," just are those experiences. All valuing of nature is built on experience too, but that does not entail that its descriptions, its "values," are just those experiences. Valuing could be a further, nonneutral way of knowing about the world. We might suppose that value is not empirical, since we have no organs and can make no instruments for it. But it could just as well be an advanced kind of experience where a more sophisticated, living instrument is required to register natural properties. Value must be lived through, *experienced,* but so as to discern the character of the surroundings one is living through.

I next work toward this conclusion by finding inadequate some lesser accounts.

Natural Value as an Epiphenomenon

Pollen is not an allergen "by nature," for nasal irritation is no part of its reproductive role. But certain pollens "by accident" evoke mistakes in susceptible immunological systems. The allergy reaction is thus a disvalue that bears no meaningful connection with the natural operation. Analogously, some natural events can (to coin a term) be "valugens," evoking positive responses without meaningful basis in a spontaneous nature. We react with a sense of beauty before the swirled flow in a pegmatite exposed in a rock cut. Again, we are enchanted by the mist sweeping in over the dell. But this is a kind of mis-taking of what is essentially there. Value is adventitious to nature, more fiction than fact, more dream than description, poetry, not prose, real in consciousness, unreal in the world.

But while partially useful, this account, if taken for the whole, leaves the human valuing subject eccentric to his world. Causal connections obtain and the relational context is required, but value is a fluke without intelligible support in its stimulus.[11] In causal cases, one may be content with any kind of *how* explanation that hooks up antecedent and subsequent events. But in the case of value one would hope for an explanation more or less logically adequate to the effect. Yet so far from enlightening us about *why* value appears, this is in fact a nonexplanation. Value is an epigenetic anomaly.

Natural Value as an Echo

Strolling on the beach, I examine dozens of pieces of driftwood, discarding all but one. This I varnish and frame for its pleasing curvatures. I value this piece because it happened to mirror the sweep and line of my subjective preference; the rest did not. Nature once in a while chances to echo my tastes. We still have an element of accident, but we can make more sense of origins. Value does not come in pleasantly allergic reaction, but rather as a reflection of my own compositions. This led Samuel Alexander to claim here that we, not nature, are the artists. "The nature we find beautiful is not bare nature as she exists apart from us but nature as seen by the artistic eye. . . . We find nature beautiful not because she is beautiful herself but because we select from nature and combine, as the artist does more plainly when he works with pigments. . . . Nature does live for herself without us to share her life. But she is not beautiful without us to unpiece her and repiece. . . . Small wonder that we do not know that we are artists unawares. For the appreciation of nature's beauty is unreflective; and even when we reflect, it is not so easy to recognize that the beauty of a sunset or a pure color is a construction on our part and an interpretation."[12]

But the more we reflect the less easy it becomes to see value as nothing but a reflection. Perhaps this is sometimes so, but as a general theoretical account we have to reckon with the felicitous echoing capacity of nature, with its stimulus and surprise. Both the epiphenomenon and echo models are unecological, not sufficiently interactive and functional. To say that when enjoying blackberries in the spring sun we are participating in anomalous value seems biologically odd. The cardinal on the wing and the *Trillium* in bloom have grace, coloration, symmetry that are structurally related to flight, flowering, and life cycles. Is the beauty here only by our selecting, not in our sensing valuative overtones that go with biological function? If I am choosing shells rather than driftwood, the color, sweep, and vault is better realized in one than in another, but seems a nisus in them all. Each attempt is an architecture under genetic control.

We are endowed with naturally selected capacities to value such things. Is the whole evolution of valuing an irrational, serendipitous afterglow? Perhaps the immunological system makes mistakes, but its development is incredible except as protection against hurts in the world. The valuational system may have fortuitous benefits, but its presence can best be accounted for in terms of an inclusive fitness to helps in the world. It would be an odd benefit indeed if it did not really better fit us to our home niche. The echoing is most often working the other way around; the human valuer is reflecting what is actually there.

Natural Value as an Emergent

Emergent phenomena occur strikingly in nature, as when first life and afterward learning appeared where none before existed. Perhaps the valuing capacity emerges to create value out of mere potential? Value is a kind of fiery excitement, and no natural scene, however complex and splendid, can have value until the precursors of value are supplemented and thickened by the arrival of human interest. Value cannot be said to have happened until present as an event in consciousness. There must be the delivery of some kind of "charge" into the valued experience. We may have little sense of manufacture or decision, but still we furnish the required awareness. Like knowing, the process of valuing goes on in the conscious mind. Like knowledge, the product, value, only exists there.

I can now give an intelligible account of the objective precedents. They are not flukes, but fuel. The valuing experience, like combustion, does indeed feed on natural properties and proceeds in keeping with their potential. Though emergent, it is not adventitious. The waterfall, the cardinal, the columbine, the blackberry, the warming sun, glycolysis, photosynthesis—all have indeed their stimulating properties, and thus are rightly valued when they are valued, but not until then does value appear. Perhaps too, valuing can fail. But everything is potential until clinched in experience. Consciousness ignites what before were only combustible materials, and value lights up. The precondition for value need not itself be a value.

To say that wood is combustible means that wood will burn if ignited, although it never nears fire. But this is a predicate of objective potential; wood might ignite in the spontaneous course of nature. But to say that wood is valuable is a predicate of subjective potential. If a human subject appears in relation, wood can be valued. This sort of dispositional predicate can be realized only in human experience. Some exception can here be made for subhuman experience. Animals may not have aesthetic, moral, philosophical, or religious sensibilities. They may be incapable of normative discourse. But they can undergo pain and pleasure; they have interested concerns. To this extent, they own values. Valuing thus dilutes across the simplifying of the central nervous system, but, if we rely entirely on the emergent account, value is never extraneural. Where there are no centers of experience, valuing ceases and value vanishes.

But neither will this account do in explanation of the main body of natural values. While it may be true that some ranges of value emerge, like the capacity for joy or aesthetic experience, these are capstone goods, but are built on valuable substructures. There are values that only come with consciousness, but it does not follow that consciousness, when it brings its new values, confers all value and discovers none.

Natural Value as an Entrance

We can best appraise the emergent account in the light of another account where value is more generously allocated to the natural world. The arriving beholder enters into the surrounding scene; it enters him. There is a two-way entrance and resulting fulfillment. Subjective experience emerges to appreciate what was before unappreciated. But such valuing is a partnership and the free-standing objective partner cannot enjoin value upon the subjective partner if it has nothing to offer. Emergence is not the whole story; there is a joining of situational value. If emergence is a *dispositional* account, we can call this a more ecological, *positional* account.

An ecologist might say that the eater realizes the potential in blackberries, but he will equally say that the eater captures nutrients instituted functionally into the ecosystem. The experienced taste is an overlay on objective food chains. The eater is waking up in the midst of events that precede and exceed her awareness. The eating of the berries, like the burning of wood, is really a matter of formed energy throughput, a physical energy onto which life has been modulated. Initially received as solar input, nature has by photosynthesis locked this energy into cellulose and carbohydrates. When humans overtake it, energy previously there is transformed in the eating and ignition. This flow-through model is a more basic one than the model of emergence. The potential is to be conceived of as a kind of capital on which we can draw a check. But the check cashing does not entirely constitute the value, even though it may reconstitute it.

We ought not to forget the noblest step, but we ought not mistake the last step for the whole history. Valuing is not apart from the whole; it is a part in the whole. Value is not isolable into a miraculous epiphenomenon or echo, even though some valued events may be happenstance. It is systemically grounded in major constructive thrusts in nature. The most satisfactory account is an ecocentric model, one that recognizes the emergence of consciousness as a novel value, but also finds this consciousness to make its entrance into a realm of objective natural value. This account works equally as well where we value things that we do not consume. When we value a thrush singing in the wild, we have a sense of entrance into events ongoing independently of our subjective presence. We cannot genuinely care here, unless we care what happens after we are gone.

Natural Value as an Education

A natural object has no frame or pedestal; much depends on how I take it. The hawk flies past, and I can follow to admire his strength and speed, or let him pass and gaze into the blue expanse, pondering his fleeting smallness in the vast emptiness. Lying on my back, resting trailside, the stalwart ponderosa pine strikes me with its strength. It has stood the wintry storms. But then a hummingbird flits on scene, and how am I to interpret this interruption? By the contrast of great and small, mobile and immobile? Or by comparison of different strengths? The bird has stood the winter by flight from it and arrives after five thousand miles over land and sea. I remark to my companion that this is a strong flight for so tiny a creature. But she has seen nothing. With eyes closed, she has been wondering whether the Swainson's or the hermit thrush is the better singer.

The Fibonacci series in the spiral nebula in Andromeda can be drawn into association with that spiral in the chambered nautilus, in weather cyclones, and waterfall whirlpools. I can dwell on the galaxy's size and age, on the nautilus' age and smallness, on the local whirlpool's being driven by the global Coriolis force. Natural objects trigger imaginative musings of discovery and theoretical recombination, depending upon an active following of the show, on cultural preconditioning, and an adventurous openness.

Natural events thus educate us, leading out the beholder into self-expression. But it would be a mistake to conclude that all values derive entirely from our *composition* and none from our *position*. There are valued states of consciousness, but some are directed from the outside in essential, though not absolute, ways by the natural objects of consciousness. The situation remains a providing ground and catalyst, and also a check on experience. We can be deceived, as we could not if we were only composing. If, through the floating mists at evening, I am appreciating the moon hanging over the summit, only to discover with a bit of clearing that this was the disc of a microwave antenna, I judge the experience to have been false and cannot afterward regain it. I may be deceived about strength in the ponderosa or hummingbird. Our value judgments have to be more or less adequate to the natural facts.

Nature presents us with superposed possibilities of valuing, only some of which we realize. It is both provocative source of and resource for value. Here fertility is demanded of us as subjects, but is also found in the objects that fertilize our experience. Nature does indeed challenge us to respond as artists, poets, philosophers, as evaluators. But rather than devaluing nature, this educational ferment deepens its valued dimensions. The self has its options where to take the experience nature launches, but only interactively with nature carrying the show forward. There is trailblazing by the conscious self, but also we go in the track of our surroundings, with consciousness a trailer of what lies around.

The notion that nature is a value carrier is ambiguous. Everything depends on a thing being more or less structurally congenial for the carriage. Promiscuous items—logs, rocks, horses—support the body and serve for a seat. Other values require rather specific carriers, for one cannot enjoy symmetry, display of color, or adventure everywhere in nature. Still others require pregnancy with exactly that natural kind, as when only the female body can carry a child. Nature both offers and constrains values, often surprising us. We *value* a thing to discover that we are under the sway of its *valence,* inducing our behavior. It has among its "strengths" (Latin: *valeo,* be strong) this capacity to carry value to us, if also to carry values we assign to it. This "potential" cannot always be of the empty sort that a glass has for carrying water. It is often a pregnant fullness. In the energy throughput model, nature is indeed a carrier of value, but just as it is also objectively a carrier of energy and of life.

In climax, the values that nature is assigned are up to us. But fundamentally there are powers in nature that move to us and through us. America became great, remarked Alfred North Whitehead, when the pioneers entered "an empty continent, peculiarly well suited for European races."[13] That suggests a vast, valueless continent, waiting to carry our imported values, although even this is belied by its being a "peculiarly well suited" emptiness. Wild America, said John Locke, was a "waste." "Nature and the earth furnished only the almost worthless materials as in themselves." The Europeans' labors added 999 parts of the value; hardly one part in a thousand is natural.[14] But under our model we ought to think of a majestic and fertile ecosystem, the natural values of which could blend with those of the immigrants. Only the ecologically naive would see the energy flow, the work done, the value mix on a farm in Locke's proportions. The farmer but redirects natural resources, soil fertility, sun and rain, genetic information, to his own advantage. Even the settlers could call the continent (borrowing a Biblical phrase) a land of promise. Indeed, we have sometimes found values so intensely delivered that we have saved them wild, as in the Yellowstone, the Sierras, and the Smokies. The cathedrals were the gems of Europe, left behind, but the national parks are the gems of America, left untouched and positively treasured for their natural value.

How shall we judge our theory that value is (in part) provided objectively in nature (T_o) against the counterbelief that value arises only as a product of subjective experience (T_s), albeit relationally with nature? Even in scientific theories, hard proof is impossible. All we can hope for is a theory from which we can logically infer certain experiences (E). If T, then E. Given these, our theory is corroborated by a kind of weak, backtracking verification. Given counterevidence (not E), we have to estimate whether the anomaly is serious. No big theory even in science, much less in value theory, is trouble free, and the theory of objective value can be stung by our seeming incapacity to know anything whatsoever in naked objectivity. But value is not the sort of thing one would expect to know without excitement. If there is objective value in nature (T_o), then one would predict it to stir up experience (E). But sometimes too that experience fails (not E), and we must presume a faulty registration and/or valueless parts of nature.

If value arrives only with consciousness (T_s) we have no problem with its absence in nature (not E). But experiences where we do find value there (E) have to be dealt with as "appearances" of various sorts. The value has to be relocated in the valuing subject's creativity as he meets a valueless world, or even a valuable one, i.e., one *able* to be *valued,* but which before our bringing value ability contains only that possibility and not any actual value. This troubles the logic by hiding too much in words such as *epiphenomenon, echo, emergent* and *potential.* They occasionally help, but in the end give us the valuing subject in an otherwise (yet) valueless world, an insufficient premise for our experienced conclusion.

Resolute subjectivists cannot, however, be defeated by argument, although they can perhaps be driven toward analyticity. One can always hang on to the claim that value, like a tickle or remorse, must be felt to be there. Its *esse* is *percipi.* Nonsensed value is nonsense. It is impossible by argument to dislodge anyone firmly entrenched in this belief. That theirs is a retreat to definition is difficult to expose, because here they seem to cling so closely to inner experience. They are reporting, on this hand, how values always touch us. They are giving, on that hand, a stipulative definition. That is how they choose to use the word *value.* At this point, discussion can go no further.

Meanwhile, the conversion to our view seems truer to world experience and more logically compelling. Here the order of knowing reverses, if it also enhances, the order of being. This too is a perspective, but it is ecologically better informed. Nor is it so stiffly humanist and antireductionist. Science has been steadily showing how the consequents (life, mind) are built on their precedents (energy, matter), however much they overleap them. We find no reason to say that value is an irreducible emergent at the human (or upper animal) level. We reallocate value across the whole continuum. It increases in the emergent climax, but is continuously present in the composing precedents.

INTRINSIC NATURAL VALUE

Intrinsic contrasts with *instrumental; subjective* with *objective.* I next map these terms onto each other and the natural world.[15] *Intrinsic* value may be found in *human* experiences that are enjoyable in themselves, not needing further instrumental reference—an evening at the symphony, or one listening to loons call. Beyond this, *intrinsic natural* value recognizes value inherent in some natural occasions, without contributory human reference. The loons ought to continue to call, whether heard by humans or not. But the loon, while nonhuman, is itself a natural subject. There is something it is like to be a loon; its pains and pleasures are expressed in the call. Those who cannot conceive of nonexperienced value may allow nonhuman but not nonsubjective value. Value exists only where a subject has an object of interest. "The being liked, or disliked of the object is its value. . . . Some sort of a subject is always requisite to there being value at all—not necessarily a *judging* subject, but a subject capable of at least motor-affective response. For the cat the cream has value, or better and more simply, the cat values the cream or the warmth, or having her back scratched, quite regardless of her probable inability to conceive cream or to make judgments concerning warmth."[16]

Centers of experience vanish with simpler animals. In the botanical realm, we find programs promoted, life courses generated and held to, steering cores that lock onto an individual centeredness. There is a kind of object-with-will even though the feeling is gone. Every genetic set is in that sense a normative set; there is some *ought-to-be* beyond the *is,* and so the plant grows, repairs itself, reproduces, and defends its kind. If, after enjoying the *Trillium* in a remote woods, I step around to let it live on, I agree with this defense, and judge that here is intrinsic objective value, valued *by me,* but *for* what it is *in itself.* Value attaches to a nonsubjective form of life, but is nevertheless owned by a biological individual, a thing-in-itself. These things count, whether or not there is anybody to do the counting. They take account of themselves. They do their own thing, which we enjoy being let in on, and which we care to see continue when we pass on. Even a crystal is an identifiable, bounded individual, a natural kind that I may wish to protect, although it has no genetic core.

But the "for what it is in itself" facet of *intrinsic* becomes problematic in a holistic web. It is too internal and elementary; it forgets relatedness and externality. We value the humus and brooklet because in that matrix the *Trillium* springs up. They supply nutrients and water for the lake on which the loons call. With concern about populations, species, gene pools, habitats, we need a corporate sense that can also mean "good in community." Every intrinsic value has leading and trailing *ands* pointing to values from which it comes and toward which it moves. Natural fitness and positioning make individualistic intrinsic value too system independent. Neither single subject nor single object is alone. Everything is good in a role, in a whole, although we can speak of intrinsic goodness wherever a point experience, as of the *Trillium,* is so satisfying that we pronounce it good without need to enlarge our focus. Here, while experience is indeed a value, a thing can have values that go unexperienced. Just as human life can have meaning of which the individual is unaware (for indeed the lives of all great persons have more meaning than they know), biological individuals can play valuable genetic, ecological, evolutionary roles of which they are unaware. If the truth could be known, not only is much of value taking place in nonsentient nature, much of value is going on over our own heads as well.

For comprehensive scope, let us speak of natural *projects.* Some are *subjects* (loons); some are individual *organic objects (Trilliums);* some are individual *material objects* (crystals). Some are *communities* (the oak-hickory forest); some are *landforms* (Mount Rainier). Every natural affair does not have value, but there are "clots" in nature, sets of affinities with projective power, systems of thrust, counterthrust, and structure to which we can attach "natures" in the plural. There are achievements with beginnings, endings, cycles, more or less. Some do not have wills or interests, but rather headings, trajectories, traits, successions that give them a tectonic integrity. They are projective systems, if not selective systems. This inorganic fertility produces complexes of value—a meandering river, a string of paternoster lakes—which are reworked over time. Intrinsic value need not be immutable. Anything is of value here that has a good story to it. Anything is of value that has intense harmony, or is a project of quality. There is a negentropic constructiveness in dialectic with an entropic teardown, a mode of working for which we hardly yet have an adequate scientific, much less a valuational, theory. Yet this is nature's most striking feature, one which ultimately must be valued and of value. In one sense we say that nature is indifferent to planets, mountains, rivers, and *Trilliums,* but in another sense nature has bent toward making and remaking them for several billion years. These performances are worth noticing—remarkable, memorable—and they are not worth noticing just because of their tendencies to produce something else, certainly not merely because of their tendency to produce this noticing in our subjective human selves. All this gets at the root meaning of nature, its power to "generate" (Latin: *nasci, natus*).

Intrinsic natural value is a term that presides over a fading of subjective value into objective value, but also fans out from the individual to its role and matrix. Things do not have their separate natures merely in and for themselves, but they face outward and co-fit into broader natures. Value-in-itself is smeared out to become value-in-togetherness. Value seeps out into the system, and we lose our capacity to identify the individual, whether subject or object, as the sole locus of value. A diagram can only suggest these diverse and complex relationships in their major zones. The boundaries need to be semipermeable surfaces, and there will be arrows of instrumental value ($\nearrow$, $\searrow$) found throughout, connecting occasions of individual intrinsic value (o). Each of the upper levels includes and requires much in those below it. The upper levels do not exist independently or in isolation, but only as supported and maintained by the lower levels, though the diagram (figure 6), while showing this, inadequately conveys how the higher levels are perfused with the lower ones.

The subjectivist claim might seem safer in view of the breakout problem, that of knowing what nonexperienced value is like. But it is just as bold, for it too refuses to shut value judgments off at the boundaries of experience. It asserts a descriptive, cognitive truth about the external world of nonexperience. It too is a metaphysical claim, going beyond immediate experience to judge what is not there. Science, strictly speaking, brings a null result here, a non-answer, not a negative answer. The subjectivist claim is certainly not simple, but rather an advanced judgment made with heavy theories replacing the primary

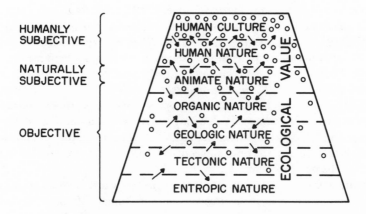

Figure 6.— Levels of Value in Projective Nature

fact of experience, where we move through a world of helps and hurts always coming at us. The logic by which one reads values out of nature is no less troublesome than the logic by which one finds values there and lets them stay.

The finding of objective value in nature is simpler and even more scientific if made with reserve. Neither native experience nor science pushes the dark back very far, but both let us in on workings that include but transcend our own existence. Immediate, middle-range experience enjoys many natural values, and one would expect this pragmatically to be locally competent. When science passes to the atomic or astronomical scales, we may wish to be agnostic. But the global sciences describe an evolutionary ecosystem where, from an inchoate planet and seed of microscopic beginnings, there progressively evolves the many-splendored panorama in which all our valuing takes place. We remain ignorant about many dynamisms and contingencies here, about what inevitability, if any, attaches to what actually did manage to happen. Nevertheless, whether rich by destiny or chance, or both, here we are embedded in it all.

Now it does not seem simple, scientific, or even safe to conceive of ourselves as subjects in metaphysical and valuational isolation from our natural launchings and underpinnings. Here value is a powerfully penetrant notion. It slips by the emergent steps back to the generating power, away from the subject over to the web and pyramid. We certainly interpret the show, experiencing redness out of wavelengths, beauty out of the patterned landscape. But we may be just as certain that the world known in sensory and intellectual paraphrase is structurally more complex than what comes through to register as fact and value. In that sense, in our knowing we are simplifying what is there, not enriching it, though, in another sense, the coming of humans enriches the drama, because valuers arrive in whom nature becomes conscious of itself.

In an otherwise admirable account, C. I. Lewis hedges and grants that natural objects carry, objectively, *extrinsic* value, in effect, the standing possibility of valuation. They actually have a potential for value, even if this forever remains unexperienced or is mistakenly experienced. When an experiencer arrives, such objects do not refer us away from themselves, but we enjoy them for what they are. Nevertheless they cannot own any intrinsic value. *"No objective existent has strictly intrinsic value; all values in objects are extrinsic only. . . . The goodness of good objects consists in the possibility of their leading to some realization of directly experienced goodness."* Value judgments are based upon facts "obdurate and compelling" and in this sense "valuation is a form of empirical knowledge." The notion that values are only subjective is "one of the strangest aberrations ever to visit the mind of man."[17]

But the word *extrinsic* suggests that essentially value is still a result of the human coming, whereas in ecological fact the human often arrives to trail naturally rooted values. There is nothing extraneous or accidental about the food value in a potato. When we overtake it, we recycle and amplify a natural value.[18] In evolutionary fact, there is nothing inessential or adventitious about those projective, pro-life forces. They inhere in the Earth itself and we latecomers inherit their work. The flow-through model of value does not find the objective side extrinsic and the subjective side intrinsic, but they are facets of one process. If, however, we revise Lewis, to use *extrinsic* to refer to that contributory role that natural things have, to their outward facing as this complements an inner facing, then in spontaneous nature things regularly have extrinsic as well as intrinsic value.

We can test our intuitions here by driving them to moral extremes. Let us imagine, in thought experiment, a parable of the last judgment. Suppose, a century hence, that in a tragic nuclear war each side has loosed upon the other radioactive fallout that sterilizes the genes of humans and mammals but is harmless to the flora, invertebrates, reptiles, and birds. That last race of valuers, if they had conscience still, ought not destroy the remaining biosphere. Nor would this be for interest in whatever slight subjectivity might remain, for it would be better for this much ecosystem to continue, even if the principal valuers were taken out. That verdict would recall the Genesis parable of the first judgment, where, stage by stage, from lesser to higher forms, goodness is found at every level.

THE ETHICAL IMPERATIVE

Future historians will find our century remarkable for its breadth of knowledge and narrowness of value judgments. Never have humans known so much about, and valued so little in, the great chain of being. As a result, the ecological crisis is not surprising. To devalue nature and inflate human worth is to do business in a false currency. This yields a dysfunctional, monopolistic world view. We are misfits because we have misread our life support system. We rationalize that the place we inhabit has no normative structures, and that we can do what we please. Afterward, this view sinks down into the hinterlands of our minds, an invisible persuader that silently shapes an ethic.

One can blunder in the old, naive view that values are known in literal, uninterpreted simplicity. But there is folly also in swinging to the other extreme. In this arrogation of value to ourselves, there is what the theologians call *hubris,* overbearing pride. It is much easier to impose our wills on the world when we believe it is otherwise of no account. Nothing stays our libido; nothing demands any human-transcending concern. But ethics too, like all aspects of life, flourishes when operating in a system of checks and balances. What if, in truth, we are not only limited by the natural facts but also by natural values? What if living well is not merely a getting of what I value, but a negotiating of my values in a neighborhood of worth? In the former belief we would forever remain juvenile. In the latter we should gain moral maturity.

There is much nobility in being self-actualizing, and nature permits us to elect some values. But such dignity is not enhanced by living as lonesome selves in a void world. There is no joy in being freaks of nature, loci of value lost in a worthless environment. The doctrine of the sterility of nature is not a boon but an evil, for it throws humans into meaninglessness, into an identity crisis. It has made much modern life sterile. At this point, there is something encouraging about the notion of relativity. Einstein introduced us, at the levels of time, space, mass, energy, to but one form of an ecosystemic principle. Subjectivity too is what it is in objective circumstances. The values we own are nested in a mother-matrix. To turn Bishop Butler on his head: everything is what it is in relation to other things.[19] This kind of relativity does not cause alienation and anthropocentrism; rather, it cures it.

Seen in this way, it is not the objectivists but rather the thoroughgoing subjectivists who commit the naturalistic fallacy, for they must either derive value at a consummate stroke out of a merely factual nature, getting it as it were *ex nihilo,* or out of something available but to no avail without us. Or they have to bring value in by skyhook from some *a priori* source. But we do not commit this fallacy because we find fact and value inseparably to co-evolve. This does not deny the mystery of emerging value, but there is value in our premises as well as in our conclusion.

We humans do not play out our drama of epiphenomenal or emergent value on a valueless natural stage. The stage is the womb from whence we come, but which we really never leave. If the enduring drama has any value, that must somehow attach to the whole plot and plasma, span over from potential to persons, even though it may be diversely distributed across events. Nature is not barren of value; it is rather the bearer of value. That both constrains and ennobles the role we humans are called to play.

NOTES

Also published in Robert Elliot and Arran Gare, eds., *Environmental Philosophy* (St. Lucia: University of Queensland Press, and State College, Pa.: Pennsylvania State University Press, 1983). For critical discussion, see Ernest Partridge, "Values in Nature: Is Anybody There?" *Philosophical Inquiry* 8(1986), forthcoming; J. Baird Callicott, "Intrinsic Value, Quantum Theory, and Environmental Ethics," *Environmental Ethics* 7(1985):257-275; Donald Scherer, "Anthropocentrism, Atomism, and Environmental Ethics," *Environmental Ethics* 4(1982):115-123; Peter Miller, "Value as Richness: Toward a Value Theory for an Expanded Naturalism in Environmental Ethics," *Environmental Ethics* 4(1982):101-114; Robin Attfield, "Value in the Wilderness," *Metaphilosophy* 15(1984):289-304.

1. William James, *Varieties of Religious Experience* (New York: Longmans, Green, and Co., 1925), p. 150. Originally published in 1902.

2. John Laird, *A Study in Realism* (Cambridge, England: At the University Press, 1920), p. 129.

3. Wilhelm Windelband, *An Introduction to Philosophy,* trans. Joseph McCabe (London: T. Fisher Unwin, 1921), p. 215.

4. Ralph Barton Perry, *General Theory of Value* (Cambridge, Massachusetts: Harvard University Press, 1926, 1954), pp. 125, 115f.

5. Samuel Alexander, *Beauty and Other Forms of Value* (New York: Thomas Y. Crowell Company, 1968), pp. 172-87. Originally published in 1933.

6. Quoted in Ernst Cassirer, *Substance and Function and Einstein's Theory of Relativity* (New York: Dover Publications, 1953), p. 356. Originally published in 1923.

7. John Wheeler, "From Relativity to Mutability," in Jagdish Mehra, ed., *The Physicist's Conception of Nature* (Dordrecht, Holland: D. Reidel Publishing Co., 1973), pp. 202-47, citation on p. 227.

8. Werner Heisenberg, "The Representation of Nature in Contemporary Physics," *Daedalus* 87, no. 3 (Summer 1958): 95-108, citation on p. 107.

9. Lubert Stryer, *Biochemistry* (San Francisco: W. H. Freeman and Co., 1975), p. 90.

10. John Dewey, *Experience and Nature* (New York: Dover Publications, 1958), p. 4a. Originally published in 1929.

11. This seems to be the view of George Santayana, *The Sense of Beauty* (New York: Modern Library, 1955) pp. 21-24, pp. 150-54. Originally published in 1896.

12. Alexander, *Beauty,* p. 30f. Alexander holds, however, that certain nonaesthetic values may exist in nature, pp. 285-99. See also *Space, Time, and Deity* (London: Macmillan and Co., 1920), 2:302-14.

13. Alfred North Whitehead, "The Study of the Past—Its Uses and Its Dangers," *Harvard Business Review* 11 (1932-33): 436-444, citation on p. 438.

14. John Locke, *The Second Treatise of Civil Government* (Oxford: Basil Blackwell, 1948), secs. 42, 43, p. 22f. Originally published in 1690.

15. I set aside a use of *subjective* which means "depending on personal judgment, difficult to get consensus on." By contrast, *objective* means "obvious to all, publicly demonstrable." Many instrumental, humanistic values in nature—our need for food—

are unarguable, while finding intrinsic natural value requires discretionary, subjective judgment. We here examine subjectivity in claim content, not that involved in verifying a claim. It is not surprising that humans reach the easiest consensus on values nearest those we subjects experience, nor that there is disagreement about objective value, since nonexperienced value is remote from the immediacy of personal life.

16. David W. Prall, *A Study in the Theory of Value,* University of California Publications in Philosophy, vol. 3, no. 2 (Berkeley: University of California Press, 1921), p. 227.

17. Clarence Irving Lewis, *An Analysis of Knowledge and Valuation* (La Salle, Ill.: Open Court Publishing Co., 1946), pp. vii, 366, 387, 407.

18. The apple, Lewis would reply, cannot realize its own value. If uneaten, it rots. So its value is extrinsic; the eater's pleasure is intrinsic. But this example is misleading unless ecologically understood. The carbohydrate stored in the overwintering potato will be used, although not experienced, by the plant in the spring. Eating it overtakes energy of value to the plant. But the apple functions as a gamble in seed dispersal. Its value is realized when birds, deer, or humans take the bait. The apple has been very successful; it has caught the man. While the apple takes care of the man, the man takes care of the apple. Its survival is assured as long as there are humans to care for it!

19. "Everything is what it is, and not another thing." Joseph Butler, *Fifteen Sermons upon Human Nature,* London, 1726; 2nd ed., 1729, in the preface.

7

Values Gone Wild

For the trip you are about to take I offer myself as a wilderness guide. Nowadays it is easier to get lost conceptually in wildlands than physically. A century ago the challenge was to know where you were geographically in a blank spot on the map, but today we are bewildered philosophically in what has long been mapped as a moral blank space. Despite our scientific and cultural taming of wildness we still wander, confused over how to value it. Values run off our maps. In journeys there, "value" changes its meaning, as does the word "wild." Travelers need pathfinding through strange places.

VALUING OUR SOURCES AND RESOURCES

Before I can lead you into the deep wilderness of values, we will have to make our way past a misguided route. It may seem to keep us oriented to value wildlands as *resources*. With soil, timber, or game the meaning of "resource" is clear enough. Humans tap into spontaneous nature, dam water, smelt ores, domesticate, manage, and harvest, redirecting natural courses to become resources. No longer wild, they come under our control. But when we try to speak of wilderness as a "resource" the term soon goes kerflooey. Notice the oddity of this resource relationship, which will prove a key for unlocking anthropocentric presumptions about value.

A park ranger may interpret the Tetons as a scientific, recreational, or aesthetic resource, but by the time she calls it a philosophical or religious resource, the term is eating up everything, as if humans have no other operating modes *vis-à-vis* wilderness. Have her notice that resources come in two kinds: the ordinary kind that are rearranged into artifacts, and the extraordinary, wild type that we impact as little as possible. The botanist in Cascade Canyon or the mountaineer atop the Grand Teton find both places important precisely as not

Reprinted by permission from *Inquiry, An Interdisciplinary Journal of Philosophy and the Social Sciences* 26 (1983): 181-207.

consumed. Contrary to typical resource use, we visit wildness on its own terms and do not reform it to ours. The conceptually wild turn is when humans, ordinarily valuing resources of the kind they can make over, here value what they will not disturb lest they devalue it. Under the standard doctrine, we wanted potatoes but the fields grew worthless brush. We wanted logs dovetailed around us as a home, but the world gave only standing trees. We labored to make value. Under the revised claim, pure wildness can be a good thing. These places change us, not we them.

Well, some reply, nature offers some resources that take no redoing or consuming, only looking and enjoying. Most are commodities to be drawn upon, but others are amenities left as is. Perhaps this revision in the logic of "resource" will solve our problem. Wilderness is important only as a resource in our society.

> Wilderness is for people. This is a principle that bears restating. The preservation goals established for such areas are designed to provide values and benefits to society. . . . Wilderness is not set aside for the sake of its flora or fauna, but for people.[1]

We must recognize various kinds of instrumental value. The commonest kind modifies natural courses, but an infrequent sort needs only to take natural things as they are. We capture wilderness instrumentally for human experience, though we never lay a hand on it and tread lightly afoot. So why is it not a resource?

Still, two deeper worries begin to loom. One is that the resource orientation is only a half truth and afterward *logically* misguided. The other is that, taken for the whole truth, it is *ethically* misguided. Unfortunately, these troubles intertwine, because everything is defined in relation to us.

We can continue by noticing how the claim, "Everything is a resource, really," parallels a more familiar claim, "Everyone is selfish, really." Here philosophers have better mapped how logical difficulties are ingrown with ethical ones. The egoist begins by citing how persons regularly pursue self-interest and then turns to apparent altruism. Mother Teresa has labored among the poor in Calcutta and Charles Lindbergh in later years turned to the defense of wildlife. But both received self-fulfillment from their efforts. The Marines who died on Iwo Jima had their families at stake, which it was in their enlightened self-interest to protect. The claim expands to digest all counter-evidence, redefining "selfish" to embrace all conduct, reinterpreting motives or imagining hidden ones until it becomes a presumption brought to experience. Afterward, there is no point in examining further cases. Willy-nilly, everything is twisted to fit the selfishness gestalt.

"Everything is a resource, really." The argument cites how humans redirect nature to their benefit, and then turns to apparent nonresources. Nevada authorities labor to save the Devil's Hole pupfish, which requires reduced water drawdown for ranching. Southwestern developers agree not to build the Marble Canyon Dam, and members of the Wilderness Society contribute money to save wilderness, some nearby which they expect to visit, and some Alaskan which they do not. But some humans are fascinated by the pupfish, run rafts down the Grand Canyon, visit the Indian Peaks, enjoy knowing the Alaskan wilds are there, and hope their children many visit them. SUPPORT WATCHABLE WILDLIFE! That slogan from the Oregon Department of Fish and Wildlife is a commendable step away from fish you catch and game you shoot, both to consume. But *watchable* wildlife is a resource for looking. In every case humans enter into some self-fulfilling relationship. What we want is high quality wilderness experience that improves human life.

Use of the word "resource" gradually changes until nothing can be comprehended outside such a relationship, no matter if the paramount emotion becomes the appreciating of these realms for what they are in themselves. One ponders the pupfish, the Supai and Redwall strata in Marble Gorge, spends a lonesome weekend amidst glacier-cut scenery in the Indian Peaks, wondering if a grandchild might ever share such feelings on Alaskan slopes, steadily stretched out of local concerns to the age-long flows of life over time. But these are resource relationships! Logically, the claim has become trivial, redefining as resource whatever one "takes in," whether food or scenery. Ethically, valuing has "gone wild" in the haywire sense because it has become so nonnegotiably anthropocentric that we cannot let values go wild in any naturalistic sense.

What if a daughter should say to her mother, "You know you are a resource, really," or a communicant, approaching the altar, were to think how the priest, in transforming bread and wine, was making better resources out of them? Before parents and the sacred, one is not so much looking to *resources* as to *sources,* seeking relationships in an elemental stream of being with transcending integrities. Our place in the natural world necessitates resource relationships, but there comes a point when we want to know how we belong in this world, not how it belongs to us. We want to get ourselves defined in relation to nature, not just to define nature in relation to us.

We Americans preserve our historical parks at Lexington or Appomattox to remember our origins, but we would be shortsighted not to set aside wilderness as the profoundest museum of all, a relic of how the world was in 99.99 percent of past time, the crucible in which we were forged. A historical park is a place to recall our sources, our national story; but we need "genesis parks" to recall our natural history. Wilderness is the first legacy, the grand parent, and offers dramatic contacts with ultimacies not found in town.

Why should it seem so logical to call even our wild natural sources a resource? To answer we must look for a still deeper presumption brought to experience: the conviction that value emerges with the satisfaction of human interest. Only positive human mental states have noninstrumental value. Take away our selection and feeling, and intrinsic value vanishes. If so, nature as the source of valued experiences must be only instrumental, and therefore a resource even if of an anomalous kind. But what if this too is logically misguided? In that case, to force everything into the all-purpose resource formula is only for those who have no better logical model for appreciating wild places. It sounds humane, yet it keeps alive a humanist illusion. But to overthrow the nature-as-mere-resource paradigm we will need a more comprehensive, nonanthropocentric theory of value.

The key idea we are following is of nature as a *source of values,* including our own. Nature is a generative process to which we want to relate ourselves and by this to find relationships to other creatures. Value includes far more than a simplistic human-interest satisfaction. Value is a multifaceted idea with structures that root in natural sources. Wilderness is valuationally complex, as it is scientifically complex. Tracking these components will require triangulation from three points, the notions of *roots, neighbors,* and *aliens.* After that, we will see whether there is any unifying systemic structure. Notice how value is indeed beginning to go wild. Extending beyond the reach of human domestication and experience, it begins to have a life of its own in spontaneous nature.

VALUING ROOTS, NEIGHBORS, AND ALIENS

We can represent the logical paths ahead, both those of discovery and justification, as in figure 1. We began with values all in the human orbit, and all outside valueless except as resources brought in instrumentally. But now values leave the human circle; they go wild. Our paths of discovery (the line arrows) follow value back into its roots, but these same evolutionary sources have generated neighbors and aliens in the planetary ecosystem we coinhabit. Paths stretch around toward these regions, zones we can also visit by crossing diffuse bound-

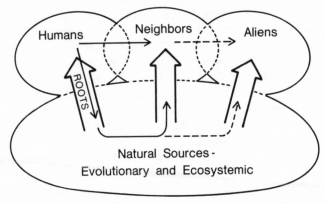

Figure 1.

aries into territories shared with these neighbors and occupied by aliens. The theory and its implications are suggested by an originating source area with three broad lines of production (the wide arrows).

On these paths leading progressively toward wilder territories, need we take any precautions about crossing illegitimately a forbidden boundary? For (some will warn) one cannot move from bare facts in nature to what is of value there, nor to what conduct persons ought to undertake, without committing the naturalistic fallacy. At this point I am going to say only that the signs posted that forbid trespassing this boundary are themselves cultural artifacts (deriving as they do from certain theories about ethics, about the moral neutrality of nature, value as human-interest satisfaction, etc.), and this guide recommends that we ignore (as wilderness travelers often do) the cultural prohibitions about where one can and cannot legitimately go. Let us undergo the wilderness experience first hand, and only then think back whether we have made any logical mistakes or gone into territory we ought not to have visited in quest of value. I have proposed to lead you into wild experiences, and only in retrospect, not in prospect, can we intelligently argue about what has happened in passing from *is* to *ought*.

Wildness Is a Place of *Roots* in Historical and Ongoing Senses

We stay oriented by thinking of a visit to the birthplace. Here historical value blends with that order of value we owe to parents. Value leaves culture to return to natal mysteries, to primitive archetypes. Wilderness is the incubating matrix that served as the production site of the human race. Stopping at a spring, I meet a salamander and am struck by its tiny fingerlike feet. As I dip water, I notice in my hand the same digital pattern, in modified but unmistakably kindred form. I catch my reflection to compare facial patterns. How far back in geologic time must go that bilateral symmetry of eyes, nose, mouth! Even now beneath my cerebrum lies a remnant reptilian brain, essential to my cognitive and emotional humanity.[2] So much of what we most radically value arose anciently in the spontaneous wild, but is presumed in the routine of culture.

Wildness does not merely lie behind, it remains the generating matrix. Laden with my pack, moving briskly along, I turn my thoughts to respiration. Present in every cell containing a respiratory chain—from microbes to humans—is is an electron carrier called the cytochrome-c molecule that evolved over 1.5 billion years ago.[3] Given that I plainly value respiration for myself, and that evolution has conserved this molecule since before plants and animals diverged, it seems some sort of wild type in value. If I become winded, my body is facing another problem. The citric acid cycle, which follows glycolysis in the processing of food molecules and is a more recently evolved skill, is not generating enough ATP for the demands of my skeletal muscle, and so my metabolism switches to make lactate rather than sending pyruvate into the citric acid cycle. The lactate leaks out of the muscle cells and is carried to the liver, which can process it.[4]

Short of oxygen and pushed for energy, my body reverts to a use of glycolysis first learned before there was atmospheric oxygen and since kept and modified for emergency situations.

Turning to the extrasomatic ecosystem, all flesh is grass, including my own, using "grass" to refer to the photosynthetic base of the biomass. All flesh is wind, remembering its nitrogen and oxygen components; there would be no protein without the nitrogen fixers, no respiration without the oxygen releasers. Resting at an overlook, I may take in the greenness, autotrophs feeding the heterotrophs, which rot to nourish the autotrophs, and realize that when higher forms evolved, the lower were not all left behind. Many remain as essentials in an ecological web. They can do without my cultures, but I cannot do without their kind of world, which forms my pyramidal community. In wildness, one learns to value the compound units of integrated biological achievement.

Such sophisticated insights, reached in biochemistry laboratories and ecological field studies, reveal the extent to which wild values surround and lie within us. But although we may learn such things in an emotionally weak sense in our cultural educations, we are prone to undervalue them. The scientific insights (cytochrome-c, ATP, the liver shift, the photosynthetic base) help us to appreciate everyday experiences (energy needs, respiration), but the uneveryday experiences in wildness help us to appreciate these phenomena as larger than ourselves, natural givens that, as we now begin to see, we share with other forms of life. The trip into wildness gives visceral intimate access to bodily experience in surrounding nature, unmediated by the protective cushions of culture. One travels *in medias res* vividly and exuberantly, like a glider pilot hung buoyantly in the air, the person lofted up over a wild world. In that sense we do not keep wildness in conservative resource use. Rather we want a radical place to be.

In the wilderness I am reminded of what culture lulls me into forgetting, that I have natural roots. I value that learning experience. But more, I value the wilderness out of which I have historically come and continue to come ecologically. Recalling our genetic roots is a valuable experience, which wilderness forces. But the wilderness here is not serving merely as resource instrumental to our experience. It is being discovered as the crucial Source of what we now intrinsically value. With this recognition, we become unwilling to stop at making it instrumental merely; wildness itself is of *intrinsic* value as the generating source. It carries value when it produces experience now in its visitors, but it has carried values historically and ecologically to these visitors. Consciously enjoying these values is an advanced form of value, taking place in humans at levels unprecedented in the unvisited wilderness. But we are also recapturing and recapitulating value in flow before we arrived and which we have inherited.

Wildness is a living museum of our roots. The experiences humans have there are to be valued because we learn where we came from and who we are. But it is crude to say this only makes a resource out of wilderness, misguided by the belief that value can appear only in human experience. We are here realizing that nature is an originating *source* of value first, and only later and secondarily a *resource*. We are *experiencing roots,* and this experiencing is to be valued, but what the experiencing is *of*—these *wild generative roots* at work before humans arrived—has delivered to us much of value, processes the benefits of which are at work within us whether we are aware of them or not.

This sort of experience moves value outside ourselves. It forces a redistribution and redefinition of value. Value is not just a human product. We realize this by learning how we humans, including much that we value in ourselves, are natural products, and are thereby alerted to look for other natural productions of value. Such nonhuman values, as we track them here, are first discovered in these roots, but the path does not end there. It leads secondly to wild neighbors and on beyond to paths more foreign and difficultly explored.

Wildness Is Place of *Neighbors* in a Sense Gone Wild

This requires a sympathetic turning to value what does not stand directly in our lineage or underpinning, but is enough like ourselves that we are drawn by spill-over to shared phenomena manifest in others. The principle of universalizability demands that I recognize corresponding values in fellow persons. But need this apply only with reciprocating moral agents? Growth in ethical sensitivity has often required enlarging the circle of neighbors, and are there no neighbors in the wild? They are not moral agents; that is part of what their wildness means. But have they no values to consider? This great natural source (figure 1) that has generated us all continues to flow in others, not into humans alone. There is a great similarity between humans and other organisms, whether at experiential, psychological, or biological levels. If I value these qualities in myself, by parity of reasoning I should likewise value them when manifested in other organisms.

Animals take an interest in affairs that affect them. They hunt and flee, grow tired, thirsty, and hot. They seek shelter, play, wag tails, scratch, suffer injury, and lick their wounds. The salamander reacts first by freezing, then fleeing. In judging such actions, we must guard against the pathetic fallacy. A moose does not suffer winter cold as we do; perhaps the warbler is not glad when it sings. But we must not commit the humanistic fallacy of supposing no naturalistic analogues of what humans plainly value. We have every logical and psychological reason to posit degrees of kinship.

Endorphins—natural analogues of morphine—are produced by human brains upon injury and stress. These compounds buffer pain, are important for emotional stability, and are implicated in certain "good feelings," like those involved in the euphoria of the wilderness experience under stress. They are found widely in the nervous systems of vertebrates—mammals, reptiles, amphibians, birds, fish—and in some invertebrates, for example, earthworms. The endorphin level in a frightened mouse rises.[5] Additionally, mice have the neural receptors for Librium and Valium. The trip into wildness, we were saying, reawakens bodily experience. There is the climb, the heat, the cold; we need water, food, shelter. We think more about endurance and fatigue, sureness and fear, comfort and pain. Such experiences bring appreciation of our own natural endowments, but if they serve that end alone, we are too humanistic. Enjoying the tonic of wildness, feeling more alive without quite knowing why, endorphin levels rising, we ought to make value judgments in kinship with all embodied being, just because we are stripped to gutsy, animal elements.

This sense of kinship need not be restricted to shared subjectivity, for it can be somatic. Consider the development of muscle and fat, both outside the central nervous system. The university-educated mind tends to value brainpower and to devalue muscle and fat, but this opinion will be challenged in the wild. Brainpower follows and coevolves with muscle. The mind is useless unless it can act, while the power to move can be of value even when governed by mere instinct. Seen at the molecular level, the coordinated muscle cells with their interdigitating fibers, A-bands and I-bands, the myosin that splits ATP to drive push-pull contractions, are hardly less an evolutionary achievement than is the nervous system. Contact with animal strength and grace, flight and fury, makes it difficult to maintain that the relevant senses of kinship here are only subjective.

Muscle cannot move without energy, and energy can be in short supply in winter. The fat cell evolves to store energy in compact form, and thus to power muscle months after energy intake. As night falls I begin to shiver, using muscle to generate heat. But some animals do not shiver. The brown fat cell, modified from the ordinary fat cell, is present in hibernators, seals, ground squirrels, bats, in the young of rabbits, cats, sheep, and newborn humans who cannot yet shiver. Brown adipose tissue appears late in evolution and forms a heating jacket that provides the capacity to survive the cold when in thermogenic response fats burn without forming ATP, thereby generating heat more efficiently.[6] If I judge that muscle and fat have no value as unfelt spontaneous processes, I begin to wonder whether I am myopically biased toward sentience. Perhaps value judgments need to be made not merely on the basis of *sympathy* for sentient kin, but on the basis of what biologists call *sympatry,* shared organic origins.

Some will find it incoherent and nonsensical, wild in a logically wayward sense, to speak of objective value in embodied being, for (say they) there is no value without awareness. Nonneural animals may have sensory receptors, but these are mere stimulus response mechanisms. But why cannot values be located outside the nervous system? In fact, at the metabolic level we gain the fullest sense of shared biological powers. The marsh hawk and the ground squirrel are enemies because they are somatically kindred; it is the protein muscle and the fat in the squirrel that the hawk can use. One could label all this so much resource use, and then stipulate that values necessitate sentient awareness. Objective organic processes form roots, precursors of value, but valueless in themselves, becoming of value only when experience is superadded. But the more one studies organic bodies, the less evidently this is the most plausible route for mapping value. It starts with a psychological or hedonic result of the biological processes, values this experiential effect, and devalues the productive causes except in terms of a late conclusion, in which, subjectively, we happen to stand. It takes a derived thing as the only thing that really counts.

In one sense, the choice between broader, objective and more restricted, subjective accounts of value does not matter. Even if value is defined as interest satisfaction, it has here become nonhuman. Intrinsic value lies in worthwhile experiences, which wild animals sometimes have, although somatically we can speak only instrumentally of the power to produce such experiences. But specify, if you wish, that muscle and fat, food and hemoglobin have only instrumental value, they are still out there in the wildlands apart from human awareness, instrumental to experienced intrinsic values that take place irrespective of human visitors, although humans do not enjoy realization of this except as they visit. But in another sense, somatic achievements such as autotrophic, muscular, or energetic self-reliance introduce us to a more comprehensive notion of value. Value arises with organic problem-solving, perceived or not, a notion we must yet refine. An achievement of this sort has value of itself, being worthwhile as a significant adventure of life, although it will inevitably also be contributory to some further achievement. But we will be better prepared for this account after making our way through some yet wilder places.

Wildness Is a Place Where We Encounter *Aliens*

The previous triangulation points (roots and neighbors) unite us with wildness, but now we turn to loving differences, even to respecting otherness we cannot love. On the first and second nights backpacking, there is a restored sense of belonging, but by the third night the country becomes foreign. Man is not the measure of things. J. B. S. Haldane was asked by some theologians what he had learned about God from biology. He replied that God has "an inordinate fondness for beetles."[7] Perhaps three-fourths of the known animals are insects, by some criteria the most successful form of life, and a disproportionate number are *Coleoptera*. God went wild making beetles. Evolution went wild in speciation. Some will stall here, but wild creatures can stretch us out of ourselves into the depth and breadth of being. We seek values that cannot be shared, altruistic encounters of the strangest kind.

Some may think it logically or psychologically impossible to value what we cannot share, but this underestimates the human genius for appreciation. Coyotes run in packs, parting and reassembling over hunting territories, with each pack having a home range. They maintain orientation and identify in-pack members and out-pack intruders with a system of scent posts, as well as with their howls. To a coyote a whiff of urine or scat contains much information about where he is and who passed that way, about mates and rivals, what to beware of and what is a waste of time. This is not a skill that I share or desire, but nevertheless one I admire. I can get a whiff of what coyote savvy must be like, since I distinguish some smells, and by inference and observation I go on to recognize and value ranges of experience I cannot fathom. All the coyote's senses are acute, and the "complexity of its total communication system seems rivaled by only a few other mammals."[8] Human experience would be the poorer for ignoring or scorning what exceeds *our* powers of sentience.

Bacteria in swamps are not disturbed by gravity, being too small to be much under its influence, but they are buffeted about by Brownian motion, rather like dust particles in air. Some bacteria orient themselves by the capture of small bits of magnetite, which they organize end on end into a built-in compass, 500 angstroms long, used apparently not to tell north from south but up from down.[9] I too use a compass, though I do not suppose that it is like anything at all to be a lost bacterium, or that the bacteria know what they are doing. Yet the bacterium values the magnetite, the coyote the orienting scent post, as surely as I value the compass. The wilderness is full of cleverness that we do not understand, of signals that we do not hear, of values that go on over our heads. We abandon our prejudices about how things are, start from scratch, and learn new scales of what ought to be.

Almost like a coyote, a jumping spider will sight its quarry at a distance, run toward it, then crouch and creep imperceptibly forward until close enough to leap upon its victim. Is there "anybody home" in this monster with eight eyes of differing focal lengths supplying wide angle and telescopic vision over color ranges perhaps including the ultraviolet? Even if we attach no subjectivity to spiderly being, is there no value in such a superbly efficient hunting unit? Its multiple eyes and legs are coordinated for alternative hunting strategies; it chooses routes to its prey, deciding on haste, stealth, and pounce, even anticipating where a fly will alight and starting its jump before the quarry has landed.[10] A philosopher, *loving wisdom,* ought to be able to love the wisdom here, for the jumping spider is certainly good of its kind, but why not a good kind in its niche?

Our duty before wildness is ambiguous. In the beginning we respect the coyote, the spider, even the bacterium by grading how much they are kin, possessing smaller amounts what we have a lot more of—biochemistry, mobility, complexity, information, skill, sentience, freedom, language, consciousness. But afterward we find this demeaning, leading to pity because they took a form inferior to our own. We insult them by calling them static lines or dead ends in the evolutionary process. What we must rather learn is to respect their own integrity, nonhuman manifestations of what Aristotle would call *arete,* excellences in kind. Wild creatures are not nature at a suboptimal level. They are humble creatures, but they can also humble humans whose values have grown too proudly provincial.

Humans are nature's richest achievement but not nature's only achievement, and in unresolved tension with our lofty rank we have to judge that diversity in being is richer than would be a world with only humans. Even if by some wizardry one could, one ought not to kiss toads into men. Nature has done that over evolutionary time, but has also taken other twists in value. These creatures improve the world just by being there, and thus alien nature is a form of wealth. We can be exalted by those of low degree; we can exalt those of low degree.

Whatever is wary, as sentient or instinctive wildness is, has a value set of its own. So the salamander first froze and then fled at the spring. The wildness by which it escapes is objective evidence of value alien to my own. But owning a value set is not merely a feature of the rapidly mobile. Every genetic set proclaims a life way, and thus makes an assertive claim over its surroundings. Every genetic set is a propositional set, a *normative* (nonmoral) set, proposing what *ought* to be, beyond what *is,* on the basis of its encoded information. So it grows, reproduces, repairs its wounds, and resists death. Wildness, activity outside the scope of human concern, is not a sign of something valueless, but of foreign freedom, of spontaneous autonomy and self-maintenance.

These things are not merely to be valued *for me and my kind* (as resources), not even as goods *of my kind* (sharing sentience or fat cells), but as goods *of their kind, as good kinds* without consideration of their kinship. At our departure value was restricted to human affairs, and later shared with neighboring organisms. With still deeper penetration into wildness, value becomes alien. Yet the human genius is such that we can nonetheless manage to cross these thresholds (through science, imagination, wilderness adventure, ethical sensitivity) and glimpse these wildest values. Value attaches to experience but also to shared somatic skills. Value attaches even to the cleverness of alien forms. Value is sometimes anthropomorphic, but can be morphic in any formed integrity. *Value is storied achievement.* With this definition we can reach a fundamental motif, which could be widely woven through culture and might be deployed even into inorganic realms, though we are tracing it here only organically. Even the inanimate planetary system is sometimes impelled, energized toward *created form,* storied developments, works of genius, and, in due course, toward the evolution of the genera and of sentient genius. Interest satisfaction is only a lately formed subset of this richer principle. Continuing our search, we must set individuals in their ecosystems and evaluate their evolutionary sources. Once again, the terrain we push through is wild and alien to the cultured mind.

SURVIVAL VALUE REVISITED—
ORGANIC AND SYSTEMIC ACHIEVEMENTS

A formidable emotion before nature is a kind of horror at the anarchy and relentless struggle in a world that opposes either by its indifference or by its hostility. Once, as a college youth, I killed an opossum that seemed sluggish and then did an autopsy. He was infested with a hundred worms! Grisly and pitiful, he seemed a sign of the whole wilderness, hardly a place of roots, hardly neighborly, but too alien to value. Each is ringed about with competitors and limits, forced to do or die. Physical nature, from which are wrested the materials of life, is brute fact and brutally there, caring naught and always threatening. Organic nature is savage; life preys on life. Perhaps we can reconcile ourselves to alien value in individuals. The opossum in its marsupial being is a good kind; even the worms defend their genetic sets and manifest biochemical skills. But the systemic source that they of necessity inhabit seems ugly, evil, wild. They do not live in a good place.

The wilderness contains only the thousandth part of creatures that sought to be, but rather became seeds eaten, young fallen to prey or disease. The Darwinian revolution has revealed that the governing principle is survival in a world thrown forward in chaotic contest, with much randomness and waste besides. The wilderness teems with its kinds but is a vast graveyard with a hundred species laid waste for one or two that survive. T. H. Huxley reacted that the values society most cherishes depend "not on imitating the cosmic process, still less in running away from it, but in combating it."[11] If so, can there be value in the wild holocaust, any reason for society to preserve or admire it?

Perhaps we will cry that there is only a survival value whose operation hurts too much for us to value it more. Everything is making a resource of something else, so far as it can, except when it is resisting being made a resource of. The jumping spider eats the fly, the worms the opossum, the coyote the ground squirrel, which eats the grass and its seeds, which grow in the rotting humus. The salamander is making a resource of the mosquito; the mosquito of me. Once again, everything is a resource, really. Only now, alas, the felicitous goodness in all this resourcing has gone bitter. Wildness is a gigantic food pyramid, and this sets value in a grim, deathbound jungle. All is a slaughterhouse, with life a miasma rising over the stench. Nothing of the compassion or morality that we value in culture is found there. Nothing is done for benefit of another, much less for human benefit, and all this is so remote from what society ideally should value. Nothing recognizes anything else's rights; each individual defends itself as an end in itself, and even in reproduction merely defends its own genes. Blind and ever-urgent exploitation is nature's driving theme. Values seem utterly wild. Can we recover a positive orientation in such a negative picture?

The diagram we need now (figure 2) modifies our earlier sketch. Small circles (o) show intrinsic values, small arrows (→) instrumental values, both as individual achievements. The three wide arrows represent what we call systemic achievement.

The cutthroat portrait does not mean there are no valuers in the wild; it portrays too many claimants contesting scarce worth. Life is never self-contained but incessantly moves through its environment, ingesting and eliminating it. Rocks attach no value to the environment, but coyotes must eat. Where anything is being made a resource of, just this claiming of the environment as nutrient source and sink reveals valuational systems in interaction. Perhaps we can return

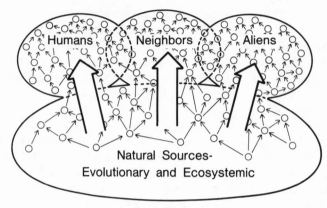

Figure 2.

to the resource notion, which at the start we had to get past, now finding it a key to the larger dynamics of the system.

The wildness can seem a great scene of disorder, but it is also a great scene of the pumping out of disorder. Indeed, all this resourcefulness has to be so understood. Now a more astonishing mystery overpowers our earlier appall. Life struggles, but has achieved so much, pumped up out of the soil, persisting on by ever novel arrivals. The marvel is how dirt spontaneously assembled itself into Cambrian worms, later into Cretaceous opossums, and still later into wondering men. In the wild, things are degraded, followed by nature's orderly self-assembling of new creatures amidst this perpetual perishing. Earth slays her children, a seeming great disvalue, but bears an annual crop in their stead. This pro-life, generative impulse is at once the most valuable, the wildest, most startling miracle of all.

To keep our bearings, we must locate individual lives on larger horizons, as goods of their kind in an ecosystem greater than they know. We can subsume struggle under the notion of a comprehensive situated fitness. Forms live on that more efficiently utilize food resources, take better care of their young, learn to form societies, fill niches not exploited by others. The survival of the fittest designs the ever more fit in their habitats. Each is for itself, but none is by itself; each is tested for optimal compliance in an intricately disciplined community. Every organism is an opportunist in the system, but without opportunity except in the ongoing system. The worms may not cripple their hosts too successfully, lest they destroy themselves. But free-living forms are just as contextually situated. What survives is never mere individuals or species, but the system containing them. Each is against the others, but each locus of value is tied into a corporation where values are preserved even as they are exchanged. From that point of view, we see conversions of resources from one life stream to another—the anastomosing of life threads that weaves an ecosystem.

Now it becomes difficult to say whether anything vital is lost at all. What seems waste in the rabbit life stream is nutrient within the coyote stream, and even the rabbit population benefits by the ongoing selection over mutants. The surplus of offspring is cut back by premature death, but this cutback is executed unawares by the coyotes so as, on statistical average, to leave the smarter, faster, more fertile, efficient, and wary. The rabbits suffer for the coyotes, but not entirely; they collectively gain from their pains. The surplus of young permits both mutational advance and the synthesis of biotic materials with higher forms at the top of the pyramid. This produces further demands on coyotes, and the coevolutionary race goes on.

Seen this way, organisms inherit value not only in their genes but from their competitors, enemies, and prey. On the short scale, values may seem hopelessly relative and impossible to evaluate, but in the whole, for all the borrowing and spending, biomass and energy are transubstantiated and recycled so that wildness is a no-waste world, frugal in its economies. We begin to get a new picture painted over the old, although some of the old picture still shows through. Wildness seemed a great struggle, and so it is; but it is also a great flowing of opposites into each other. Wildness is a complex tapestry of value on the one side, though it can seem a jumble of values on the other. Comparatively, there is as much wasting of resources in culture, and the more advanced the culture the greater the waste. The checks and balances that pull conflict into ordered existence are as successful in nature as in culture.

Over evolutionary time, these individual searches for advantages steadily yield systemic advancements. Wildness builds life up across perpetuated millennia. The cycling of values becomes the spiraling of stories. Once there were simple things, later complicated things. Fins become flippers, then feet, then fingers. Once there was no smelling, swimming, hiding, gambling, making mistakes, or outsmarting a competitor, but all these appear by trial and error. Through attempting and discarding, nature learns to build eyes, wings, photosynthesis, hemoglobin, muscles, fat, nerves, and brains.

Nothing knows what it is becoming, so much transcends the individual. The selective system must be capable of producing additional values, beyond those entertained by any individual organism, because it has long done so. We get higher forms. Natural selection edits to leave those forms that are justified in at least a right-for-life sense, and perhaps partly in some increasing right-to-life sense. Wildness as a jungle of exploitation becomes a theater of adventure and improvisation. Some forms merely track through stable environments, but others grow more clever in the same, changing, or new environments. Some persons may call this the luck of wildness, but it seems rather a lust for more life, even a lure that elaborates ever higher values.

Nature treats any particular individual with a momentary life, but life is a propagating wave over time. Located in individuals, value is also consigned to a stream. Even species regularly come and go, typically over five to fifty million years. Some become extinct without issue, but over longstanding trends nature transforms others to increase the numbers of species present in each later epoch, as well as their richness. Even the few crashes and mass extinctions, though setbacks, have reset life's directions, as happened at the ends of the Permian and Cretaceous periods. Retrenchments in the quantity of life were followed by explosive inventiveness in its quality. The mammals came into their own, triggered by wiping out the dinosaurs, even while reptiles and amphibians, and their descendants, the birds, remain important in our ecosystems. So I have at once to respect salamanders and to be glad nature sacrificed cold-blooded forms for hot-blooded developments beyond.

Wildness is an unquenchable, pro-life force in this respect, however groping, blind, and unmerciful it may otherwise seem. Survival value has its upstrokes, and we reach the paradox that out of seeming disorder order comes the more. There flows this great river of life, a strangely wild flowing because it flows as it were uphill, negentropically from nonbeing to being, from nonlife to objective life and on to subjective life. Nature is full of crooked, winding paths. Some are wayward lines; some prove routes to interesting places, and some are ascents to summits. Wildness is a place of new arrivals, as much as of survivals.

An individual's life is a defense of its value set, a concrete attempt at problem-solving, instantiating an intrinsic value. But an individual's death, by which such value collapses, is a contribution to values being defended by others who recycle its materials, energy, and information. Overall, the myriad individual passages through life and death upgrade the system. Value has to be something more, something opposed to what any individual actor likes or selects, since even struggle and death, which are never approved, are ingredients used instrumentally to produce still higher intrinsic values. Things good in themselves and of their kinds are not permitted to have such integrity alone, but are required to be good in their niche, good corporately. This can seem in morally wild disregard for their individuality, treating each as a means to an end. But the whole system in turn generates more and higher individuality. Problem-solving is a function of the system too as it recycles, recovers from setbacks, speciates, increases sentience and complexity, pulls conflicts into harmony, and redeems life from an ever-pressing death. The systemic source interblends intrinsic and instrumental values.

As we earlier met it, value is what makes a favorable difference to an organism's life, whether microbes using compasses or humans enjoying their wilderness roots, no matter whether instrumentally or intrinsically conceived. But as we now enlarge it, value is what makes a favorable difference to an ecosystem, enriching it, making it more beautiful, diverse, harmonious, intricate. Here a disvalue to an individual may be a value in the system and will result in values carried to other individuals. Intrinsic value exists only as embedded in instrumental value. No organism is a mere instrument, for each has its integral intrinsic value. But it can also be sacrificed in behalf of another life course, when its intrinsic value collapses, becomes extrinsic, and is in part instrumentally transported to another organism. When we interpret this transfer between individuals systemically, the life stream flows up an ecological pyramid over evolutionary time. The incessant making use of resources unifies the intrinsic and instrumental distinctions (the small circles and arrows of figure 2) and the result is the broad arrows of storied achievement by the great wild Source. Value as storied achievement is a property alike of organisms and the evolutionary ecosystem. Against the standard view that value requires a *beholder*, we see how value requires only a *holder*, which can be an individual, but can be also the historic system that carries value to and through individuals.

There is nothing secondary about instrumental value. When resource use is found omnipresent in the system, it loses its sting. Although there is something wrong with making everything else a resource for humans, there is nothing wrong with something being an instrumental resource for others. We think that a person is narrow and selfish who cultivates intrinsic worth and withdraws from seeking any instrumental value in the community. A person's intrinsic worth—for example, creative ability—is not separable from the power to confer a benefit on others. Excellence does not consist in what a thing is merely for itself, but in what it is for others. This is true of persons, animals, and plants. Excellence is not a matter of encapsulated being, but of fittedness into a pervasive whole.

Like instrumental and intrinsic values, the *is* and the *is good* have evolved together, and are even now experienced together. The recommendation that one ought to value these events follows from a discovery of their goodness in place, which is not so much by argument as by adventure that experiences their origins, structures, and environmental locations. We find value holders defending their values and fitted into the larger narratives of life. Natural *facts* of this kind are *storied doings* (Latin: *factum*, a deed) with their *value* (Latin: *valere*, to be worth) integral to their having managed to happen. In such a story every achievement is to be viewed intrinsically and instrumentally.

A wilderness guide can only exhibit examples from nature and then ask what reasons remain for asserting that storied achievement is not of value. The reason traditionally so called is that value lies in (human-) interest satisfaction. But that now seems only a stipulation born of prejudice or shortsightedness. Interest satisfaction is one among other values, and this better theory retains all we want from the narrower predecessor. Approbation and pleasure are only later parts of the story, and storied achievement can take place using, in the absence of, in indifference to, and even in opposition to interest satisfaction. Wildness first seems a chaos where nothing is given but everything is fought for. But afterward we learn how in the struggle everything vital has been given. In one sense wildness is the most *valuable* realm of all, the struggling womb *able* to generate all these adventures in *value*, whether involving roots, neighbors, or aliens. Thus the experienced wilderness traveler finds that the no trespassing signs posted between the *is* and the *ought* are nothing but cultural artifacts.

TRANSVALUING NATURE AND CULTURE

The trip home is almost as unsettling as the trip out. The giddy, wild experience of valuing nature shed of culture has led us through alien values and threatened chaos, but we have transformed a negative evaluation into a positive one. When we now swing round to return to culture, we find that we have a shaky trip home, this time shifting from a positive to a more negative evaluation. Culture is a good thing, fulfilling our human-interest satisfaction, but how far has it occurred in blind insensitivity to the storied achievements in nature? Some of what we have imagined was cultured in the good sense has in fact been valuationally wild in a haywire sense.

A key axiom in our culture declares it good to master nature. For this we have managed even to revise our justifications so as to maintain the ethic over shifting worldviews. The dominion thesis can be monotheistic, or it can be scientifically based. By the Darwinian creed, every species struggles to take over as much of Earth as it can, and humans evolve as dominants in the ecosystem. Huxley followed neither Genesis nor Darwin, still he advised us to combat the cosmic process. Freud psychoanalyzed humans to judge that we form civilization to conquer a fearful nature, and Marx saw in nature a thesis for which culture was an antithesis, with nature to be humanized in a final synthesis as labor imposes value on a valueless nature. The American's manifest destiny was to tame the continent. Across changing theories about how nature *is* constituted, we have derived the same *ought*—cultural exploitation of the environment—because we kept the same value theory. But it is time to take stock of the anti-wild policy itself. Can values sometimes be pro-wild? Here changing canons of judgment erode what we think of our own behavior.

Only about 2 percent of the contiguous United States remains wilderness; 98 percent is farmed, grazed, timbered, hunted over, dwelt upon, paved, or otherwise possessed. Not to put the remaining wildlands to some use seems un-American. It is as though a football team were to carry the ball 98 yards and walk off the field, as though an evangelist were to convert 98 of the folk in a village and decide to leave the last two pagan. To have islands of wildness deliberately in a sea of culture seems to let values go wild, out of our disciplined control. Even small amounts left as valuable are anomalies that force us to rethink the major ethic. That is why calling everything a resource seems so comfortable logically and psychologically. It prevents cognitive dissonance. An *ad hoc* auxiliary hypothesis protects the main policy—conquest and reclamation—by accommodating a little wildness transformed into a cultural good. There is minimal challenge to the triumphant Americanism. Even the wilds carry values at and for our pleasure. Userless nature is useless nature.

But if we face the epistemic crisis, the main paradigm is being overthrown. When the wildness is almost conquered, we begin to awake to error in the mastery theory. Not all value is labored for, assigned, or realized at our coming.

The anomalous 2 percent that we will to keep wild, and then realize to be valuable without our will, reveals that the theory of value that has governed our handling of the 98 percent is flawed, only an approximation over a certain range. Newton explained a high percentage of the observations of motion, especially at middle ranges, but could not handle an anomalous fraction of these. Einstein transcended and even falsified the old mechanics by showing that the classical theory was only approximate, on larger scales not corresponding to the world structures. In value theory, the human-interest satisfaction theory, with its corollary, the dominion thesis, works at a certain pragmatic home range, but it cannot handle wild values, and thereby stands revealed as incomplete if taken for the whole. The better theory relativizes what had seemed so absolute.

We can still give the conventional justifications, but we will be operating with a "Newtonian" view, true only locally. We will not have the "Einsteinian" view until we can also give nonanthropocentric justifications for why we ought to have wilderness in our midst. Thereupon we find that our new perspective over the last 2 percent casts some shadows over what we have done to the 98 percent conquered. There has been some savagery—greed, insensitivity, lack of control and compassion—in the civilized state. We have preyed on the natural areas we have sacrificed. We are parasites with this difference from the worms in the opossum: we had moral and conscious options for an evaluation of our roles, while they did not.

Let us perform a wild thought-experiment. What if the founding fathers by democratic resolution had resolved to set aside as natural wonders all major springs and caves, all natural lakes, summits, passes, gorges, water gaps, cascades, waterfalls, all headlands, capes, spits and half the shorelines and offshore islands? What if they had preserved a natural beltway along each river and major stream? What if the Bill of Rights had included an article governing the biotic rights of species? What if we had zoned each county and state to preserve one-fifth of the land public and wild, to include all rare ecosystems and ample representatives of the prevailing habitats? America would have formed a saner, more sensitive culture. It would be a different kind of country.

Let us put beside that practices from which we are only now recovering. For most of our national life we used bison and passenger pigeons for target practice. For almost a century, the Park Service at Yosemite would build an enormous fire on the lip of Glacier Point at dusk. "Indian Love Call" was played, and the fire pushed over the cliff to the ahs! of spectators. In the early 1960s I visited Yosemite to find the firefall stopped as an inappropriate activity. I had moral sense enough to agree, but a day later thought nothing of driving through a giant sequoia, stopping to let my wife take a photograph. I now see something of the Yahoo in myself for such zany comedy. There should be no more drive-through sequoias; they mutilate for whimsy a majestic living thing. We can rather learn why sequoias attain such age and size, or why this relict species has survived geological changes that destroyed its relatives.

In Yellowstone park officials long put soap into geysers to break the surface tension and time the eruptions conveniently for tourists. Old Faithful needed colored floodlights and background music between eruptions. Royal Gorge and Grandfather Mountain needed improvement, and so we built those touristy bridges that deface the gorge and the summit. Were what we did to Mount Rushmore and Stone Mountain good things? Or only grown-up versions of a little boy carving his initials on a maple tree? Reagan's and Eisenhower's faces carved on Yosemite's Half Dome would be a national disgrace. Colorado has 54 peaks over 14,000 feet, and we have built highways to the summits of only two, Mount Evans and Pike's Peak. But that is quite enough. Summit roads disfigure the peaks and scar the tundra. They compromise the "purple mountains' majesties" and easy access makes for inferior perceptions. Access roads and pleasuring activities should yield to some sense of natural norms to which we adapt our uses.

We fell into these cheap appreciations of our landscape because we had no sense of admiring respect for nature itself, a legacy of the policy that nature even left in a rude state exists as our park and pleasuring grounds. So we mislocated the thrills, and could not see the sequoia and bison, the mountain community or the geyser basin as excellent achievements in spontaneous nature. Development has sometimes been a good thing; the theory of wild value need not contest that. It only insists that development take place with some sense of sacrifice to be argued against wild values. We should not unilaterally assault nature. Development against wildness plots on a curve of diminishing returns; it is a relative and not an absolute thing. You can have too much, and lose your bearings on a horizon of wild goods, the more valuable when they are threatened with extinction. The place where values go wild in the berserk sense is in a nation which, having destroyed 98 percent of its pristine wilderness, having paved more area than it has designated wilderness, can consider the remaining 2 percent and wonder if it has too much. The world's cultures have grown wild in a cancerous sense when, continuing on their present courses, they can destroy one tenth of Earth's species in a generation.

On the other hand, a modest moral maturing can be seen in those names that, over the years, we have attached to wild places. Besides lands for the "Bureau of Reclamation," we formerly had only "National Forests" and "National Parks," work places and play places for multiple use and as pleasuring grounds. Later, we established "Wildlife Refuges" and "Sanctuaries," which, less evidently "National," are places where bighorn sheep and pileated woodpeckers can have their own territories, not exclusively our property. More recently still, we have designated "Wildernesses" and "Natural Areas," and now the label "National," though kept to designate federal administration, seems almost imperialistic. These are not really American places at all but enclaves with a sovereignty of their own "where the earth and its community of life are untrammeled by man, where man himself is a visitor who does not remain."[12] These are realms where Americans value freedom so highly that we give even the wilderness the freedom to run itself. At least here, humans elect to leave wildness unclaimed. We need a new, strange kind of foreign policy, an almost self-contradictory wilderness management where what we really manage is those who visit it, so as to arrange for noninterference and compensate for interferences previously unmanaged.

Wildness is a bizarre place where our conventional values get roughed up. We learn the relativity and subjectivity of what in civilization can seem such basic rules. Wild nature doesn't know my frames of reference and can't in the slightest care about my deepest cultural norms. In wildness there is no time of day; it is not 10:00 a.m. Eastern Daylight Time, nor is it Tuesday or July. There are no board-feet, BTUs, meters, miles; the lines of latitude and longitude and elevation contours do not really exist. There is no English or German, no literature or conversation. The numbers and words are gone, and we know them for the cultural improvisations and mathematical overlays they are. One leaves money in the car and enters a different economy. There are no artifacts and labor is fleeting. There are no deeds, statutes, or police—this is what makes boundaries, regulations, and rangers so disruptive of the wilderness experience. In wildness there is neither capitalism nor socialism, neither democracy nor monarchy, science nor religion. There is no honesty, justice, mercy, or duty. There are no human resources, because, like targets or pests, these do not exist as such but only become so awakened by interest. We do not even term these places a wilderness except negatively, a place where humans are not.

So what, if anything, is positively of value there? There is light and dark, life and death. There is time almost everlasting and a genetic language two billion years old. There is energy and evolution inventing fertility and prowess, adaptation and improvisation, information and strategy, contest and compliance, display and flair. There is muscle and fat, nerve and sweat, law and form, structure and process, beauty and cleverness, harmony and sublimity, tragedy and glory. Wildness is the projective and selective system that spins the embracing story. Wildness is the primal ground, the prime mover, as nearly as we can approach such things in phenomenal experience. In this light, a test of a consummate culture is not whether it can consume all nature, but whether it is wise enough to choose its social values, let natural values stay wild, and appreciate nature as the generating source of storied achievements.

DISTINCTIVELY WILD VALUES, DISTINCTIVELY HUMAN VALUING

Two final elements enrich the story, one emerging in spontaneous nature, one in culture, both distinctively yet differently wild.

Wildness is nature in what philosophers call idiographic form. Each wilderness is one of a kind, so we give it a proper name—the Rawahs, the Dismal

Swamp. We climb Mount Ida or canoe on the Congaree River. Even when exploring some nameless canyon or camping at a spring, one experiences a concrete locus never duplicated in idiosyncratic detail. In culture, there is but one Virginia and each Virginian has a proper name. The human differences include conscious self-affirmations and heritages for which nature provides little precedent. But nature first is never twice the same. Always in the understory there are distinctive landscape features—the Shenandoah Valley or the Chesapeake Bay—with which the Virginians interact, each with a unique genetic set. Before culture emerges, nature is already endlessly variable. This feature is crucial to what we mean by wildness.

Storied achievement is a unitary idea, but diffracts into plural lives and diverse communities. We do not want order at the expense of spontaneous variety, too much system and too little story. We want constancy with contingency. Just this final wildness, which might threaten to make nature chaotic and thus perhaps to upset storied achievement, proves rather to enhance it, adding excitement and novelty. What seems fortuitous is also fortunate and valuable. By making each location different, wildness makes a favorable difference. It makes each ecosystem historic, the more excellent because no two are alike. Wildness proves of further value just for everywhere making these differences.

If you have seen one mountain or redwood, you have not seen them all. The sunbather at the shore sees all herring gulls as alike, but Niko Tinbergen found each gull different.

> It is quite a thrill to discover that the birds you are studying are not simply specimens of the species *Larus argentatus* but that they are personal acquaintances. Somehow, the colony becomes much more interesting when you realize that it is composed of individuals that you know personally. Somehow, you feel, you are at home, you are taking part in their lives, and their adventures become part of your own life. It is difficult to explain this more fully, but I think everybody who has studied animal communities will understand how we felt.[13]

Tinbergen felt bound to recognize this individuality but could not incorporate it into ethological science.

Science gives us statistical nature, abstractly and theoretically modeled, but wilderness is historically particular. A scientific law never changes, a trend seldom changes, but wilderness ever changes. Our sciences are unable to predict or systematize this element. Each river or gull is a one-time event in the mixtures of forces, laws, and happenstance that shape its course. Sometimes this yields only a kaleidoscopic recombination of old materials. Much variation is an unfolding of causal chains too scrambled for us to follow. A rock loosened by frost heave thaws and rolls down a hillside just as a coyote is set to pounce on a ground squirrel. This distracts the predator, alerts the prey, and the squirrel escapes. All this is causal enough, but wild in the impingement of unrelated causal lines, so that we can never write laws about these messy interactions and are repeatedly surprised by them. Beyond this, there is openness, option, and decision, as when a random mutation appears, or a moose confronted by a wolf decides not to run but to stand his ground. Genuine wildness with its empirical individuality at each native locus always escapes scientific specification.

Mere order has little story in it, but wildness makes an idiographic narrative out of what otherwise might be universal repetition and law, less storied achievements. After the laws have explained what they can, there is a residue of wildness. We value this detail, which is wild of the very laws it obeys. In that sense, the "ideal" is not the uniform and predictable. More unbroken sameness would not be as valued as the wilder nature we in fact have, the more ideal because the more storied. A second natural place is never redundant, because never reducible to a first one; each is irreplaceable. No text that narrates one place fully describes another. The system that earlier might have seemed to swamp out individual integrity is now seen to resist being so systematized that uniqueness vanishes.

Physics and chemistry are thought to be about fundamental nature, but they ignore wildness—unless perhaps we see some beginnings in quantum randomness, fluid turbulence, vortex streaking, stochastic elements, margins of error, or probability patterns. As sciences of law and order, they bring nature under laboratory control, being relatively exact sciences because they denature nature of its accidental and historical eventfulness. More wildness begins to appear in geology; and in geomorphology or meteorology we reach an earthen system that has uniqueness in each Mount Saint Helens explosion or Big Thompson flood.

Biology is still more inexact because closer to wildness. Generalizations abound, but in textbooks that simplify what is going on in the field. Physics and chemistry have repeatedly made predictions out of their theories. Neptune and helium were predicted, then found. Relativity theory predicted time dilation, and quantum mechanics the neutrino. But biology has seldom been able to do this. The cellular structures—mitochondria, chromosomes, plasmids—were only found without advance expectation. Before a visit to Lake Baikal, no one could predict its flora and fauna; 1500 of its 2000 species are unique. The most telling lament against evolutionary theory is that it explains only in retrospect, and then stutters over why the birds invaded the skies when they did, or why only a few primates grew larger brains.

A physicist or chemist predicts that reactions known on Earth hold uniformly on Jupiter or Sirius, but an exobiologist would be foolish to do more than speculate what life must be like elsewhere, because elements of historical uniqueness are much advanced over anything in the nonbiological sciences. One can progressively say less of what must happen until after things are already happening. Biologists find dependable biochemistries, phylogenies, and genetic dynamics. But they also know that wild nature is more and less than their models. Ecologists trace generalized food chains, mineral cycles, and plant successions, but also find a site-specific and situation-specific character that forces its best practitioners to say that the only thing they know for certain is that nothing is certain. Their models only approximate nature's robustness, because they leave out wildness.

Everyone has hiked into a place, topographic map in hand, to be surprised how different it was from anything expected. Maps and earlier experiences leave out the vicissitudes of this new locale. To go to nature guided by science manuals is to go in ignorance of its provincial integrity. The texts only describe bristlecone pines, not the gnarled sentinel where the Bierstadt trail breaks out on the tundra, only oak-hickory forests, not the floor of Linville Gorge. They describe foxes in their predator-prey relations, not the vixen at Brown's Lake that jumped higher than I expected and stole the food cache I had strung up. Wilderness areas are unique in that appreciating them, and the sorts of experiences that can be had in them, cannot be reduced to any of the established sciences. Wildness is to be valued both for its generating of idiosyncratic human experiences and in itself as generating ever varied topographic integrities and the singular stories that take place at such loci. Although we have often appealed to the sciences for insight into events of wild value, in the end there is in wildness a value that is uncaptured by science.

There is no narrative in biology text, but a trip into wildness is always a story. One comes back with tales to tell. The storm broke when supper wasn't cooked. The whippoorwills sang so loud one couldn't sleep. The squirrel watched at the cliff missed its jump and fell to its death, and there were fourteen fairy slippers within an arm's reach a half mile east of Donner Pass. Last summer in the Mount Zirkel Wilderness I found a northern species of *Bryum,* which is disjunct 1300 miles south of any known station for that species.[14] This element of surprise supplies adventure, and is part of values gone wild.

In closing, we turn to the human side. When our values go wild, there is the emergence of an utterly new kind of caring. The animal takes an interest in its own affairs, vitally interested in food or predator, valuing its life and kind with zeal, but unconcerned beyond. I do not entirely deny animal curiosity; nevertheless, only humans can take a sustained interest in sectors of the environment not their own. So Tinbergen studied gulls, Lindbergh defended wildlife, and you and I have taken this trip into the wildlands. For the first time, a form of life values something outside its own niche, cares intensively or comprehensively beyond its own pragmatic sector.

A singular feature of human psychology and morality is how we can value wild things not for ourselves, but for what they are in themselves, estimating our own place in nature when so doing. Animal species, though out there in the wild, cannot appreciate wildness beyond their own territories. But humans can value wild roots, neighbors, and aliens independently of whether a particular phenomenon affects our survival, well-being, or convenience. Resource relationships are set aside, and we look at the world with moral judgment. Nor is this merely at the individual level, valuing kinds in themselves, but it is also at the global level, for we alone are able to see past the atomistic struggles into the production of value in the evolutionary ecosystem. We do not have survival value revisited, but survival value transcended. We have a novel arrival indeed. We reach an almost supernatural altruism, unprecedented on the planet.

Humans are disjoined from nature not merely because we form cultures and dramatically rebuild our environment. We are still more unnatural creatures when we post boundaries for our cultures and designate wilderness that we resolve not to rebuild. At this point, I do want to grade the human excellence over the other creatures. On the one hand, this human evaluation of the world expresses itself as a late-coming consequence of, rather than claiming itself as an exemption to, a value-generating creativity inherent in nature. On the other hand, this human excellence is exceptional. Nature takes a wild turn, an idiographic and historic one in ethical achievement. The story comes to a head in humans, although the story is vastly more than its heading in humans. Persons count, but not so much that nothing else counts; and persons count for more when they can count something else.

It is not surprising that humans should come to care for their own kin and kind, for, astonishing as is the emergence of morality, sympathy can be shown to have survival value. It is not surprising that humans care instrumentally for wildlands. Novel as is the coming of mind, to calculate one's interests in the natural system makes simple good sense. But all these ways of valuing that we can plausibly unfold by extensions from spontaneous nature are entirely superseded when we meet this creature who can value at a distance. In a final paradox, when we humans recognize values outside ourselves, we realize within the subtlest value of all. Valuing wildness does not bring any dehumanizing of ourselves or reversion to beastly levels. On the contrary, it results in our further spiritualizing. We become nobler spirits, encompassing the wild other for itself and in the whole, not humanistically. Nature surpasses herself to generate the most exceptional novelty yet. We praise the productive source, and praise the values found instrumentally and intrinsically among the myriad natural kinds. We cannot produce ourselves and must value the system that has. But the systemic source cannot reflectively evaluate what it has produced; only we can. In humans, an evolutionary ecosystem becomes conscious of itself.

Before wildness I realize that I have yet more valuational work to do. I become surprisingly more human and also enjoy being surprisingly wild myself. If we humans can rightly learn to value wildness, that will be a still more sophisticated storied achievement.

NOTES

For critical discussion see Anthony Weston, "Beyond Intrinsic Value: Pragmatism in Environmental Ethics," *Environmental Ethics* 7(1985): 321-339.

1. John C. Hendee, George H. Stankey, and Robert C. Lucas, *Wilderness Management* (Washington: USDA Forest Service Miscellaneous Publication No. 1365, 1978), pp. 140-41.

2. Paul D. MacLean, "The Triune Brain, Emotion, and Scientific Bias," in Francis O. Schmitt, ed., *The Neurosciences Second Study Program* (New York: Rockefeller University Press, 1970), pp. 336-49.

3. Lubert Stryer, *Biochemistry* (San Francisco: W. H. Freeman & Co., 1975), pp. 351-52.

4. Ibid., pp. 373-74.

5. J. Alumets, R. Hakanson, F. Sundler, and J. Thorell, "Neuronal Localization of Immunoreactive Enkephalin and β-endorphin in the Earthworm," *Nature* 279(28 June 1979): 805-806; K. A. Miczek, M. L. Thompson and L. Schuster, "Opioid-Like Analgesia in Defeated Mice," *Science* 215(1982): 1520-22.

6. Olov Lindberg, ed., *Brown Adipose Tissue* (New York: American Elsevier Publishing Co., 1970); Julie Ann Miller, "Getting Warm," *Science News* 111, no. 3 (15 January 1977): 42-43.

7. Quoted in G. E. Hutchinson, "Homage to Santa Rosalia, or Why Are There So Many Kinds of Animals?" *American Naturalist* 93 (1959): 145-59, on p. 146.

8. Philip N. Lehner, "Coyote Communication," in Marc Bekoff, ed., *Coyotes: Biology, Behavior, and Management* (New York: Academic Press, 1978) pp. 127-62, citation on p. 158.

9. R. B. Frankel, R. P. Blakemore, and R. S. Wolfe, "Magnetite in Freshwater Magnetotactic Bacteria," *Science* 203(1979): 1355-56; T. H. Maugh II, "Magnetic Navigation an Attractive Possibility," *Science* 215(1982): 1492-93.

10. Lyn Forster, "Vision and Prey-Catching Strategies in Jumping Spiders," *American Scientist* 70(1982): 165-75.

11. T. H. Huxley, *Evolution and Ethics* (New York: D. Appleton & Co., 1894), p. 83.

12. *Wilderness Act of 1964*, sec. 2c. (U.S. Public Law 88-577).

13. Niko Tinbergen, *The Herring Gull's World* (New York: Basic Books, 1960) pp. 84-85.

14. Holmes Rolston, III, "*Bryum knowltonii* New to the United States," *Bryologist* 85(1982): 420.

III. ENVIRONMENTAL
PHILOSOPHY IN PRACTICE

Perhaps when philosophy goes wild, it loses all civil utility. Can environmental ethics speak to our social policy and economy? Can it put its theories into practice informing decisions? Two essays that follow show how environmental ethics operates in the worlds of business and government. A third asks for a rationale for the preservation of endangered species. We do not here seek to make actual decisions in the specific detail faced by corporate executives, professional resource agency personnel, or legislators. We seek guidelines that orient decisions in a coherent and reasonably functional way; we want help setting policy through what we shall call middle-range maxims.

The multiple maxims that we here propose to guide business decisions, therefore, pragmatically mix human interests and a complementary concern for natural things in their own integrity; they mix instrumental and intrinsic values, morals and prudence, present and future, financial and legal concerns, individual and species. The result is a many-faceted effort to seek justice in business where business encounters nature. Further, policy decisions in government are no less complex. The second essay returns to the question of value, first to analyze its levels—economic, social, individual, organismic, and the like—and then to recall, in variant form, the types of values that arise in human encounters with the landscape, its fauna and flora. The third essay probes the human relationship to and responsibility for endangered species in their ecosystems. All this is directed toward a policy for making decisions about remnant wildlands. Once again, there are practical maxims to orient those who make environmental decisions.

8

Just Environmental Business

INTRODUCTION

Since business began, some ways of making money have been judged morally unacceptable. But only in the last two decades has business been pressed to cope with environmental prohibitions. Consider for instance the following cases, and notice how what may first seem to be routine and nonmoral environmental matters, just business, turn out to involve deeper ethical puzzles about what is just in business. Notice too that the justice we are here called upon to think through is not abstract and impractical; it concerns everyday affairs in the business world.

1. Case Studies

Case 1. Allied Chemical Corporation, operating an eastern Virginia plant, was charged with intentionally violating environmental protection laws by releasing Kepone into local waters. Denying the charges, the firm pleaded no contest, but was fined $13.2 million, the largest fine ever imposed in an environmental case. Judge Robert R. Merhige, Jr., wrote: "I disagree with the defendants' position that all of this was so innocently done, or inadvertently done. I think it was done because of what it considered business necessities, and money took the forefront. . . . Allied knew it was polluting the waters."[1]

Case 2. Daniel K. Ludwig, the wealthiest American, has been bulldozing much of 5,800 square miles of Amazon rain forest, replanting it for silviculture and agriculture, producing mostly rice, paper pulp, and newsprint. His Jari project is welcomed by many as a model for the whole Amazon basin. But this rain forest is the richest biological system on Earth, and how many thousands of

Reprinted by permission from Tom Regan, ed., *Just Business: New Introductory Essays in Business Ethics* (New York: Random House, 1984), pp. 324–359. Copyright © 1984 by Random House.

plant and animal species Mr. Ludwig and other Amazon developers are destroying cannot be known because the fauna and flora there are very incompletely studied. Hugh H. Iltis, a leading contemporary naturalist, has condemned Ludwig in a presidential address to the National Association of Biology Teachers for his part in "the enormity of this crime," among the biologically most dangerous and destructive events of this century.[2]

Case 3. Cyprus Mines Corporation, owned by Standard Oil of Indiana and Westinghouse, has proposed a uranium mine, the Hansen project, thirty-five miles northwest of Canon City, Colorado. Permitting agencies have been indecisive over disposal of tailings, above grade or below grade, more or less expensive to handle depending on trenching involved and isolation from the ground water. Though the uranium is removed, daughter radionuclides remain, long-lived radium that steadily emits short-lived but mobile radon gas, decaying into further contaminants. By dust, wind, leaching, runoff, irrigation, wildlife movements, these make their way into air, water, food. Some studies find that revegetated soil cover would slow this, others find that plant intake moves radon into the air faster than would a rip-rap cover. Radiation and health risks are debated. The project has stalled.[3]

The sorts of issues raised in these three cases will unfold as we proceed, but right at the start we begin to see how environmental questions have recently awakened us from our ecological slumbers. The Environmental Protection Agency and related regulatory agencies have become major federal powers. There are many state and local environmental rules. Environmental regulation is a daily fact of business life. But business leaders ought not be concerned merely with obeying the law. They will want to be sensitive to the right and wrong that underlie, or should underlie, the law. Debates about new laws or less regulation will turn on what is just. But how can we decide right or wrong in such cases? That is the central question that demands our attention.

2. Two Kinds of Environmental Ethic

Two kinds of environmental ethic are possible. The obvious kind is anthropocentric. Right and wrong are determined by human interest. This ethic (let us call it the humanistic ethic) is secondarily an environmental ethic; concern for the environment is entirely subsidiary to a concern for *humans,* who are helped or hurt by the condition of their surroundings. The other type (the naturalistic ethic), held perhaps more intensely by fewer advocates, is directly about *nature.* It holds that some natural objects, such as whooping cranes, are morally considerable in their own right, apart from human interests, or that some ecosystems, perhaps the Great Smokies, have intrinsic values, such as aesthetic beauty, from which we derive a duty to respect these landscapes. Both types have new moral applications to think through, but the naturalistic ethic is more radical. While few deny that humans have duties to other humans, many puzzle how nonhuman nature can be the object of duty. Nevertheless, a novel happening in current normative ethics is the emergence of serious thought about the possibility of a nonanthropocentric, naturalistic environmental ethic. Is there moral awakening going on here, analogous to that of the days when we awoke to the evils of slavery or of child labor? People in business are by custom bound to consider the anthropocentric ethic, but not the naturalistic one. But those in the world of business eventually will encounter the principles and implications of the latter ethic and, as the proverb has it, there is no time like the present to begin to do some thinking here. This is not only because some of the most vigorous critics of business have these deeper concerns, but because even those who operate out of humanistic motives may find that they sometimes share sympathies with, and find some logic in, what the naturalists recommend.

We will begin with a sketch of some of the main principles or operating rules of a humanistic environmental ethic (secs. 3-12) and follow that with a sketch of some main rules in a more naturalistically oriented environmental ethic (secs. 13-22). In a third and final part (secs. 23-32), we note how the ethical interplay between business and the environment is an especially complex thing. Owing both to the nature of business in our industrial society and to the nature of environmental interactions, complications arise that require us to make ethical judgments in less familiar and more demanding contexts than ethicists sometimes face. Our final group of guidelines offers some advice for the business-person in the midst of the complexities of environmental affairs. A mosaic of ideas—humanistic and naturalistic concerns, individual and corporate responsibility, obligations to future generations, shared risks, and so forth—has here to be kept in focus if we are to form a clear picture of "the facts" and "the values." Stand too close and we see some details but lose the overall design. Stand too far away and we see the shape but lose the substance. The challenge is to command a clear view.

A further word is appropriate about the style of presentation. Our overall argument does not run like the links of a chain, for extended formal argument is seldom possible in ethics. Rather, what unfolds is a series of maxims, or injunctions, together with explanations and illustrations sufficient for the reader to see what is demanded. This invites critical reflection. So far as readers find, on reflection, that these "commandments" make sense, they will tend cumulatively to support an over-all ethic, as multiple legs support a large table. These maxims will be what moralists sometimes call middle-level rules, that is, neither very general nor very specific. We will give each one a name, so that we do not forget it too easily.

BUSINESS AND A HUMANISTIC ENVIRONMENTAL ETHIC

Environmental ethics connects us with a problematic theme: how to harmonize the sometimes dissonant claims of private interests and public goods. An old ambivalence in the Judeo-Christian mind about profit-making and how this mixes doing unto oneself with doing for others has reappeared in recent discussions about the social responsibility of business. If moral philosophers have nearly agreed to anything, they agree that ethical egoism (I ought *always* do what is in my enlightened self-interest) is both incoherent and immoral. If ethically enlightened executives have nearly agreed to anything, they agree that profit-making cannot be the *sole* business of business, however much it is a necessary one, and however unsettled the extent of their social responsibility. In a narrow sense, the personal ethic most opposed by ethicists seems to be the bottom line of all business. But in a broader sense, much business is possible that simultaneously serves private interests and public goods. It is hard for a large business to stay in operation, whatever its profits, unless the managers and employees bring themselves to believe that the firm is contributing to the public good. Else, negatively, they must regard themselves as trapped or bury themselves in their own anxiety. But, positively, this means they will try to choose a route that at once serves their profit and the public good, more or less. That much agreement, admittedly rough, reconciles business and moral philosophy enough to let us apply this in environmental ethics.

"Environmental and other social problems should get *at least* as much corporate attention as production, sales, and finance. The quality of life in its total meaning is, in the final reckoning, the only justification for any corporate activity."[4] That demand, with its emphasis, comes from the former chairman of the board of the world's largest bank, Louis B. Lundborg. What would it mean to write environmental ethics into company policy? If that ethic is humanistic, the following ten maxims would be first considerations.

3. The Stakeholder Maxim: Assess Costs Suffered by Persons
Not Party to Your Business Transactions

Social costs do not show up on companies' or customers' books, but someone pays them sooner or later. Dumping pollutants into the air, water, and soil amounts to having free sewage. A business exports pollution, more or less of it depending on how much one can get past current regulations. The EPA classifies over half of the fifty thousand market chemicals as being hazardous if inadequately disposed of, with perhaps only ten percent being safely handled. Divide or multiply their figures by two or three, and the threat is still serious. Someone has to suffer impaired health, a blighted landscape, and reduced property values, and pay clean-up bills or medical costs. The acid rain falls downwind at home or abroad. Governor George Wallace once remarked, as the winds blew east to waft pollution through the Alabama capitol's corridors, that the odor wasn't so bad. In fact, it was "sweet" because it was "the smell of money."[5] He could more accurately have said that it was the smell of money changing pockets from the hapless victims, who must pay for the damages, to those of the business operators who profited the more from their free sewage.

Here, a good company will follow the urging of Henry B. Schacht, chairman of the board at Cummins Engine Company, to consider the stakeholders as well as the stockholders.[6] But it is easy to forget this because of the concentrated benefits and widespread costs. The costs are heavy but too thinly dispersed to keep focused against the lesser but concentrated benefits. Lots of persons are hurt, but they may not be hurt very much, or be able to show very easily the origin of their hurt. Individuals may be too scattered to organize themselves well against the offending company. The stakeholder maxim enjoins concern about all this.

The Kepone fine (see Case 1) shows how legal penalties are developing because business has been notoriously slow to police its spillover. The Superfund legislation of 1980 provides large sums to clean up a hundred orphaned sites inherited from (knowingly or unknowingly) irresponsible practices of earlier years. Many chemical and petroleum companies backed this legislation, a bit grudgingly, perhaps hoping thereby to deal with the tip of an iceberg. They will get off cheaper this way than if the full extent of old costs hidden at fifty thousand sites ever becomes evident. One business by itself can only partially (to use an economist's catchword) internalize these externalities, but every business can as a matter of policy work in concert with others here. Almost every reader is carrying in his body some of the burden of this problem, so there ought to be none unwilling to weigh the moral burden here.

4. The Countryside Maxim: Do Not Assume that What's
Good for the Company Is Good for the Country

The aphorism of Charles E. Wilson, a famous GM executive, that, "What's good for General Motors is good for the country," is half true, even mostly true.[7] But its untruth comes out well in environmental affairs, where we give the word "country" a grassroots twist to include people in their urban and rural places. The United States automakers have steadily resisted stronger pollution standards and fuel-efficient cars, foot-dragging all the way. This is true even though the cleaner air was good for the city, the countryside, and all inhabitants thereof, and though smaller cars would have been less demanding on petroleum reserves. Their reason has been that compliance took extra work and put a crimp in the industry's profits. Every developer, realtor, purchaser of minerals and fibers, user of energy, and disposer of wastes will find some ways of doing business better, some worse for the countryside, and here one ought to love his country more than his company. Each business, like each person, lives, eats, and breathes in and on a public reservoir. In this sense there is no such thing as a private business. Garrett Hardin has described in a sad phrase, "the tragedy of the commons," how individuals and their companies can each do what is in their own immediate self-interest but all together gradually destroy the public domain, "the commons," including their neighborhood and countryside, its air, water, soil, forests, resources. They end by destroying themselves.[8]

5. The Sunshine Maxim: Do Not Keep Company Secrets that May
Vitally Affect Those from Whom the Secrets Are Kept

This permits a healthy outside environmental audit. A company has a limited right to keep trade secrets and to classify its affairs, but there is a lamentable tendency under this guise to conceal information that might prove detrimental to the company. The reluctance to count spillover costs or the trouble distinguishing the good of company and country make it important to get the facts, and lack of them, out for the purpose of open debate. This is especially important if those who may be hurt are to have the chance to defend their own interests. It took the Freedom of Information Act to disclose that (in 1976) eight thousand pounds of plutonium and bomb-grade uranium were unaccounted for in the United States, enough for the construction of hundreds of nuclear weapons. A corporate polluter once claimed that the amount of sulfuric acid his company dumped into the Savannah River was a trade secret; others have claimed that the public had no right to know what was coming out of their smokestacks. The National Science Foundation's Panel to Select Organic Compounds Hazardous to the Environment sent a survey to industries in 1975 and found that only twenty-eight percent of the industries gave replies that were usable as answers in compiling data, owing largely to the tradition of secrecy in the chemical industries.[9] Subpoenaed documents have often shown companies to be telling less than the whole truth.

Love your "enemies" here because they are, in the long run, your friends, unless you really don't care whether you harm innocents. Company policy should volunteer relevant files cooperatively, even if this may reduce company profits. It forces you to more care, but the threat of potential harm to innocents overrides reduced profits by operators. The sunshine maxim also requires individual employees to reverse, even to violate, policy that maliciously, tacitly, naively, makes truth the first casualty in an environmental contest. It may require whistle-blowing. The secrets here are sometimes about secrets. For example, the administrators of a nuclear reactor may fail to reveal that they do not know the extent, and cannot diagnose the threat, of contaminants released in an accident. It is hard to maintain credibility when ignorance and mistakes are exposed, but still harder to recover it when once it is found that you have lied or mismanaged the news.

6. The Legacy Maxim: Do Not Disclaim Responsibility in Inherited Problems

Many mistakes were made before hazards were understood. When an individual

joins a firm, he or she inherits all its problems (often coinciding with its opportunities) proportionately to his or her influence with that company, the degree of
which may advance over time. When a firm enters the market, it inherits all its
problems (also its opportunities) proportionately to its share of the market. Both
individuals and firms will find themselves with problems for which *they* are not
responsible. *Other* actors produced the present situation. We have a rationalizing
tendency to conclude that we are not responsible *in* the inherited mess if we are
not responsible *for* it. The employee may not have been born or the company in
business when the now-orphaned wastes were carelessly dumped. But present
operators, both one company and all in concert, can do something about reversing these conditions, as the firms backing the Superfund illustrate. Creatively
doing what we can is our responsibility. When we wake up to sufficient environmental deterioration to alarm us morally, the problem is well underway. It is not
"our" fault, if we restrict the scope of "our" to present employees and firm, but it
is still "our" problem. Voluntarily to join a company is voluntarily to assume
responsibility for the effects of its past decisions.

7. The No-Discount Maxim: Do Not Discount the Future Environmentally

We now place a moral check on the practice, used wisely enough in limited
places in classical economics, of discounting the future. Initially a function of the
interest rate, discounting is philosophically defended because future needs are
uncertain and resources shift with developing technologies. We excuse our
present consumption by saying that what persons desire varies over generations,
and that future persons will have to look out after themselves. Nor do we
altogether use up natural resources; we partly convert them to capital, which
others inherit.

Such justifications make some sense, but fail when we begin to tamper with
what have hitherto been the natural certainties. Perhaps we are not obligated to
supply future generations with oil or timber, for they may not need these as
much as we do. But water, air, soil, genes, even landscapes are not in this class
of resources, because they are more timeless and irretrievable. They define everything else, and there are no substitutes. There is a difference between cutting off
a person's paycheck and cutting off his air supply, between eating the harvest
and eating the seed corn. We have no duty to leave our grandchildren wealthy,
but we ought to leave them a world no worse than we found it, like campers
who use a campsite.

The issue is deceiving because we only gradually push the troubled skies and
poisoned soils over onto the next generation. When the fifty-five-gallon drums
storing our wastes rust out, their labels gone, what then? Toxic substances in
ground water are nearly impossible to remove. If the pharaohs had stored their
plutonium wastes in the pyramids, these would still be ninety percent as lethal as
when stored. Radiocontaminants for uranium tailings will be mutagenic for

generations. Our books may be black, the GNP up, but how much of this is because of what we have charged to future generations? One shouldn't make debts for others to pay, and especially when there is no foreseeable way for them to pay such debts.

But concerns here are not merely those of safety and a decent environment. They are also about freedom to enjoy the natural amenities. What if the executive's grandchildren prefer warblers, eagles, parks, the seasonal rhythms of a countryside, over the aging shopping centers and hydroelectric plants he leaves them? They might complain that he bequeathed them no capital. They are more likely to complain that he took away their options in wildness, and that business and technology can provide no authentic substitutes. Thou shalt not steal the natural basics from tomorrow.

8. The Unconsumption Maxim: Maximize Nonconsumptive Goods

Consumption is what business and even life is all about, for we all consume to live. But in another sense, consumption is a kind of wasting disease, one of ineffective use. Perhaps permitted levels of consumption can rise gradually over time, as broader resource bases, recycling methods, and energy techniques are discovered. Then the luxuries of the fathers can become the necessities of the children. Nevertheless, at any given decision point, it is better to favor the least consumptive alternative. Some things can be used without being used up, the difference between a cloth and a paper towel. A trophy hunter brings the buck back with him, a wildlife photographer leaves him there for others to enjoy. So, fiscal concerns being equal, an optics manufacturer might prefer telephoto lenses to crosshair scopes. Often, the less consumptive a good is (a day spent hiking the Appalachian Trail), the higher its quality. Amenity use tends to be nonconsumptive, while commodity use tends to be consumptive. A realtor who resolves to keep goods as public and permanent as possible will not seek to convert into posted, exclusive cabin plots land suitable for a state park or essential to the Trailway.

One alarm clock may last two years, another twenty. In our lavish yet cheap, throwaway economy, business has hardly urged efficiency upon its customers. The market is full of planned obsolescence, with far more time spent hooking the gullible buyer into consumption than is spent considering alternative, possibly equally profitable ways of making goods more durable. We too often have (adapting a computing term) a gigo economy, garbage *in*, garbage *out*, because the stuff is not only junk when finished, it is junk when sold. There are some goodies too that should hardly have been made at all. It is unlikely that electric carving knives have really benefited one in a hundred of their purchasers. The advice to eliminate consumptive goods is ridiculous, but the effort to maximize consumptive goods is equally so, and unethical as well.

9. The Reconsumption Maxim: Maximize Recycling

Make it so it will last, but then again, make it so it won't. When junked, can it be remanufactured? Of otherwise comparable materials, which one may be more economically reused? General Motors has had a task force looking for ways to improve the recyclability of cars by changing the materials. Ecologically, one material may be biodegradable, another not. The hamburger must be eaten, but does it need to be wrapped in so majestic a petroplastic carton, used for twenty-five seconds to carry it from the counter to the table, then tossed to lie in a trash heap for decades? The hamburger is digested and eliminated, the nutrients recycled; the wrapper, indigestable by man or microbe, outlasts the life of the burger eater. For that matter, does the hamburger even need to be wrapped, if this requires Mr. Ludwig to sacrifice the Amazon rain forest? (See Case 2.) The soda pop consumed on the trail is soon gone, the aluminum tab tossed there lasts nearly a century. It might have been manufactured affixed to the can, and the can packed out and recycled by deposit or buy-back incentives. A single wood-handled carving knife will outlast half a dozen electric ones; it gives its user needed exercise and no expense. If it ever wears thin, the wood can rot and the steel be remelted, while the plastic from the electric gadgetry lies useless at the dump.

An economist needs to be mindful of what an ecologist calls "throughput" in the system, the movement of energy and materials so that the valuable constituents nowhere choke up, but keep being reutilized in the systemic flows. From one viewpoint this is a matter of expediency and efficiency, but from another it is also a moral concern. How do we spend a resource so as to keep it from being spent forever? How do we recycle value? Nature's bounty and invisible hand once took care of these things reasonably well, but no longer. So business has a new duty.

10. The Priority Maxim: The More Vital an Irreplaceable Resource, the More Worthwhile the Use to Which It Should Be Put

No resources should go through the economy too cheap to meter, but some are dear enough to need metering by more than market supply and demand. Of those nonrenewable and difficult to recycle, some are more crucial than others. The more one does business in this type of resource, the less one ought to manufacture transient, trivial goods, the more one ought to lock it into the capital of the economy. Molybdenum is in relatively short supply, its ores are uncommon. An area known as "Oh Be Joyful" near Crested Butte in Colorado high mountain country, desirable for wilderness, for watershed, for ski development, is believed to have high potential for ore. The large Mount Emmons mine is already being planned nearby. Retained as wilderness, the area would be used nonconsumptively, or it could be developed for skiing and lightly used with high public turnover. If prospected and later mined, as urged by AMAX, the area has to be destroyed, with drastic social effects as well on the small town.

Now what becomes of the molybdenum? It goes into solar collectors, which help toward energy independence. It goes into ICBM's, but do we have enough already? It goes into sporting rifles, so trophy hunters can shoot up their game, and into electric carving knives, of which we have too many already. As wilderness, the area is in short supply; but the molybdenum is needed, so it might be sacrificed for true but not for false progress. Solar development, though destroying the wilderness, might be more important than skiing, which doesn't. But if the wilderness is to be destroyed, then the vital mineral should not be indifferently used. Unfortunately in our present capitalist economy (as socialists rightly lament), there is no one to ration the use of such a resource. Until this comes, perhaps by selective taxation, the business community needs to develop some conscience about priority use for our more critical resources. That is admittedly a difficult assignment, and many will shrug their shoulders and say they can do nothing about the demand for and uses of their products. But that is only to acquiesce in an unjust and clumsy market system.

11. The Toxic-Threat-Is-Trumps Maxim: An Ounce of Permanent Toxicity Is Worse Than a Ton of Passing Goods

The Business Roundtable lobby has complained that federal authorities are overly biased in favor of health protection.[10] There is room to discuss what counts as acceptable risk, especially since minute pollutants are the most expensive to remove, but surely one wants a moral bias in favor of health, over the production of extra goods, public or private. Given the recalcitrant sloth of leaky businesses, one wants lots of such bias. They have preferred to pollute until damage was evident, and impossible or expensive to reverse. They have scoffed at risks, later to eat crow while the public eats their contaminants. Especially in view of time lags here, the margin of error ought to favor those who breathe, not those who pollute. Even in small amounts, such long-term toxicity is foisted unwillingly upon millions not party to the business. The aerial spraying of pesticides, which involves nearly two-thirds of their use, mostly on fiber crops, not food, increases the risk of disease of those downwind, who may derive little or no benefit from the spraying, and take the risks involuntarily. This can happen while short-term goods are sought willingly by the customers, and profits by the operators. If you can't survive without polluting at toxic levels, then you should go out of business; society cannot afford your kind of business. Life shortened and life crippled is life taken; and thou shalt not kill.

The Kepone in the James River will gradually flush out, but toxicity levels are unknown, and when eventually ingested the carcinogen has a latency period up to twenty-five years. (See Case 1). Here, the more permanent the poison, the more it counters large amounts of immediate goods. The radioiodine in my thyroid kills me and moves on to others afterward. Plutonium remains lethal for fifty times longer than any civilization has yet survived, five times longer than *Homo sapiens* has survived. Even the brightest engineer must have a dull conscience to say, with Mr. Micawber, "Oh, well, something will turn up to detoxify it. My decade needs the extra energy." So he builds his nuclear plants, risks the plutonium use, and ships his noxious freight down the road out of sight. In view of accidents, terrorism, and even "permissible" exposures, are not the chances better that someone will get hurt by it? Over the long haul, some violations in environmental ethics are more dangerous than those in traditional ethics, because of the threat to so many generations. Since a toxic threat erodes life and health, a little overrides a lot of the pursuit of happiness. In repeated surveys the public prefers environmental protection over lower prices with pollution by about two to one, and a majority in all walks of life will say that environmental integrity at critical points must be maintained regardless of cost.

12. The Steady-State Maxim: Accept No-Growth Sectors of the Economy

Some sorts of growth may occur forever, as advancing technology makes new products possible. Our supply of materials is finite (short of space mining); but materials can be recycled and substituted and energy in principle is in generous supply, although in practice difficult to get cheaply. The growth of know-how may be unlimited, given the ingenuity of hand and brain. At the same time, some sorts of growth have limits, and here the ethical economist mixes savvy with conscience to know what growth to stimulate and what to subdue, before limits are thrust upon him. There are sixty-nine dams on the Tennessee and Cumberland river systems, and perhaps there should be no more. The chamber of commerce might better be of a Lesser, not a Greater Seattle. Perhaps there never need be three televisions in every home. Our United States cars should never have been the two-ton, tail-finned dinosaurs they were in the sixties. Think steady, when enough is enough. Think small, when less is more. A sign of the adult state, surpassing juvenile years, is that physical growth is over, and a more sophisticated intellectual and social growth continues. In these years physical growth may be nonfunctional, even cancerous.

BUSINESS AND A NATURALISTIC ENVIRONMENTAL ETHIC

A humanistic ethic may be viewed as a matter of fouling or feathering our own nest. It has insisted on considering a public, not merely a company nest. But ethical concern deepens with the claim that we have comprehensive duties to consider the natural community and its diverse sorts of inhabitants. In this community we humans no doubt have our interests, but these interests are, as it were, investments in a bigger corporation. Here we humans are major but not exclusive stockholders. The place of lesser subsidiaries has to be recognized. In a humanistic ethic, we had only to pull environmental concerns under social values already more or less in place. But with a nonanthropocentric, naturalistic ethic we have to pull social values under an inclusive environmental fitness. When human interests are the sole measure of right and wrong, nature is but the stage upon which the human drama is played. When nonanthropocentrism comes to the fore, the plot thickens to include natural history. The humanistic ethic will still be needed, but if exclusive, it will be pronounced shallow. Any business is wrong that asserts self-interest at cost to the whole public welfare. We have already conceded that. Now we move the argument one step up. The whole human business is wrong if, likewise, it asserts its corporate self-interest at the expense of the biosystemic whole, disregarding the other stakeholders. We need some enriched moral calculus reconciling human and natural systems, economic and ecological ones.

What values would a naturalistic environmental ethic recognize and seek to foster? That is what the next list of maxims attempts to identify. These value judgments will affirm the worth of objective characteristics in nature (for example: life, rarity, complexity) and deny that nature is in the usual economic sense merely a collection of resources. But adding to our moral puzzlement, we will find that nearly all these maxims have a humanistic rider. Some benefits may come to humans who recognize the natural excellences. This fits the age-old observation that to respect the integrity of another person is often to gain a benefit from this. Nevertheless the benefit is often nebulous and iffy, softer and more intangible, never very impressive before hard, immediate economic pressures. Humanistic motives are here weak and subordinate. They must combine with some appreciation of nature to bring you to endorse a maxim. This leaves us confused about our motives and principles, but it may nevertheless leave us with operational guidelines so that when in business we can do business with ecological satisfaction.

13. The Reversibility Maxim: Avoid Irreversible Change

We do our business in a many-splendored natural system, one where life has so far prospered. It vastly exceeds our mastery, is incompletely understood still, and its mysterious origins and dynamics are perhaps finally unfathomable. All evolution is irreversible but moves very slowly. Here humans want to avoid precipitous irreversible changes, or even minor ones we later regret. This commandment mixes respect and fear. This natural system, though sometimes hostile, is one in which we have been generated and now flourish. We should respect it as our home soil and be reluctant to do anything that might make it worse for ourselves, worse because we have tinkered with what is already a pretty good Earth.

All business alters nature, and any experimental venture runs some risks.

But we should not disturb an ecosystem so that we cannot, if we later wish, put it back as it was. "To keep every cog and wheel is the first precaution of intelligent tinkering," warned Aldo Leopold, a forester and one of the first environmentalists, writing a generation back.[11] We should leave room to reconsider; we should avoid radically closing options. Choose that business that allows us to redeem our mistakes. Any change is to some extent irreversible, but recent technology has made some quite irreversible—the extinction of species, the loss of critical habitat, the shrinking of breeding populations, the introduction of exotic pests, poisons and mutagens in soil and waters. The chestnut and the passenger pigeon are gone forever, the starling and the English sparrow are here to stay. What next with our effluents in the salt marshes, with our acid rain over the Adirondacks, with our bulldozers in the Amazon? What links are being cut, what gene pools overshrunk, what eggshells are becoming too thin?

14. The Diversity Maxim: Maximize Natural Kinds

Nature creates lots of niches and then puts evolutionary and genetic tendencies to work, filling these with a kaleidoscopic array, as glancing through a butterfly guide will show. It would be a pity needlessly to sacrifice much, if any, of this pageant, especially if we get in return only more good like that of which we already have enough. Variety is a spice in life. That says something about human tastes, but not so as to overlook the natural spices. There are twenty-two recreational lakes on which to water-ski within sixty miles of the Tellico Reservoir. There was but one rare, small snail darter population before it was drowned by the dam and scattered by hectic attempts to transplant it. The darter had no use, but it could have made the place interesting. This is not an axiom to maximize kinds unnaturally, but only to preserve diversity where we find it naturally, so far as we can, and unless we can find overriding reasons why not.

Often more is at stake than tonic and interest. Natural ecosystems are resiliently interwoven, usually so that when one thread breaks the whole fabric does not unravel. They absorb interruptions well, as when the chestnut was replaced by oaks. But with the advent of monocultures (single crops grown over wide areas), we push the whole surrounding rural system toward a fragile simplicity. Factory forests, growing timber species only, and artificially revegetated mine lands are easy to operate, bring high yields, and lower costs. But they have low stability and high vulnerability to insect pests, diseases, droughts, and erosion. Even when diversity adds no evident strength, some of the natural kinds may have uses of which we are unaware. The remarkable medicinal properties of curare were found in 1940, but there are further stories of Amazon basin plants that dissolve gall and kidney stones, heal burns, staunch bleeding, and provide long-lasting contraception. Some of these plants are common, others endangered, and Mr. Ludwig ought not to destroy the Amazon forest before we know whether those stories are true. (See Case 2.)

At least one can maximize diversity in quality, with all sorts of habitats located so that many persons have access to them. Nothing here depreciates business-built environments. We only insist that some wild ones be kept too. We have no business impoverishing the system. Yet industrial expansion has accelerated the natural extinction rate a thousand times, and we have only a fraction of the wildness we had a century ago, when our population was a fraction of what it is now.

15. The Natural Selection Maxim: Respect an Ecosystem as a Proven, Efficient Economy

Business and labor use resources resourcefully, and this effort spent transforming nature sometimes leads us, unreflectively, to see raw nature apart from human occupation as a useless wasteland. But an ecosystem is an economy in which the many components have been naturally selected for their efficient fitness in the system. There is little waste of materials and energy. Wherever there is available free energy and biomass, a life form typically evolves to fill that niche and exploit those resources. The economies we invade are durable, they have worked about as they do for tens, even hundreds of thousands of years, and in this sense each is a classic. Nature is a sort of tinkerer, adapting this onto that, seldom starting from scratch, but by trial and error experimenting with odds and ends on hand, pragmatically insisting that a thing keep working, surviving, or tearing it up and making something else. There is relentless pruning back by a sort of cost-efficient editing process, so that only the fittest survive. Detroit engineers do a lot of this sort of tinkering, pressed toward efficiency, defeated if their trials are structurally or functionally unsound. Even business in general operates much like this.

When we step in, we need to be careful with our massive, irreversible, simplifying innovations, because the chances are that our disturbance will have some unintended bad consequences. Even Ph.D's in engineering can be like the foolish natives who slash and burn, and wonder why the desert advances and their economies fail. With their forests gone, the Brazilians may soon be asking why their lateritic soils have lost their fertility. (See Case 2.) One analyst even warns, "The survival of man may depend on what can be learned from the study of extensive natural ecosystems."[12] That is perhaps extreme, but it is likely that our economy can be improved by attention to the efficiency of nature's economy. Again, appreciation of what nature objectively is has a spin-off. Those who prefer to say that the effect on human welfare is all that is valuable here may nevertheless endorse this maxim, only giving a more pragmatic twist to the word "respect." Even in modern business we can ponder an aphorism coined long ago at the start of the technological age by the English philosopher Francis Bacon, "Nature is not to be commanded, except by being obeyed."[13]

16. The Scarcity Maxim: The Rarer an Environment,
the Lighter It Ought to Be Treated

Nature's habitats are unevenly distributed. Grasslands are common, gorges infrequent, geothermal basins rare. Human development has increased the rarity of them all; we have only scraps of once-common ones. The Little Tennessee, now feeding a lake at the Tellico Dam, was one of the last really wild rivers in the East. The rarer an environment, the more carefully we ought to do business there. This will impose minimally on business in general, though it will vitally affect the few companies who work in rare environments. Weyerhaeuser, "the Tree Growing Company," with a generally positive environmental record, owns timberland areas collectively as large as Massachusetts. A few holdings are subalpine forests interfingered with alpine meadows; others are cathedral groves of virgin growth. The former were always relatively rare, the latter are now. Weyerhaeuser has been clear-cutting both, and their director of environmental affairs, Jack Larsen maintains that, while there is a public interest in preserving such forests, this is "not the responsibility of the private land owner," but "a function of government."[14] But this is too simple a shifting of responsibility. Proportionately as these forests are rare, they ought to be cut by selection or remain uncut, whether or not the government is alert about this. The managed, regrown forests that may slowly succeed the primeval ones will not be the equal either for wilderness experience or for scientific study of the rare, virgin forests sacrificed for a quick crop.

The rare environments are not likely to be essential to regional ecosystems, and hence we can do without them. But they may serve like relics, fossils, and keepsakes as clues to the past or to alien and twilight worlds. They are planetary heirlooms that hark back to the wonders of nature, to our broader lineage. Their serendipitous benefit is that, as environments under special stress, they are often good indicators of the first negative effects that humans introduce, good laboratories of exotic survival. Given our bent for radical technologies, it is hard to predict just where the next stress points will appear, and what will be the best laboratories in which to study them.

17. The Aesthetic Maxim: The More Beautiful an Environment,
the Lighter It Ought to Be Treated

Every businessperson has stood at some scenic point and been glad for the pristine, unspoiled beauty. Teddy Roosevelt exclaimed before the Grand Canyon, "Leave it as it is. You cannot improve on it. The ages have been at work on it, and man can only mar it."[15] The really exceptional natural environments do not need any business development at all. Tastes in beauty differ, but a survey of what most people think will usually do for business decisions. In tougher cases, the witness of experts with enriched aesthetic sensitivities can be sought. Some art is priceless, and all art is awkward to price. Here natural art is not really an economic resource, but is better understood in romance. The technological, businesslike relation of humans to nature is not the only one; and sometimes we wish not to show what we can do, but to be let in on nature's show.

Where natural places are not left alone, we ought to work in and on them in deference to their beauty. The philosopher Alfred North Whitehead lamented a half-century ago, "The marvelous beauty of the estuary of the Thames, as it curves through the city, is wantonly defaced by the Charing Cross railway bridge, constructed apart from any reference to aesthetic values." Society suffered the loss of natural beauty here because "in the most advanced industrial countries, art was treated as a frivolity," and "the assumption of the bare valuelessness of mere matter led to a lack of reverence in the treatment of natural or artistic beauty." In any socially progressive business, "the intrinsic worth of the environment . . . must be allowed its weight in any consideration of final ends."[16]

18. The China Shop Maxim: The More Fragile an Environment, the Lighter It Ought to Be Treated

Natural ecosystems have considerable stamina, but not equally so. Industrial society developed in Europe and the eastern United States where (and in part because) the soils were fertile, the climate temperate, the waters abundant. This sort of ecosystem is especially self-healing and those environments took a lot of punishment and offal. Society moved into the arid West; industrial expansion went multinational, seeking raw materials even under the tundra and sea. We have discovered, often sadly, that old ways of doing business will not transplant to fragile soils. The Alaska pipeline crosses eight hundred miles of arctic vegetation. Some gashes will be there long after the oil is burned, even after the men who made them are dead. The oil shale found in the plateaus of western Colorado is proving difficult to extract without mutilating the terrain. The shale has to be heated, and if this is done above the ground the spent shale is hard to revegetate, given the low precipitation and chemical changes in the retorting. If it is done underground, the chemicals prove toxic in the limited water in the aquifers that feed the few creeks and watering holes. Technologies that might work with thirty inches of rain cannot be used with an eight-inch rainfall.

All this is, in the first instance, the prudent preventing of a boom-and-bust cycle. But it can be a reluctance to go bulldozing in a china shop, lest what is busted be "ruined," perhaps because of its beauty or rarity, perhaps to avoid irreversible change, or to maintain diversity, or to appreciate the extra regimen in an economic system so soon subject to our distressing it. Fragility alone, like rarity, is hardly a value word. But it has a way of figuring in a constellation of natural qualities; and in the whole pattern we may find some respect for the integrity of a natural place. We may resolve to do our civil business with less insult, less savagery. Vandalism is possible on nature, even in a businesslike way.

19. The CNS Maxim: Respect Life, the More So the More Sentient

The capacity for quality of experienced life parallels the sophistication of the central nervous system (CNS). Pleasure and pain become more intense as we go up the phylogenetic tree. It has seemed self-evident to moral philosophers that pleasure by itself must be a good thing and pain by itself must be bad. But if evil for persons, then why not for sentient animals? It will not do to say: "Because they are not persons." That indeed is inhumane anthropocentric insensitivity! As Jeremy Bentham, an eighteenth-century English philosopher, accurately saw, "The question is not, Can they *reason?* nor, Can they *talk?* but, Can they *suffer?*"[17] Important differences need to be marked out between domestic and wild animals; the former would not even exist without human care; the latter sometimes suffer terribly in their natural ecosystems. Those who build an environmental ethic on animal rights and those who build it on the characteristics of natural ecosystems do not always agree. But we need not consider such problems here in order to conclude that one ought not needlessly increase suffering. Does not the Golden Rule reach at least this far?

Animal suffering might sometimes be justified by sufficient human benefits. Even then, we ought to do business so as to cause the least pain. We should, for instance, choose the least sentient animal that will do for the purposes of our testing and research. Some human goods may not justify the suffering they require. A pharmaceutical firm, Merck Sharp and Dohme, applied for a permit to import chimpanzees as the only known animal in which a vaccine for Hepatitis B can be tested. But chimps are a threatened species and known to be highly intelligent social animals. The capture of a juvenile chimp requires shooting the mother, and caged chimps are much deprived of their natural life. One analyst concluded, "The world has a growing population of 4 billion people and a dwindling population of 50,000 chimpanzees. Since the vaccine seems unusually innocuous, and since the disease is only rarely fatal, it would perhaps be more just if the larger population could find some way of solving its problem that was not to the detriment of the smaller."[18] The permit was denied, largely for ethical reasons.

Calves are confined in constricted stalls and, except for two daily feedings, kept in darkness for their entire lives, in order to satisfy a gourmet preference for pale veal, neither more tasty nor nutritious than darker veal. In the Draize test, cosmetics are tested by dripping concentrates into the eyes of unanesthetized rabbits until their eyes are swollen or blinded. The gourmet, the restaurateur, and the perfumed lady who know these things might be less callous. Faced with growing public criticism, Revlon, Inc., has funded a $750,000 grant to find a substitute for the Draize test. Ducks feed on spent shot that falls into their ponds, needing grit for their gizzards, and afterward die slowly from lead poisoning. The manufacturer, the sporting goods retailer who knows this should prefer steel shot instead.

20. The Life-Specific Maxim: Respect Life, the Species More Than the Individual

Three-quarters of adult Americans (the customers and stockholders of business) believe that endangered species must be protected even at the expense of commercial activity. That alone makes it good public relations to do business protecting rare and endangered species. We have already met some of their reasons: Extinction is irreversible, we lose diversity, beauty, a genetic resource, a natural wonder, a souvenir of the past. But more underlies these, really a religious reason. Life is a sacred thing, and we ought not be careless about it. This applies not only to experienced life, but to preservation of the lesser zoological and the botanical species. Species enter and exit the natural theater, but only over geologic time and selected to fit evolving habitats. Individuals have their intrinsic worth, but particular individuals come and go, while that wave of life in which they participate overleaps the single lifespan millions of times. Nature treats individuals with brief lives, but prolongs the type until it is no longer fit. Long-lived survival trends are at work here. Lost individuals can be replaced, but the species is irreplaceable, and the loss of critical habitat and a shrinking breeding population dooms a species.

Between one and three species vanish every day, and within a decade that could be one per hour. If the accelerated extinction rate is unabated, twenty percent of all species on Earth could be lost within twenty years. About half these losses result from tropical deforestation, in which Mr. Ludwig is so vigorously taking part (see Case 2), and the second greatest cause is pollution. Such a threat cuts to the quick in our respect for life. The question now is not, Are they sentient? but, Are they rare? "We had to decide which was more important: saving a rare bird, or pumping more oil and gas from an area which is that creature's only known nesting place in North America. I decided in favor of the bird."[19] So reported Walter Hickel, secretary of the interior, in a 1970 decision for the California condor. "For the birds!" The oil tycoon will say that derisively. "For the birds indeed!" The naturalist will say it too, but more respectfully.

21. The Nature, Inc., Maxim: Think of Nature as a Community First, a Commodity Second

That ecosystems are intricate communities is an established biological fact, a principle of ecology, which those doing business in nature often run into, sometimes to their regret. In the Pacific Northwest, loggers have clear-cut forests to discover, on some sites, that the forest cannot be regenerated. They did not understand the undercover shielding needed for seedling regrowth, provided by the cooperation of multiple species, sometimes weedy ones, or they did not understand the nitrogen economy, failing to recognize that seemingly useless lichens, found primarily on old growth trees, were critical fixers of nitrogen, which fertilized the forest. In southeastern pine forests mycorrhizal root fungi are similarly crucial. The picture we get is of a community where parts fit together in what is called symbiosis.

Nature operates its economies in a cooperative mode, if also in a competitive mode. This does not mean that the individual members of the community are even aware of this process, much less endorse it, only that natural systems are selected to form a kind of togetherness. The strivings of the parts are overriden to insure cooperative behavior and functioning in a symbiotic whole. After Darwin, some might have said that nature is a jungle, a free-for-all where issues are settled by pulling and hauling. But after ecology, we get a revised picture of checks and balances that pull the conflicts into an interdependent community. This continues but goes beyond seeing natural systems as tight and proven economies, a fact that we recognized in an earlier maxim (sec. 15). We think now of a community, a web of life, of life forms as flourishing only when interlocked in biological pyramids. In terms of the root metaphor of the word "ecology," a root shared also by "economics," we all live in a *household* (Greek: *oikos*).

Does any ethic follow from all this? Those who accept the prevailing, anthropocentric ethic will still treat things like property and resources, only they may become more prudent in extracting resources or eliminating wastes. But there are others, more naturalistically inclined, who can endorse the natural principle of life-in-community not only as a given but as a good. This account runs as follows. Even in humanistic ethics it is always individuality-in-community upon which ethics rests. There can be overly atomistic views that posit only self-interested individuals looking out for themselves, and some may think that business should be like popular conceptions of Darwinian nature, a field of competition where the fittest survive. But surely a more appealing view is one that can generate some sense of the individual welfare as inseparable from the good of the community, recognizing on a moral level in human affairs what we called symbiosis in biology. We have a doubtful ethic where an individual treats all fellow persons like so many commodities, forgetting how his life is in a community.

But when we turn to natural systems, we find the same sort of thing. The competitions take place in a cooperating community, not a moral or conscious one, but a good one, and when we humans come to do our business there, the principle of community membership, known already in human affairs, is to be continued because it fits well with the biological patterns we find: that life is always life-in-community. This may not derive ethics from natural facts, but it at least tries to fit an ethic to natural modes of operation. In nature there are movements of self-interest that are quite properly present, but these are superintended nondeliberately in ecological systems by nature's overriding hand in favor of an interdependent whole. When humans, as moral beings, enter to evaluate this, they continue by endorsing the principle of interdependent life. We have the right to treat nature as a resource, but also the responsibility to respect the community in which all life is sustained. A business needs prudently to recognize the limits imposed by ecological laws. But it is even better for it to be fitted by moral temper for its place in the whole natural community of which it is a part. Nature is really the ultimate corporation, a cooperation, into which we ecologically must and morally ought to fit.

22. The Parental Earth Maxim: Love Your Neighborhood as You Do Yourself

The surrounding countryside is, as Augustine said of God, that in which we live, move, and have our being. We should not be either irreverent or provincial about this. The local neighborhood is our nearest responsibility; there a business's impact for good or ill is likeliest to be felt. But the successes of big business and the revelations of science have shrunk the world so that our neighborhoods are larger and interlocked. The ultimate neighborhood is the parental Earth, seen so hauntingly in pictures from space. This Earth has generated us and continues to be our life support. It should be the object not only of our prudent care but of our love.

This maxim is rather philosophical and general, but there are immediate, practical applications. We give local care to natural items that have become cultural symbols of home (the Shenandoah, the Mississippi, the bald eagle) but also to landforms just because they are the home in which life is set, to life forms just because they are our "neighbors"—in the Biblical sense. For the average American, already well-heeled and comfortable, from here on these natural things are increasingly worth saving, and if a business continues to destroy them, what benefits it provides are not likely to outweigh the harm it does. Even for the average world citizen, who has real physical needs that business ought to meet, the quality of life cannot really be raised if the quality of the environment declines thereby. Sooner or later, ethics and business must attend to the appropriate unit of survival, and that cannot be less than the whole Earth, the womb of all.

ETHICAL COMPLEXITIES IN BUSINESS AND ENVIRONMENTAL CONCERNS

Moral responsibility in environmental affairs is as complex and novel as any responsibility a business executive is likely to face. This demands decisions that weigh technical, fiscal, social, and moral judgments, often made over long hauls

and in the face of unknowns, breaking new ground with an amalgam of humanistic and naturalistic interests. We face two kinds of ethical difficulties. One is
where we know what ought to be done but not how to get the company to do it.
The other is where we do not know what is right. We do not know how to
attach values to facts, or how to trade this good off against that one. Decisions
will not be ideologically pure, but rather messy. (See Case 3.) But there is some
good news with the bad. The business executive will never be replaced by a
computer on which these decisions are programmed. There will be an increasing
need for business heads that can do hard thinking.

Someone may object that the maxims given so far are useless, because too
general and imprecise. It is well to recall that ethics is not geometry, and that we
should not expect of one what we require of the other. Remember that a
principle or warning can have value even though somewhat general. Though we
cannot derive from these maxims concrete solutions for every case, nevertheless
they provide a background against which we can explore and assess our practical
decisions. Those who share some or even most of them may disagree in practice
in some cases, but still they have reference points against which to work, a
background against which to sketch the shape of their differences. These maxims
have to be brought into cross-play between themselves and more traditional
injunctions. One rule may collide with or sideswipe another. These are not
maxims from which we can compute exact solutions, but neither are they empty.
They lay moral constraints on available options. For actual decisions, we have
further moral work to do. But these *prima facie* directives clearly preclude some
wrong choices. We cannot eliminate but we can reduce ambiguity by maxims
such as these.

Notice that whether an act is *expedient* or *moral* needs to be specified with
reference to the actor, the affected class, and the time span. All these are
complicated in business morality. Here individuals, who are morally responsible,
act for the company, which is owned by themselves, by employers, by stockholders. The company itself has some explicit or tacit policy, and serves the
community over both short and long terms, a community populated with changing individuals. A particular decision may be immoral but expedient for stockholders this year, its reverse, a decision that is moral though inexpedient now,
may prove expedient five years hence, given ensuing public opinion and governmental regulation. Meanwhile the body of stockholders has somewhat changed,
and different persons fill some company jobs, "offices." As a rule of thumb, the
farther one looks ahead, the broader the group considered within the company,
and the more effective social critics are, the more the moral and prudent will
coincide. As a rule, too, the bigger and more long-lived the corporation, the
more fuzzy the line between private and public concerns, which increasingly
interlock. Thus it tends to become true for such businesses that what is ethical is
self-serving, but not in the way that ethical egoists maintain, but because smaller,
shorter-range individual concerns fade into bigger, longer-range corporate and

social ones. Meanwhile also, no businesses and no persons within them escape immediate short-range pressures that sometimes pull them toward making short-sighted decisions.

Where moral decisions become complex, they often cease to be absolutely and unambiguously right or wrong, and we seek to judge what is the best of competing but mutually incompatible goods or to choose the least of evils. There is some good to be accomplished on either alternative, some profit, which too is a good, but some products delivered and services rendered that fill public needs. We need the power, the pesticide, the plastic, the paper pulp, but then again can we really afford it at this social cost and consequence? Someone is going to get hurt on either alternative. Here it is tempting to deliver the goods, give persons what they want, or seem to want, and let *them* assume the responsibility. But here, even more than in traditional ethics, the good is the enemy of the best. One has to watch for and compensate for what is called "the dwarfing of the soft values,"[20] that is, where values that are quite important, even of the highest kind, but dispersed and soft, get trampled down before values that are not really any more important, but concentrated and hard, easy to get into calculations and marketable. We have to trade off clear scenic vistas against smoggy ones with cheaper power. Sometimes too persons' actions can be well-intended and still, when their actions combine with others, do ill environmentally. Nevertheless, at other times a great deal of environmental carelessness and even crime stems from rationalizing selfishness. Neither a humanistic nor a naturalistic ethic allows the abdication of individual and corporate responsibility, and the following maxims will help one to maintain a sense of responsibility despite the complexities of environmental concerns, in which it is easy (and sometimes convenient) to get lost.

23. The Buck-Stopping Maxim: Do Not Use Complexity to Dodge Responsibility

Environmental causal links are multiple, incremental, and long term. Their discovery is slow. Any verification is more or less partial, probabilistic, and backtracking. One can steadily deny that the sulfur dioxide from his smokestack had anything to do with the acidity of a pond two hundred miles away. One can point to closer plumes that sometimes blow that way, cite better-buffered watersheds where the fish still flourish, notice that volcanoes emit some SO_2, and for perhaps a decade debunk the evidence. As one is forced toward compliance, lag times for design, delivery, and installation of anti-pollution technology are easy to use for delays and confusions. With compliance mandated, one can build the stacks higher, if this is cheaper than scrubbers, airmail the contaminants further downwind past the local monitors, and claim that this dilutes them to a now-harmless level. Then the dispute has to start over whether this is so.

Add to this the complexity of the corporation, its business links, and its role in society. Various levels of management can deny authority, since this is often partial, and management can claim to be only agents, not principals, to work for stockholders, whose will seems to be known (to optimize profits by recalcitrant compliance) but who are too diffuse a body upon which to fix responsibility. Compliance will require financing, but will the lending agencies attend to the soundness of the projects they finance? Most banks resist the claim that they have any environmental responsibility; these matters are too complex for them to get involved in. The John Hancock Life Insurance Company, the Equitable Life Assurance Society, and Aetna Life and Casualty have, however, paid considerable attention to the environmental impact of projects they have financed, and sometimes voted the stock of companies in which they have holdings with this in view. Of course causal links and corporate responsibilities need to be clearly defined, for there is no single cause or villain, but the complexity ought not be a hiding place used to postpone responsibility or to subvert the law.

24. The No-Cosmetics Maxim: Do Not Use PR to Confuse Yourself or Others

Every company lives and dies not only in the market but also by its image. Here it is tempting to opt for symbolic solutions rather than substantive ones, then to advertise this legitimate but minor cleverness, while ignoring—deliberately or tacitly—the major environmental problems that lie still unsolved. The company builds a model new plant, while continuing to run thirty in noncompliance. It can exaggerate the cost of sound solutions, plead foreign competition, the unlikelihood of better technical solutions, feature the jobs lost in a plant closure, its solicitousness for employees, low profits in that subsidiary, and through it all so advertise the good will of the firm as to look better than it actually is, if management were to be honest with themselves. Diversionary PR only fools others about your worthiness; perhaps it even fools you. The ethical person insists on judging the reality behind the image, and, more than that, judges phony image-seeking to be unethical.

Diversionary PR is not only directed outside the company. The deep need of employees to believe that they are contributing to the public good can be a virtue. But it can also be a vice, because, owing to their need to believe this, employees are easily deceived by company pep talks about its environmental awareness, about its progressiveness before obstructionist Luddites, elitist bird-watchers, and canoe freaks. Here the need for personal self-justification coincides with the company's need for a positive image. This gives employees a tendency to rationalize and adds further to the company tendency to contrive token solutions and cover things up with rhetoric. But all this only confounds the problem. At the core of management, those in charge know the intricacies, possibilities, and costs of environmentally sound business better than the agencies who are regulating them, or the environmentalists who are suing them, and if they don't then they *ought* to—an *ought* with elements of both job competence and morality. A nuclear power consortium should focus on these things, rather than publish a promotional pamphlet that exclaims that God must love nuclear reactors because in the stars he made so many of them,[21] which only diverts attention from whether we ought to build this reactor three miles, not ninety-three million miles, from an elementary school.

25. The Second-Mile Maxim: Morality Often Exceeds Legality

"There's no law on the books that says we can't." But environmental novelties are still unfolding, they ignore jurisdictions, and one can expect here a lag time between legislation and the developing conscience. Nor will the law at its best ever embody more than the minimum negative public ethic. It forbids the most serious violations, but it cannot command the second mile of good citizenship. Even the conservative Milton Friedman, doubtful of any social responsibility for business, recommends that business "make as much money as possible while conforming to the basic rules of society, both those embodied in law and those embodied in ethical custom."[22] That recognizes the gap between the legal and the moral, but is too conservative, because in environmental ethics what is already embodied in ethical custom, beyond the law, is likely to be archaic. Unprecedented sorts of damages may be done before the law and public opinion wake up, but the managers of an offending business may be able to sense and correct trouble much sooner. In this ethic, a business leader is called to live on the frontier. The best will be ahead of government, which itself is often subject to delay and malfunction. Law and politics can be quite as flawed as can business, often more so; and the moral businessperson will not take advantage of outdated law or a do-nothing legislature.

That may seem too much challenge, but consider the alternative. If a company announces that it intends to make all the legal profits it can, though it concedes modest attention to ethical customs, this waves a red flag in warning. Everyone knows that such a business has to be watched like a hawk, past good faith in law and custom, so as to push it toward any deepening ethical insight. People will assume that it will become less ethical with increasing market insecurity. It will only increase its morality at the irritation of its critics, and such a firm can expect to do business in an atmosphere of hostility. The courts, public interest groups, and the press rightly conclude that they will have to drag such a firm along by steady legal and social pressures, lest it fling its legal acid into the wind or clear-cut whatever is legal in Oregon or Brazil, always in the rear, always callous in attending to the fragility or beauty of the environment, to rare species and amenities. Is this the reputation business wants? Unless a firm really is out for pure black profit, it is better to move voluntarily toward compliance and even to go the second mile, especially in those cases where you are soon going to be forced to it anyway. Both those within the firm and those without it will feel better about a morality that exceeds legality.

26. The Burden-of-Proof Maxim: Recognize a Shifting
Asymmetry in Environmental Decisions

From 1941 through 1977 the volume of manufactured synthetic chemicals increased 350 times, with many of these quite toxic to natural systems and to
human biology. Even the most resilient local ecosystem cannot absorb our
exhausts, pesticides, and herbicides. Even global currents cannot flush out aerosol
fluorocarbons and SST exhausts. The more massive the manipulative power,
the nearer one approaches the carrying capacity of the commons, the more the
unintended, amplifying consequences are likely to be far-reaching. Such chemicals, unlike persons, are not innocent until proven guilty, but suspect until
proven innocent. So the burden of proof shifts, and it is now up to the industri-
alist to dispatch it. This puts one again on the frontier, technologically and
morally. Formerly nature's "invisible hand" ruled over these things, but this is
no longer so.

One might have hoped that as our competence increased, risks would diminish. But the depth of upset advances even more, and we remain ignorant of our
reach. Uranium was mined by the Climax Uranium Company (now AMAX)
from 1951 through 1970 on the south edge of Grand Junction, Colorado. The
tailings, containing eighty-five percent of the original radioactivity but thought
harmless, were widely used as construction materials in thousands of homes, in
schools, and in sidewalks. Not until 1970 did physicians noticed a marked
increase in leukemia, cleft lip and palate, and Down's syndrome. These causal
links are still vague, but established enough for federal and state governments to
take emergency action. What are the unknowns at the Hansen mine? (See Case
3.) The regulatory authorities could have made better guesses if they had had
the latest report of the National Research Council's Advisory Committee on the
Biological Effects of Ionizing Radiations (BEIR III), but during their delibera-
tions that had not been published, because of the inability of members of the
committee to reach a consensus.

With ever-higher technology, it seems that our power to produce changes
overshoots increasingly our power to foresee all the results of our changes. The
latter takes much more knowledge. It is easier to make Kepone than to predict
what it will do in the ecology of the James River estuary, easier to mine
uranium and make reactors than to predict where the mutagens in the tailings
will end up and what damage will result. In a way, our ignorance outpaces our
knowledge. So we are asking for trouble unless we slow down the introduction
of potentially more potent novel changes with adequate pretesting. The unforeseen consequences outnumber the foreseen consequences, and the bad unforeseen
consequences greatly outnumber the good unforeseen consequences. Serendipity
is rare in high technology. Adding to the problem, many persons in business are
paid to introduce changes, new products, the quicker the better. But few are
employed to foresee adverse consequences and caution against them. So the

government regulates to widen by the law the margin of safety. But caution is also a moral requirement in these circumstances.

DDT causes cancer in mice, but it is difficult to show that it does or does not in humans, for we cannot experiment much on them, and everyone is already carrying a DDT load from its previous use. So does one conclude that, since there is no hard evidence, we should continue to use it anyway, at least where it is legal, outside the United States? We would, in effect, be experimenting on humans that way too, and making a profit during the experiment! Or does one accept the burden of proof to show that although carcinogenic in mice it does not cause human cancer? This might perhaps be done by experiments on more anthropoid mammals, by comparative studies with synthetic chemicals that humans regularly contact, but that we have no reason to think are carcinogenic in humans, and yet that do prove to be carcinogenic in mice. It might be done by comparing more refined measurements of cancer rates with existing DDT loads as these fluctuate within diverse populations, or as they flush out across a period of years. The point is that it is moral to err on the safe side, and that business has the responsibility to argue that the risks are minimal, not to presume so, and to chance the damage. Our grandfathers when in doubt could risk a new fertilizer, but we as conscientious grandchildren must increasingly refuse to act until we prove the limits of our effects. This applies to life's necessities, but also to risks of the natural amenities, which have never before been so threatened.

27. The Full-Circle Maxim: Extend Moral Judgments Through the Whole Event in Which Your Business Plays a Part

While the buck should not pass outside of a given company, the scope of judgment should not stop at the boundaries of that business. One should think as far outside one's business as one can. We cannot tell just by looking at the effects of our own actions, considered in isolation, whether we are acting well. Each of us is a link. Parts tied into wholes cannot be judged themselves, but have to be judged in the resulting pattern that they constitute.[23] Hitherto an entrepreneur could skimp on this principle, because the results of his enterprise were reasonably evident to immediate parties, and any unintended consequences were likely to be neutral.

But we can no longer assume that new technology or more growth is likely to be positive, or even neutral. What might look good in itself, what has always been good in past contexts, may be bad when seen full circle. Even when technology succeeds, the promised sweetness increasingly comes with much that is sour. The workers have jobs, but for miles around all suffer a blighted health and landscape. Almost invariably when high technology fails, the benefits are lost and their opposites arrive with a vengeance. We need to consider what's left economically, if the gamble doesn't pay off. The Kepone was intended for better crops and a stronger economy, but the result is a crippled company and a poisoned James River basin. (See Case 1.) The failed reactor can no longer deliver its power; worse, the legacy is expensive and even impossible to clean up. Society is not in the black, nor do we go back to zero, we are deep in the red.

Ethical judgment needs to reach for the compound unit. There is no point surviving on a sinking ship, little point prospering in a deteriorating environment. We might formerly have thought that the relevant unit to consider was merely the company and its customers. Now with sophistication and a sense of danger, it needs to be society, the country, the global Earth!

28. The Grandchild Maxim: Think for Decades

There are strong pressures to see what the charts look like this quarter, even this week. Some say that the successful business eye has to be myopic. But this is never entirely so, and increasingly less so with the size and longevity of the modern corporation, where collective interests overleap even the lives, much less the interests, of individuals who play company roles. The Weyerhaeuser timber cycle is a half a century. No big company can afford less than telescopic vision. Nor do stockholders care only about the next dividend. Most are holding their investments for ten or twenty years; the more dynamic the corporation, the more likely they intend to retire on these investments and bequeath them to their children. They want the firm to make it through the year, but in such a way that the long outlook is promising. They will take reduced profits if they believe the company is innovative and that this increases the quality of the environment in which they retire and in which their children, who inherit those investments, will live. Commercial and home loans are for twenty or thirty years. Why should the lending company think their clientele uninterested in the business stability and the quality of the neighborhood during and after the time that these loans are being repaid? Environmental spending, like that for military defense, is immediately a nonproductive cost; its benefits are general and longer range.

The corporate and composite character of the big firm can permit exactly the demanded time scale. The company itself needs what is also required by social and naturalistic concerns. Beyond our grandchildren, future generations may not have much moral or biological hold on us, but if one can see as far as grandchildren, that will do operationally in the present case. Meanwhile the company need not age and die at all, it can be revitalized forever. Couple this with the fact that many of its owners and operators are on board for decades; couple that with the tendency of expediency and morality to coincide over time, and a good business head will think for decades.

29. The Do-To-Yourself-First Maxim: Impose on Others
Lower Risks Than You Yourself Are Taking

Some fishermen work both the James River and uncontaminated tributaries, mix both catches for public sale, but carefully take home a batch of the uncontaminated ones. They represent a multitude who own and operate businesses that require a hazardous waste site but who refuse to live near one, who demand power but from faraway reactors and coal-fired plants. They want goods but not risks. But no one should buy goods and not bear risks. In fact, we should do this risk-bearing without consideration of fiscal costs and their distribution. My profit never permits your poisoning—the toxic-threat-is-trumps maxim. (See sec. 11.) But set profit aside. How then do we divide the risks that remain? You ought not impose on others risks you are unwilling to take yourself, in view of public benefits. We have to consider not just degrees of risk, but whether these are distributed equally and voluntarily or involuntarily.

Most persons do not wish to live within one hundred miles of a hazardous waste dump or nuclear plant, and these folk ought not to demand power or goods that requires others to do so. A company that sites dumps or plants any closer to a local population will impose upon them, and operators ought not to do so unless they live within this radius. Removing pollutants escalates in cost with the percentage removed and zero risk is impossible. Some risk is unavoidable, more risk profitable, and there will be cost pressures to set tolerances high. So let the maximum permissible concentration be set by researchers, themselves among the susceptible, who are ignorant of costs and who must long breathe the air whose toxicity they define. Business is now playing with toxins, mutagens, carcinogens. Let all those involved join in the risks proportionately to the public, but never merely private interests. Without consent, one doesn't gamble with somebody else's happiness, not if the odds are one in a hundred. Nor with someone else's life, not if the odds are one in a thousand. A risk imposed on others should be several orders of magnitude below one for which you will volunteer.

30. The Togetherness Maxim: Work for Benefits
that Can Be Had Only in Concert

There is not much point in removing the sulfur from one stack if a hundred remain. One developer may drop an area upon finding that the Nature Conservancy is trying to get an option on it, but a dozen others still bid. Not only is the intended effect lost by the noncooperation of others, the environmentally sensitive firm is disadvantaged in the market. You cannot always do the better thing and survive, while others do wrong cheaply. Competitiveness here becomes a vice because it encourages gain by eating up the commons. But what one firm cannot afford, all together can. Both the environmental and the economic con-

texts require that businesses act in concert. Moral success depends on the interplay of many wills. Associations of manufacturers, power companies, and real-
tors often have considerable persuasive force for broad policy-setting.

Still higher, there may be governmental regulation, zoning codes, pollution
standards, taxes, quotas. The historical tendency of free enterprise has been to
resist these. But surely they are morally required where the alternative is private
profit at public loss. The capitalism that cannot incorporate working-for-bene-
fits-in-concert is doomed, sooner or later, to fall before socialism, if not into
totalitarianism. If the association of firms proves to be only the self-interest of
companies all over again, a lobby rather than conscience in concert, then we can
expect again the social antagonism met earlier for announced legal profiteering.
(See sec. 25.) One should work for "mutual coercion, mutually agreed upon."[24]
Perhaps no industry can be trusted entirely to police itself, perhaps we need to
recognize this for ourselves and our successors as we face unknown pressures
ahead. No company is an island; the bell that tolls for one, tolls for all.

31. The Question-Authority Maxim: Stay Critical of Corporate Pressures

A corporate structure tends to deaden and fragment moral awareness. This is
because of the individual's partial involvement there, because of a firm's limited
functions and claims, because of its collective impersonal nature, because our
paychecks lie there, and even though a corporation's long-lived semi-public
character permits more moral reach than the individual can have. For many,
morality goes off when the business suit goes on, when the time card goes in.
We may be given, and want, a job description with sharply defined responsibilities. There are some questions we may not be encouraged to ask; you get the
message that nobody here can handle them, you are socialized to forget it and
get on with the job. The corporate climate may foster more interest in loyalty
than in truth. Perhaps we get moral fatigue, our nerve fails, but what we ought
to do is to ask all the questions we would as a parent, citizen, or consumer and
give them the answers we would if we were not working for the company.

Some say that philosophy makes a person unfit for business, but this is
rather only for unfitting sorts of business. Philosophy urges business by "one
able to judge" (Greek, *kritikos*), and judgment is a high-class business skill.
Like the university, government, or church, the corporation that cannot welcome
and include its critics will grow dogmatic and archaic. There can be reformation
only by those who question authority, and, if the critics stay noisy, the moral
and the expedient tend to coincide over time. Rachel Carson was right about
DDT, Ralph Nader was right about automobile exhausts and air pollution. Our
cars, towns, and countryside are the better for them. The Alaska pipeline is
better built because of its critics. Conservative business operators said, a century
back, they could not afford the abolition of slavery and child labor. They say
now they cannot afford environmental responsibility. But the more philosophical

executives are setting this right. The profit pressures do need moral watching. Whitehead remarked, "A great society is a society in which its men of business think greatly of their functions."[25] That has now come to include "thinking environmentally."

32. The Greening Maxim: Remember that the Bottom Line Ought Not to Be Black Unless it Can also Be Green

There is no such thing as a healthy economy built on a sick environment, and we can rewrite an earlier, faulty slogan. What's good for the countryside is good for the company. Not for all companies, but we use this to test for the good ones. Running in the black is not enough if this requires our running out of the green, green being here the color of the natural currency. T.V. Learson, former president of IBM, argues for "the greening of American business," and concludes, "in the end, therefore, the whole question of the environment boils down to a value judgment, a priority setting, and the will to do something about it. Most businessmen I know have made that value judgment. They want a cleaner environment as much as anyone else. I believe they will have the *will* to press on for it too, and to help, through business leadership, in stiffening the national will."[26]

This demand for bottom-line green is because the oceans, forests, and grasslands are the lungs of the Earth. But the reasons are more than obvious pragmatic ones. Business relations are only one of our manifold human relations with nature. This should not preempt the others that go on after business hours, or when we are no longer consuming. These other ways of pursuing happiness are scientific, recreational, aesthetic, appreciative, pastoral, and philosophical. Both in order that business may continue and in order that we may live well after business is done, we need an environment clean enough to be green. *Clean* has two meanings, here: clean in the nonpolluted sense, and clean in a noninterrupted sense. Some areas ought to be absolutely and others relatively clean of human management and intervention. Some spaces should remain rural, some wild. There should be mockingbirds and cottontails, bobwhites and pristine sunsets, mountain vistas and canyonlands. There should remain much of that sort of business which went on for the millions of years before we modern humans arrived. In this sense green is the color of life, the most fundamental business of all.

BUSINESS AND NATURE

Every organism must "earn its way" consuming its environment, and business activity follows the natural imperative that we must labor for food and shelter. This much of what *is* the case we can also endorse as what *ought* to be. What nature requires (that we work), what is the case (that we must work), we also morally command (one ought to work). Otherwise we cannot flourish and, in extremes, we die. That much of a bread-and-butter "work ethic" properly opposes a romantic naturalism that wants to leave nature untouched. It can celebrate how marvelously labor and management have brought the environment under our control. At the same time, every organism must be a natural fit, integrated into a life-support system. In the wild, misfits cannot flourish and are eventually eliminated. However much human business revises spontaneous nature, primarily by deliberately adapting the environment to humans rather than humans to the environment, we do not escape the fundamental requirement of inclusive fitness to our surroundings.

Thus, though we must and should work, not all our working is equally appropriate. Any business activity that contributes, even incrementally, to the reduced fitting of humans into the natural system does not really contribute to a better standard of living; it may even imperil our survival. An upset of Earth's carrying capacity is a prospect for today and tomorrow that was seldom a fear for business yesterday. Here labor and management must become sober environmentalists. Again we move from what *is* the case (how life is ecologically grounded) to what *ought* to be (how, given a humanistic environmental ethic, business ought to be environmentally alert and sensitive). Both human ecology and human ethics are inescapably environmental affairs. Locally and globally, humans are interlocked with their Earth, with material and energy inputs, throughputs and outputs, so that here too balanced budgets are required, not less than in accountants' offices. In that sense *economic* activity sooner or later must be and ought to be deeply *ecological* activity, both adjectives having the sense of life prospering in a home place.

Bertrand Russell claimed, "Every living thing is a sort of imperialist, seeking to transform as much as possible of its environment into itself and its seed."[27] But that is an overstatement, which, taken alone, leads to a social Darwinism thrusting atomistic egos and their firms into aggressive competitiveness, with nothing more. Nature has not so equipped or inclined any one form to transform very much of the environment into itself and its seed. Each life form is specialized for a niche, limited to its own sector but woven into a web so that it depends on many other species in a pyramidal, flowing biomass. Recent biology has emphasized not so much aggression and struggle as efficiency and habitat fittedness. Many animal populations limit themselves to suit their resources. If not checked from within, a species' genetic impulses are checked from without by the "natural corporation" that keeps every living thing in community.

All this is premoral, so what are we to say when, at the top of the pyramid, there emerges *Homo sapiens,* so powerful and unspecialized that, culturally evolving to where we are now, we almost can transform the Earth into ourselves and our seed? The answer lies in nature's simultaneously equipping us with a conscience, not given to nonhuman creatures. Perhaps this conscience can now wisely direct the magnificent, fearful power of the brain and hand. A naturalistic ecological ethic seeks to realize how conscientious human activity, business included, ought to be a form of life that both fits and befits, however much it also extends, what has previously, premorally been the case. Each life form is constrained to flourish within a larger community. The planetary system carries humans most gloriously, but it cannot and ought not carry humans alone. The best of possible worlds is not one entirely consumed by humans, but one that has place for the urban, rural, and wild. Only with moral concern for the whole biological business can we do our work of living well. This ethic defends human life by balanced resource budgets. But more, it defends all life in its ecosystemic integrity.

Whether Earth was made for us is a question we leave to the theologians, who are not likely to say that it was made for us to exploit. We can meanwhile say that we were made for Earth (if not also by it), and this gives us both the power and the duty so to act that we continue to fit this Earth, the substance, the sustainer of life.[28]

NOTES

1. October 5, 1976. U.S. District Court, Eastern Division of Virginia, Richmond. Judge Merhige's statements were made from the bench at the time of sentencing. The fine was technically reduced to five million dollars when Allied placed eight million dollars into a fund to reduce damages.

2. Hugh H. Iltis, "The Biology Teacher and Man's Mad and Final War on Nature," *American Biology Teacher* 34(1972):127-37, 201-21, especially p. 201f. While this article was in press, the Jari project passed into the control of a consortium of Brazilian operators, owing to Mr. Ludwig's age and to financial difficulties. The environmental outlook of the new owners remains to be seen.

3. For details of the Hansen project I am indebted to an unpublished paper by Thomas J. Wolf.

4. Louis B. Lundborg, *Future without Shock* (N.Y.: W. W. Norton, 1974), p. 128f.

5. Compare a report by Marshall Frady, "The View From Hilton Head," in *Harper's Magazine* 240, no. 1440 (May 1970):103-112, on p. 103.

6. Henry B. Schacht and Charles W. Powers, "Business Responsibility and the Public Policy Process," in Thornton Bradshaw and David Vogel, eds., *Corporations and Their Critics* (N.Y.: McGraw-Hill, 1981), pp. 23-32.

7. See *Time*, October 6, 1961, p. 24. More accurately, Wilson once reported, "For years I thought that what was good for our country was good for General Motors, and vice versa."

8. Garrett Hardin, "The Tragedy of the Commons," *Science* 162 (1968):1243-48.

9. *Final Report of the National Science Foundation Workshop Panel to Select*

Organic Compounds Hazardous to the Environment (Washington, D.C.: National Science Foundation, September 1975), p. 8.

10. *Cost of Government Regulation Study for the Business Roundtable* (Chicago: Arthur Andersen and Company, 1979); *The Business Roundtable Air Quality Project* (November 1980).

11. Aldo Leopold, "The Round River," in *A Sand County Almanac* (N.Y.: Sierra Club/ Ballantine Book, 1970) p. 190.

12. H. E. Wright, Jr., "Landscape Development, Forest Fires, and Wilderness Management," *Science* 186 (1974): 487-95, citation on p. 494.

13. Francis Bacon, *Novum Organum, Works* (N.Y.: Garrett Press, 1968) 1:157; cf. 4:47.

14. Quoted in Robert Cahn, *Footprints on the Planet* (N.Y.: Universe Books, 1978), p. 107.

15. Theodore Roosevelt in a speech delivered there, recorded in the *New York Sun*, May 7, 1903.

16. Alfred North Whitehead, *Science and the Modern World* (N.Y.: Mentor Books, New American Library, 1925, 1964), p. 175.

17. Jeremy Bentham, *The Principles of Morals and Legislation* (1789) (N.Y.: Hafner, 1948), ch. 17, sec. 4, p. 311.

18. Nicholas Wade, "New Vaccine May Bring Man and Chimpanzee into Tragic Conflict," *Science* 200 (1978): 1027-30, citation on p. 1030. See also Paul R. and Anne Ehrlich, *Extinction* (N.Y.: Random House, 1981), pp. 60-61.

19. Walter J. Hickel, *Who Owns America?* (Englewood Cliffs, N.J.: Prentice-Hall, 1971), p. 151. The decision halted further oil and gas leasing in the Sespe Condor Sanctuary, March 9, 1970.

20. After Laurence Tribe, "Trial by Mathematics: Precision and Ritual in the Legal Process," *Harvard Law Review* 84 (1971): 1329-93, on p. 1361.

21. William G. Pollard, "A Theological View of Nuclear Energy" in the *Let's Talk About* series interpreting nuclear power to the public, published by the Breeder Reactor Corporation, an association of 753 electric systems, Oak Ridge, Tennessee.

22. Milton Friedman, "The Social Responsibility of Business Is To Increase Its Profits," *New York Times Magazine,* September 13, 1970, pp. 32-33, 122-126, quotation on p. 33.

23. To adapt a more technical ethical distinction, this requires a teleological concern against a deontological naiveté. One cannot judge the rightness of an act in itself, but has to consider the outcomes of it.

24. Hardin, "The Tragedy of the Commons," p. 1247.

25. Alfred North Whitehead, *Adventures of Ideas* (New York: The Free Press, 1967), p. 98.

26. T. V. Learson, "The Greening of American Business," in *The Conference Board Record* 8, no. 7 (July 1971): 21-24, quotation on p. 22.

27. Bertrand Russell, *An Outline of Philosophy* (N.Y.: New American Library, Meridian Books, 1974), p. 30.

28. The author wishes to thank Richard D. Steade of the Colorado State University College of Business for a number of helpful suggestions.

REFERENCES

Vincent Barry, "Ecology," ch. 9 in *Moral Issues in Business* (Belmont, Calif.: Wadsworth, 1979).

Tom L. Beauchamp, and Norman E. Bowie, "Environmental Responsibility," ch. 8 in *Ethical Theory and Business* (Englewood Cliffs, N.J.: Prentice-Hall, 1979).

Herman E. Daly, ed., *Economics, Ecology, Ethics: Essays Toward a Steady-State Economy* (San Francisco: W. H. Freeman, 1980).

D. J. Davison, *The Environmental Factor: An Approach for Managers* (N.Y.: John Wiley and Sons, Halsted Press, 1978).

Jean Dorst, *Before Nature Dies* (Boston: Houghton Mifflin, 1970).

Nicholas Holmes, ed., *Environment and the Industrial Society* (London: Hodder and Stoughton Educational Services, 1976).

H. Jeffrey Leonard, J. Clarence Davies III, and Gordon Binder, eds., *Business and Environment: Toward Common Ground* (Washington, D.C.: The Conservation Foundation, 1977).

George F. Rohrlich, *Environmental Management* (Cambridge, Mass.: Ballinger, 1976).

Donald Scherer and Thomas Attig, *Ethics and the Environment* (Englewood Cliffs, N.J.: Prentice-Hall, 1983).

Presson S. Shane, "Business and Environmental Issues," in *Ethical Issues in Business: A Philosophical Approach,* Thomas Donaldson and Patricia H. Werhane, eds., (Englewood Cliffs, N.J.: Prentice-Hall, 1979).

Manuel G. Velasquez, "Ethics and the Environment," ch. 5 in *Business Ethics: Concepts and Cases* (Englewood Cliffs, N.J.: Prentice-Hall, 1982).

Sec. 1. There is more detail on the Kepone case in Beauchamp and Bowie (see reference above). See also Marvin H. Zim, "Allied Chemical's $20-Million Ordeal with Kepone," in *Fortune* 98, no. 5 (September 11, 1978): 82-90, and Frances S. Sterrett and Caroline A. Boss, "Careless Kepone," in *Environment* 19, no. 2 (March 1977): 30-37, and references there. For a discussion of the Jari project see William M. Denevan, "Development and the Imminent Demise of the Amazon Rain Forest," *The Professional Geographer* 25 (1973): 130-35; A. Gómez-Pompa, C. Vázquez-Yanes, and S. Guevara, "The Tropical Rain Forest: A Nonrenewable Resource," *Science* 177 (1972): 762-65; Norman Gall, "Ludwig's Amazon Empire," *Forbes* 123, no. 10 (May 14, 1979): 127-44; Philip M. Fearnside and Judy M. Rankin, "Jari and Development in the Brazilian Amazon," *Interciencia* 5 (1980): 146-56. For radiation risks from uranium tailings see D. G. Crawford and R. W. Leggett, "Assessing the Risk of Exposure to Radioactivity," *American Scientist* 68 (1980): 524-36. See also a suggestion for sec. 26.

Sec. 3. For more on stakeholders, see Schacht and Powers, note 6 above. For a survey of environmental concerns in corporate policy see Leonard Lund, *Corporate Organization for Environmental Policymaking* (N.Y.: The Conference Board, 1974), Report No. 618.

Sec. 4. Mobile Oil's ad, "The $66 Billion Mistake," in *The New York Times,* February 1, 1973, p. 35, favoring California over federal standards, illustrates corporate foot-dragging. Du Pont's extensive lobbying and advertising against fluorocarbon aerosol bans, despite mounting evidence of their depletion of the ozone layer, is illustrated by an ad in *The New York Times,* June 30, 1975, p. 30. The Reserve Mining Company case discussed in Beauchamp and Bowie (reference above) is another example.

Sec. 5. See David Burnham, "The Case of the Missing Uranium," *The Atlantic Monthly* 243, no. 4 (April 1979): 78-82. For examples of corporations dodging release of information about waste emissions, including the Savannah River case, see the *Freedom of Information Act Oversight: Hearings before a Subcommittee of the Committee on Government Operations,* House of Representatives, July 14, 15, 16, 1981 (Washington, D.C.: U.S. Government Printing Office, 1981), testimony of Ralph Nader (p. 330), and James M. Fallows, *The Water Lords* (N.Y.: Grossman, 1971), especially ch. 9. See also *Toxic Substances and Trade Secrecy* (Washington, D.C.: Technical Information Project, 1977), containing the proceedings of a conference supported by the National Science Foundation, especially the article "Toxic Substances and Trade Secrecy: Rights and Responsibilities" by William Blackstone, reprinted in Scherer and Attig, *Ethics and the Environment* (see general references).

Sec. 7. For the pros and cons of discounting, especially with reference to natural amenities, see Anthony C. Fisher and John V. Krutilla, "Resource Conservation, Environmental Preservation, and the Rate of Discount," *Quarterly Journal of Economics* 89 (1975): 358-70.

Sec. 11. See for instance the dismal record of U.S. Steel, itemized by John R. Quarles, Jr., "American Industry: We Need Your Help," in Leonard et al., *Business and Environment: Toward Common Ground* (reference above). For public opinion on environmental issues and business, see "The Public Speaks Again: A New Environmental Survey," *Resources,* No. 60 (September-November 1978): 1-6. See also suggestions under sec. 20.

Sec. 12. For steady-state economics, see Herman Daly (reference above).

Sec. 14. For estimates of little-known and unknown Amazon plants that may prove medically useful, see Nicole Maxwell, "Medical Secrets of the Amazon," *Americas* 29, nos. 6-7 (June-July 1977): 2-8. For how little we really know even about the lands North Americans have long inhabited, including New England and the Midwest, see Wright, note 12.

Sec. 18. For the difficulties of heavy technology on fragile land see *An Assessment of Oil Shale Technologies* (Washington, D.C.: U.S. Government Printing Office, 1980), prepared by the Congressional Office of Technology Assessment.

Sec. 19. For the treatment of animals, see Peter Singer, *Animal Liberation* (N.Y.: New York Review Books, 1975), with discussion of the Draize test on p. 50f, and veal calves, pp. 127-35. For lead versus steel shot, see U.S. Fish and Wildlife Service, *Final Environmental Statement: Proposed Use of Steel Shot for Hunting Waterfowl in the Unites States* (Washington, D.C.: U.S. Government Printing Office, 1976). The report finds no adverse crippling with steel shot.

Sec. 20. Attitudes of Americans toward endangered species are reported in *Public Opinion on Environmental Issues,* Resources for the Future Survey for the Environmental Protection Agency, et al. (Washington, D.C.: U.S. Government Printing Office, 1980), p. 18. The alarming acceleration of extinction rates is discussed in *Environmental Quality—1980,* Eleventh Annual Report of the Council on Environmental Quality (Washington, D.C.: U.S. Government Printing Office, 1980). See also *The Global 2000 Report to the President,* Council on Environmental Quality and Department of State (Washington, D.C.: U.S. Government Printing Office, 1980). See also Norman Myers,

The Sinking Ark (Oxford: Pergamon Press, 1979) and Paul and Anne Ehrlich, *Extinction* (note 18).

Sec. 23. For environmental policies in banking and finance, see Cahn (note 14), pp. 124-40, who reports that only six in thirty of the major commercial banks have environmental policies, none of these very specific, but found also the positive records of John Hancock, Equitable, and Aetna.

Sec. 26. See the *Progress Report on the Grand Junction Uranium Mill Tailings Remedial Action Program*, prepared by the U.S. Department of Energy's Division of Environmental Control Technology, the DOE Grand Junction Office, and the Colorado Department of Health, February 1979, and available from the National Technical Information Service. The report of the Committee on the Biological Effects of Ionizing Radiations, *The Effects on Populations of Exposure to Low Levels of Ionizing Radiation: 1980* (BEIR III), has since been published (Washington, D.C.: National Academy Press, 1980), but the much-troubled report was never released without dissent among committee members. The ozone threat involves uncertain but drastic and far-reaching environmental degradation. Du Pont has persistently claimed that the connection between fluorocarbons and ozone depletion is not yet proved. The details of this case (given in the Velasquez reference above) provide a good discussion of the necessity for a shifting burden of proof.

Sec. 29. Public opinion about living near risk sites is recorded in *Public Opinion on Environmental Issues* (reference under sec. 20. above), p. 31.

Sec. 30. See Kenneth R. Andrews, "Can the Best Corporations Be Made Moral?" *Harvard Business Review* 51, no. 3 (May-June 1973): 57-64.

9

Valuing Wildlands

About 2 percent of the contiguous U.S. is wilderness (1.2 percent designated; 1 percent under study); 98 percent is developed, farmed, grazed, timbered, designated for multiple use. Another 2 percent might be suitable for wilderness or semiwild status—cut-over forests that have reverted to wilderness or areas as yet little developed. Decisions are being made about how to value these relict wildlands. Since they are almost entirely public lands, these are political decisions; but they are also taking place in the midst of a philosophical reassessment, coupled with ecological concerns, about how humans should value nature. They are political decisions entwined with reforming world views.

Since these are public land-use decisions about wild nature, there is a tendency to think that the most useful principles and strategies are likely to be economic: that the nearest thing to an adequate theory of "resource use" is going to involve an estimate of benefits over costs in dollars; that wise use will be "efficient" use. Decisions ought to be democratic, since they are political and about public lands, but pitfalls in the democratic process are many. Those with political clout and savvy, those with concentrated high-order interests, a lot to gain or lose, outshout or outmanipulate the disorganized majority whose interests are diffuse and low-leveled. Organized small groups typically outact large latent groups; legislators react to pressure groups and defend their own interests. Agencies grow bureaucratic and sluggish; citizen preferences are difficult to register and aggregate; voters never have the options they prefer presented at the ballot box; and so on. One way to minimize these pitfalls is to insist on a decision analysis which is more systematic, more scientific, which often means, more economic.

While it is widely recognized that some "amenity values" or "environmental values" are recalcitrant to quantification in dollars or other units, nevertheless, the effort to see how far cost-benefit analysis introduces some sense of order into an otherwise sprawling dispute over values continues. Legislators and government professionals are always sensitive to the charge of misusing public funds

Reprinted by permission from *Environmental Ethics* 7 (1985): 23-48.

and resources, and if they can make economically based wildland decisions, they think that their decisions will then be as nearly scientific and democratic as can be. They believe that one sure route into human caring is by pricing, not in all cases, but routinely in matters of resource use. Some consideration of the just distribution of such costs and benefits will be needed, but that can come later. Initially, they say, an economic assessment of what these relict wildlands are worth is all that is required.

In the discussion to follow I challenge this strategy. My discussion is not a criticism of the utility of cost-benefit analysis, only an inquiry into whether the sorts of values to be protected on relict wildlands can be captured in economic terms. In section one I outline several levels of value, applicable independently of wildland decisions, followed by twelve types of value associated with wildland use. In section two I question whether efforts to register these values in monetary terms succeed. In section three I suggest several philosophical principles that might improve wildland decisions. Section one is descriptive; section two is critical; section three is partisan; all sections are analytic.

A TAXONOMY OF VALUES

In the taxonomic levels and types narrated here, there is no reason to think of mutually exclusive categories, but there is every reason to think of identifiable dimensions of value that need to be factored into any complete analysis.

Meaning Levels of Value

(1) *Value*$_{ip}$ = *individual preference value*. Value$_{ip}$ is what individuals prefer in contexts of choice. Valuing and its product, value, lie in the experience of interest satisfaction. In this sense valuing is subjective—valuing brings value into being within subject-owners, typically in their relationship to the world. Mere objects, including organisms that have no psychological life, no felt preferences, can have no preference value, though they may be resources for preferences. In our private case, for normal adults, what we ourselves prefer is reasonably evident from introspection coupled with action. The values$_{ip}$ of others can be known from verbal preferences and behaviors, although some situations compel discrepancies between attitude and action. Where there are constraints, it may be difficult to ferret out true values. We also have to separate goals from failed performances, latent from manifest preferences, etc. Value$_{ip}$ has seemed to many to be the motor force of all value, from which all the rest are derived.

(2) *Value*$_{mp}$ = *market price*. Often an illuminating way out of the subjectivity of value$_{ip}$ is to look to the market, which, though produced by value$_{ip}$, has empirical objectivity. Articles and services are regularly exchanged on the market, which in nonbarter societies invests them with a going price, a public, observable

quantity, resulting from many individuals estimating the worth of having these commodities. Value$_{mp}$ is a derivative of usefulness, rarity, labor, advertising, government regulation, etc., but in the end things are traded instrumentally to satisfy human interests, and their price must reflect preferences. If no one desired these things, the market would collapse. In wild nature, no monetary or barter economy exists, but humans, nevertheless, buy and sell natural things incessantly. They labor, trade, and own property, using nature for interest satisfactions, and this brings wild nature into the economic sphere.

Value$_{ig}$ = individual good value. If valuing is just preferring, one can hardly make mistakes about what one has valued, any more than one can be mistaken about having made a target of something, though mistakes abound with regard to whether what is preferred really brings satisfaction. We can make choices and purchases that are not in our best interest, not really. They bring momentary goods, or none at all, and soon leave us worse than before. Value$_{ig}$ is what is in a person's interest, whether or not the individual chooses it. Preferences need to be constantly revised accordingly in terms of it. There is something raw about untutored preferences; individuals need education (even perfect knowledge) before they can competently say what (all) their goods are. Many things happen (such as the rain) that are of value whether we welcome them or not. Biological processes (photosynthesis) are vital even in our ignorance of them. Values$_{ig}$ may not involve exercising preferences, much less marketing.

Value$_{sp}$ = social preference value. Through politics, ethics, religion, etc., individuals express a social will, often conflicting with some particular wills. Value$_{sp}$ is what a society prefers when optionally allocating its time, resources, skills, energy, and money. Values characterize groups, not just individuals. Value$_{sp}$, a social trait, represents some amalgamating of value$_{ip}$, a psychological trait, though it is not clear how this does, or should, take place. Sociologists debate whether there is any social whole above the individual-person parts who compose it. Society itself has no center of experiences; only individuals do. Society is not capable of interest satisfactions; it enjoys no pleasures, suffers no pains. Such considerations lead many to claim that value$_{sp}$ is some kind of fiction, a pragmatic operational concept (like a center of gravity) which is only apparent. Still, some social preferences seem to serve society at large, beyond the fact that, or regardless of whether, they satisfy individual interests. Social preferences, unless oppressive, seem to command more importance than particular individual preferences. At least they are relatively more enduring.

(5) *Value$_{sg}$ = social good value.* Society can err about what contributes to its well-being. Social choices too can be out of touch with reality. Further, given the prevailing pluralism, a negotiated consensus of values$_{sp}$ is likely not to be consistent. Even if only individuals have a well-being (society being an aggregate of related individuals), at least society functions and dysfunctions. The vague, beguiling slogan, "the greatest good for the greatest number," can mean "what most prefer on average" (value$_{sp}$) but usually means "what is on average func-

tional in society" (value$_{sg}$). Part of the worth of a practice is whether it keeps society functioning smoothly, regardless of whether this agrees with the corporate will. The "open space" of the Indian Peaks Wilderness serves as a pressure release valve for the Denver-Boulder metropolitan area, and it might be more functional for Colorado society to maintain it so, even though the legislature voiced a preference, reflecting polls, that federal managers log the area for jobs and firewood.

(6) *Value$_{or}$* = *organismic value*. Value is not just an economic, psychological, social, and political word, but also a biological one. Value$_{or}$ is what is good for an organism, and all preferences and goods of humans are really subsets of this more comprehensive notion. Various instrumental organic and environmental goods contribute to an organism's well-being, and that well-being is for the organism a telic end state, an intrinsic value, not always a felt preference. Survival value, lies at the core of evolutionary adapation. Genetic information is of high organismic value, but has no necessary connection with sentience, experience, preference satisfactions, or markets. Wild creatures defend their lives as if they had goods of their own. An organism grows, repairs it wounds, resists death, and reproduces. Every genetic set is in this sense a (nonmoral) normative set, proposing what *ought to be* beyond what *is*. At this level, wild nature is a place of values prior to human decisions, and one thing the reforming world view asks is whether any concern for wild organismic value limits human decisions about land use.

(7) *Value$_{es}$* = *ecosystemic value*. Like persons in society organisms live in ecosystems, with a parallel between the good of the system and that of the individual. Persons are good in the roles they serve—mothers, wildlife biologists. Organisms fill niches and sustain a flourishing system, though not intentionally, perhaps unwillingly. Songbirds, which have intrinsic value$_{or}$ in themselves, have instrumental value regulating insect populations. Ecologists too (coached by sociologists?) have doubted whether ecosystems exist as anything over their component parts. Value$_{es}$ is even more convincingly a kind of fiction than value$_{sg}$, because in ecosystems there are no policy makers, no social wills, no goals. Though the ecosystem can seem more biologically real than the social system, it less evidently has a locus of value. Nevertheless, in some way that we poorly understand, some creativity (accidental or not) in the evolutionary ecosystem has formed all its organic species and processes, and we as humans are now much concerned with keeping these ecosystems running as they do. Some events can be better, some worse for the integrity of a biological community, as in the choice for a biodegradable pesticide.

Types of Wildland Values

(1) *Market value*. Wildland products have value$_{mp}$. Individuals value$_{ip}$ them, a use expressed in the social will, value$_{sp}$. The goods of individuals and society are

thereby increased. Nature can be used instrumentally to render human existence more materially comfortable. Humans have no options about some consumption of nature in our economy, but we have options concerning how much. Until recently, especially in the vast undeveloped New World, nature seemed an almost unending resource. By an increasingly competent use of natural resources our economy could grow forever. Lately however, in a revising world view, we are decreasingly confident about the myth of inexhaustible resources. We seek renewable resource use, or expect rationing of nonrenewable resources, perhaps because of rising value$_{mp}$, and hope for substitutes. Growth pressures have increasingly forced market values into competition with all those values to which we next turn.

(2) *Life support value.* So far as culture is entwined with ecosystems, our choices (value$_{ip}$, value$_{sp}$) need to be within the capacities of biological systems, paying some attention to value$_{es}$. But the latter are not values that go on in the human mind. The central goods of the biosphere were in place before humans arrived, though they have lately become our resources. Further, such things as air flow, water circulation, sunshine, nitrogen-fixation have never figured much in market prices, individual preferences, or collective choices. They were just natural givens that supported everything else. Lately, however, the scope of human activity has increasingly threatened crucial life support functions (soil depth, the ozone layer, groundwater purity). One reason for managing wildlands with care is that their cumulative impact on hydrologic cycles, photosynthesis, biomass decomposition, insect regulation, and pollution scrubbing is considerable. Another is that we want to know what the unmolested system was in order to fit ourselves more intelligently in with its operations when we do alter it.

(3) *Recreational value.* Wildlands have two kinds of positive recreational value. We want (a) to see what we can do (activity) and (b) to be let in on nature's show (contemplation). Wildlands are valued$_{ip}$ for sports (fishing, skiing) that demonstrate skills in the challenge of the wild. Nevertheless, people also enjoy watching wildlife and landscapes with the focus on nature as a wonderland, a rich evolutionary ecosystem where truth is stranger than fiction. There are trails to be hiked, a rare bird or fern to be admired, or just a hypnotic vortex below a waterfall to capture our attention. The continuing existence of an outdoor gymnasium and theatre is valued by two-thirds of Americans, especially by the young and educated, as a matter of preference and well-being. There is even a push-pull effect. Not only are persons drawn to the wildland, they escape to it, driven from the city. Wildlands absorb a kind of urban negative disvalue, a tandem effect.

(4) *Scientific value.* Nature is a laboratory for the pursuit of science, good not just because individuals like it (value$_{ip}$), but because society gains pure knowledge, which enlarges our understanding of the world and our roles in it, and gains better applied science, which enables us to manage and rebuild our environments (value$_{sg}$). These benefits to "science" are vaguer than economic or

recreational benefits, where the affected citizens can be easily identified. They do not belong merely to Americans but rather enter the global culture. Although it is hard to say whether they are individual or social, they are not minor. The most juvenile natural science is ecology; the least known level of organization is the mosaic of communities that compose a biome. We have no theory of evolution at the ecosystemic level; biologists are divided over whether interspecific competition is a minimal or a major force in evolution, indeed we are not very clear on what the natural successions are over a few hundred years. Relict wildlands are the only places where these disputes can be settled. Destroying wildlands is like burning unread books.

(5) *Genetic diversity value.* Humans eat remarkably few plants in any volume (about thirty), and still remarkably fewer come from North America (one or two). With the loss of fifteen cultivars, half the world would starve. Ten species provide 80 percent of the world's calories. Given increasing pressures from agriculture (monocultures, pesticides, herbicides, hybridized strains, groundwater pollution), given increased mutation rates from radioactivity, the nuclear threat, exotic blights, it seems important to preserve the genetic reservoir naturally selected here, just in case we need to crossbreed against such microorganisms as produced the corn blight of 1970, or to turn to food stocks adapted to North American habitats. Such resources, presently unknown, cannot be well protected *ex situ* (in zoos, seed depositories), but only *in situ* by preserving natural ecosystems. Nor can laboratory genetic recombinations substitute for wildlands; we need natural diversity for the startpoint materials.

(6) *Aesthetic value.* Nature's problem solving yields works of grace—an eagle soaring, a snake slithering, a coyote on the run, the fiddleheads of ferns, even mud flats with their 120-degree stress fracture symmetries. On small scales and large, both ensemble and individual, nature's patterns can please the eye. Further, the sense of abyss overlooking a gorge is aesthetic, as is the eerie chill when, nearing a stormy summit, one's hair stands on end in the charged air. So also is the thought that in one cone lies a possible forest. All are experiences unlikely to be had in the Metropolitan Museum. We do not need to settle whether or how far beauty is in the eye of the beholder; it is enough that such experiences come. But we do need to notice that sensitivity to this value takes an educated eye. Plain places (as may be judged swamps and flatlands) have a coherence and completeness of which plain persons never dream. Here, familiarity breeds no contempt. Valuing wildlands is vastly more than soaking up scenery, as one travels slowly in intimate contact with the environment.

(7) *Cultural symbolization value.* The bald eagle symbolizes national self-images and aspirations (freedom, strength, beauty), as does the bighorn ram, a "state animal" for Coloradoans. The pasqueflower is the state flower of South Dakota; the alligator a symbol for Florida. Natural areas enter local cultural moods—Grandfather Mountain in western North Carolina; Natural Bridge and the Shenandoah in central Virginia. Horsetooth Mountain, overlooking the city,

provides the logo for Fort Collins, Colorado. Culture commingles with land-scape and wildlife in places named after geomorphic, faunal, or floral features: Tinkling Springs, Fox Hollow, Aspen, Crested Butte. We want some wildness preserved because it comes to express the values of the culture superimposed on it, entering our sense of belongingness and identity. This involves value$_{ip}$, but even more value$_{sp, sg}$. What would be the impact on American hopes if the bald eagle became extinct? On the perceived quality of Colorado life with the death of the last bighorn?

(8) *Historical value.* Wildlands provide historical value in two ways, cultural and natural. America has a recent heritage of self-development against a diverse and challenging environment, seen in pioneer, frontiersman, and cowboy motifs. Forests, prairies, and ranges ought to be preserved as souvenir places for each generation's learning (however secondarily, playfully, or critically) of our fore-father's moods, learned there quite as much as in the Minuteman Historical Park. They provide a lingering echo of what we once were, of a way we once passed. There is nothing like the howl of a wolf to resurrect the ghost of Jim Bridger. A wilderness trip mixes the romance and the reality of the past in present experience, lifting historical experience out of books and recapturing it on a vivid landscape. But wildlands also provide the profoundest historical museum of all, a relic of the way the world was in 99.99 percent of past time. We are relics of that world, and that world, as a tangible relic in our midst, contributes to our sense of duration, antiquity, continuity, and identity. We passed that way once too.

(9) *Character-building value.* Wildlands are used by organizations that educate character—Boy and Girl Scouts, Outward Bound, and church camps. Similar growth also occurs in individuals independently of formal organizations. What is valued is the challenge of self-competence, in teamwork or alone, with reflection over skills acquired and one's place under the sun. Wildlands provide a place to sweat, to push yourself more than usual, perhaps to let the adrenalin flow. They provide a place to take calculated risks, to learn the luck of the weather, to lose and find one's way, to reminisce over success and failure. They teach one to care about his or her physical condition. They provide a place to gain humility and a sense of proportion. Such growth experiences can be sought (value$_{ip}$), as with the goose pimples and quickened pulse of the first solo back-pack. They can also be unsought and even traumatic (caught in a storm, injured or ill in a remote location). Still, integrated into character, they increase well-being (value$_{ig}$), and the social good (value$_{sg}$) is benefited by having such citizens.

(10) *Therapeutic value.* An entirely normal use of wildlands, reported by a majority, is for semi-therapeutic recreation. A minority use, less well explored, is as a setting to treat psychologically disturbed persons. For the mentally ill, the ambiguity and complexity in culture can be disorienting. It is hard to discrimi-nate friends, enemies, and the indifferent, hard to get resolve focused on what to do next, or to predict the consequences of delay. But in the wilds supper has to

be cooked; one needs firewood. And it is getting dark. Exertion is demanded unambiguously; accomplishment is evident in a low-frustration environment. The self is starkly present and the protocol is simpler. One really is on his or her own; one's friends are few and he or she utterly depends on them. All this can mobilize the disturbed for personal recovery. So far as humans have been selected over the evolutionary course to need challenge, adventure, exertion, and risk, society must provide avenues for such archetypal emotions, or expect deviant behavior—gangs and rebels without a cause. Wildness may provide a "niche" that meets deep-seated psychosomatic needs.

(11) *Religious value.* The wilderness works on a traveler's soul, as well as on muscles and character. Mountaintop experiences, sunsets, canyon strata, or a meadow of dogstooth violets can generate experiences of "a motion and a spirit, that impels . . . and rolls through all things."[1] Wildlands thus become something like sacred texts. Whether in the majority or minority, the rights of such "users" are to be protected. For wilderness purists intensely, and for most persons occasionally, wildlands provide a cathedral setting. The wilderness elicits cosmic questions, differently from town. Some of the most moving experiences attainable are to be had there. Those who do not attend religious services can value nature more than those who do. Church leaves them cold; they are pantheists or nonecclesiastical monotheists. They have a diffuse naturalistic religion, not a supernaturalistic creedal one. They do not like indoor liturgies, but prefer outdoor awe, solitude, vastness. Since the constitution protects religious freedom, so far as wildlands are essential for or facilitate this, they need preserving.

(12) *Intrinsic natural value.* Each preceding type makes nature tributary to human experiences, but several hint at more. They recall how, on the concluding two levels, wild organisms have goods of their own (value$_{or}$), how they are selected (blindly, but nevertheless effectively) as good fits in their environments, so that a spontaneous ecosystem is typically healthy (value$_{es}$). All this occurs premorally, but when humans appear with their reflective consciences, do they have some duties toward these storied natural achievements? Typically such convictions mix a derivative anthropocentric prudence (recreation, genetic vulnerability) with an ethical concern, often inarticulate, that grizzly bears, pileated woodpeckers, even wildernesses, have a right to continued existence for what they are in themselves as neighbors and wonderlands on Earth. Two-thirds of Americans doubt whether humans ought intentionally to destroy endangered species or rare environments. Diffuse but deeply felt, such values are difficult to bring into decisions; nevertheless, it does not follow that they ought to be ignored.

CONTINGENT VALUATION OF WILDLANDS

Can the preceding array of value levels and types be reduced, wholly or in part, to economic terms, as a prerequisite for a cost-benefit analysis? J. V. Krutilla and A. C. Fisher noticed the difficulty and suggested some categories. "In confronting the need to evaluate preservation benefits, we find that there are a number of aspects of such benefits that we do not know how to estimate quantitatively. These are the value of natural environments that have remarkable qualities for scientific research; the value that individuals place on retaining an option when faced with actions having irreversible consequences; and the value that some individuals place on the knowledge of the mere existence of the gifts of nature, even when they feel certain they will never have or choose an opportunity to experience them *in situ*."[2]

Taking up the challenge, there have been a number of proposals to make economic estimates of various wildland values, typically (1) scenic value, (2) recreational value, (3) option value, (4) existence value, and (5) bequest value.[3] *Option value* is the value of retaining options that a set of natural entities, threatened with erosion or destruction by development, provides now and henceforth to a prospective user. *Existence value,* separable from option value, is the satisfaction to an individual of just knowing that the wild set exists, even if unvisited by himself (or others?). *Bequest value,* thought also separable, is the value that an individual places on bequeathing a wilderness to children and future generations.

The most plausible of the five to be measured economically is recreational value. Recreation is sold elsewhere on the market and can perhaps be shadow priced. Though wilderness experience is unsold, it costs something—gas, meals, lodging enroute, fishing licenses, gear (?), campground fees. Access costs are typically $10-15 per day. Does this represent the value of the visit? Difficulties arise. Wilderness is a free good provided by Mother Nature, like fresh air and sunshine. Wilderness is a nonmarket service provided by governments, like the military and public schools. The wilderness experience is an atypical recreational experience and what the user actually spends poorly reflects its value.

To overcome this difficulty, contingent valuation is proposed. We can discover what users would be willing to pay. "The applicable rule to follow . . . is to use that procedure which appears to provide the best measure of expression of willingness to pay by the actual consumer of the recreation good or service."[4] "Techniques of benefit estimation have been developed sufficiently to make benefit-cost analysis fully applicable to appraisal of recreation alternatives on public forests. Willingness of users to pay is the appropriate way to measure benefits, and can be estimated from either the participation behavior of recreation users or by surveying a sample of participants to learn their preferences."[5] From what the users (think they) are willing to pay, we now subtract access costs for the net benefit supplied by the government, the "consumer's surplus," a value$_{ip}$ received but not paid for.[6] Aggregated over multiple visits and visitors, the total renders objective the otherwise subjective (though real) wildland recreational value, which can be compared with timber sales.

This is imaginary money, which the users pay no one and which also does not remain in their pockets. Still it might provide a reliable estimate, provided users have a congenial context of judgment. But on wildlands there is little reason to ask willingness to pay except under the shadow of protecting wildlands from alternative uses, and in this context the answer becomes a competitive bid. Rather ill-defined, it is something akin to a proposal that we take from them what they have had by tradition, public benefit, or right, and then ask what they are willing to pay to defend it. The precise status of any "right" to recreation, scenic views, open space, wildlife encounters, religious experiences (all integrated with recreation) on public lands is obscure, and, of course, developers also have "rights" on "lands of many uses." But citizens have long been told that these are "your national forests" (as the signs say on entry), which they are encouraged to use, managed by public servants whom (directly or indirectly) they have elected. They are wholly unaccustomed to paying to keep developers out; their presumptions are the other way round: that the developers who gain (and not the losers) ought to bear the full cost of what they remove from the public till.

The better question might be what the users would accept in payment to give up their recreation. But now we are asking a quite unfamiliar question. Although it does presume a willing seller rather than a defender of a threatened good, the user is made the owner of a good—a unit of recreation (integrated with historical, cultural symbolization, or life support values)—that he is ill-adept at selling. It introduces a host of concerns (examined below) about whether a citizen can entertain the thought of selling, corporately with others, a public good for private gain, *x* dollars. The upshot is that in these surveys economists are unsure whether to ask willingness to pay or to accept payment. Even if they have theories about what should be the starting reference point, their survey respondents do not operate out of these theories.

Clever respondents might bid or sell high to save the wilderness. (Or should they bid low to prevent entrance fees?) They could misrepresent to gain the outcomes they value. However, strategic scheming seems beyond most respondents, and can (in part) be checked against by alternative questions that put all on a limited budget. A better grounded fear is of nonstrategic pricing. If they think their estimates are not going to set any policy, they will not care what they say, especially if busy or puzzled. They must not simply be preferring but helping to project what will take place. The incentive for being responsible is the same as that for bias. Even if earnest, one is being asked to price what one has little clear strategy for pricing. This is especially true in the package of up to a dozen goods, some of which (re-creation beyond recreation, aesthetic experience, religious experience, amateur scientific study, character building) make it difficult to differentiate recreational value in isolation from the rest.

The difficulties are compounded if we try to price aesthetic value. (Is this a subset of, or something else than, recreational value?) "This is a national park, to be affected by a proposed coal-fired power plant nearby. How much additional entrance fee would you pay to have for thirty days a year (of relevant atmospheric conditions) a scenic visibility of 25, 50, 75 miles? What would you sell such views for?" This supposes that an individual in private trade might gain or sell a public good such as air quality or scenic vistas, more or less murky. It asks him to translate a good that is collective and nonmarket (scenery) into a good which is private and market (consumer dollars). It asks an individual to presume the right to sell (not only on his part but implicating others) what he thinks of as a nonexclusive, nonrival public good. "This wilderness has coal under it. How much would you pay (taxes, utility hikes?) not to lose x encounters with elk, coyotes, brown creepers?" (Is this an aesthetic value or respect for value$_{or}$ mixed with value$_{es}$?) These questions suppose a voluntary exchange (power for scenery, dollars per wildlife encounter), but in fact the exchange will be individually involuntary; it will be an agency decision levied upon all. The sets of persons who lose the vistas and the wildlife are really quite different from the persons who gain the power or the operators who profit.

The frequency of "infinity," "zero," or "not for sale" responses indicates that for many (up to half) the question is in one way or another off the map.[7] Persons expect to pay for some good produced, an artifact or service, some material that has been or can be labored over. But here on wildlands there is no "producer" or "supplier" whom it seems right to compensate.[8] No one has labored over anything, and why should anyone pay or be paid? In a way, the "victim-must-pay" inquiry is like paying to prevent the theft of a good one thought he had by democratic process or by gift of nature. It is something like paying for protection on the streets of Chicago, hardly a free market. It forces the user to be a consumer and compromising pragmatist in a decision context in which he ought to be a citizen, esthete, philosopher, and ethicist.

The format allows no account of what the recreator thinks in the fuller dimensions of his person about the larger benefits of public wildlands, free goods provided by nature and preserved by the government, about income constraints, the inequitable distribution of wealth, or the best things in life being free. The respondent is blinded to such considerations as the need for diverse options in recreation, rights of minority users, future trends, needs of future generations, intrinsic natural values, the psychological or social desirability or the quality of various forms of recreation. He must skip all historical, therapeutic, or cultural symbolization values. Already a victim who must estimate his willingness to pay to defend something he owns, the citizen is further victimized by the narrowed context into which he must squeeze his preferences. Only dollar answers count.

If we try to press beyond recreational and scenic values to option, existence, and bequest values, the problems rapidly grow worse. While some economists caution that we do not know how to price these values, others suppose that here too willingness to pay is the appropriate measure. A Colorado household is willing to pay, on average, about $4.04 annual option value, $4.87 annual existence value, and $5.01 annual bequest value, for a total of $13.92 annually for 1.2 million acres of wilderness. This sum rises to $18.75 for 2.6 million acres

($5.44 option value, $6.56 existence value, $6.75 bequest value). For 5 million acres, the total willingness to pay is $25.30 ($7.34 option value, $8.86 existence value, $9.10 bequest value). Multiplied by the number of Colorado households, we calculate the benefits to the state.[9] But why not use willingness to sell here? Perhaps because no one could seriously imagine that compensation would be paid the sellers. In any case, what have such numbers measured?

Such categories as existence, option, and bequest values promise to package up a fuzzy assortment (roughly the range of types 2-12, minus some recreation), but as values grow intangible, social and ecosystemic, the individual's capacity to price them becomes progressively poorer. All the problems met with in pricing recreational or scenic value return with a vengeance. As consumers, respondents are being asked to express their convictions in dollars about things over which they have no market experience, and dollars are, after all, units that have their everyday home in markets. Even as citizens voting in referendums they are accustomed to answer "Is-it-worth-it-in-dollars?" kinds of questions that have to do with the purchase of market materials and services (bombers, library books, real estate, building construction, man-hours of police time). They are unaccustomed to citizen "purchases" of genetic diversity, wildlife encounters, scenic vistas, or wild cultural symbols, especially on lands that the citizens already own and in situations where no money changes hands.[10]

The respondent has never operated in any market vaguely resembling these kinds of goods. How do we price, for instance, "the value that some individuals place on the knowledge of the mere existence of the gifts of nature, even when they feel certain that they will never have or choose an opportunity to experience them *in situ*"?[11] Since biological diversity, a value we are only learning to appreciate, is not something on the market, how can one price it? Does one include it somewhere with option, existence, or bequest values, or is it omitted in such a survey? Might it be that for $3.00 per person Americans will sell the whooping crane into extinction? Most respondents do not know how to resolve questions of extinction even within their own hierarchy of personal needs, much less to price these for social policy. Does it matter whether the respondent is ignorant about the intricacies of the ecosystem he judges, whether the estimator of scientific value is a scientist? Even allowing, as economists often do, that some environmental values remain uncaught, how do we know which ones are left out and not confusedly stated somewhere in the dollar amounts for option, existence, and bequest values?

It might first seem to help to cast the whole question into a citizens' rather than consumers' orientation. Respondents are cautioned that they must not think of their replies as consumer purchases, despite the fact that their dollar figures go into cost-benefit equations, and even though a frequent economist's term for the value so captured is "consumers' surplus." They must think of them more like citizen votes, using dollars as a kind of proxy, indicating what they think citizens ought to pay for wildland benefits, comparably to the way they pay for law courts or military protection. The survey is a citizen's device only partly to cooperate with but more to counter the real market. Willingness to pay levied taxes will have more citizen orientation than individual entrance fees, purchasing a day's recreation, or utility hikes, consumer-style transactions. But the payment of extra taxes does nothing to eliminate the victim-must-pay distastefulness of the procedure.

Willingness to pay becomes a kind of game, used not so much to imagine anything on a consumers' market as to elicit citizen choices, preferences stated in monetary amounts in order that these can be weighed into the equations, competing with alternate uses that do involve marketed goods. Despite appearances, we are not asking a "What's-it-worth-to-you-personally?" question, where each bids dollars depending on tastes and purchasing power. We are asking, "What's it worth to citizens on average, yourself included, in tax dollars, if all pay fairly proportioned amounts, and if all have the same nonconsumptive access to these public benefits that we cannot expect the market to supply?" In terms of the value level analysis, we are not asking a $value_{mp}$ question, despite the dollar appearance of the answers, nor even a $value_{ip}$ or $value_{ig}$ question, but a $value_{sp}$ and $value_{sg}$ question.

The difficulty now is that the question is not what it appears, and even if the respondent comes to understand the pretending involved, he has no rules by which he can translate $value_{sg}$ into $value_{mp}$, none by which he can integrate value types 2-12 on a scale commensurate with the market value of wildland products. The more he operates as a citizen, the more the privatized form of the question is remote from what he is really trying to indicate, and the less his capacity to do any pricing. He may also feel that he is being forced to play this game, in the sense that no answer eliminates his opinion, and wonder whether zero bids or infinity demands (or others that the interviewer considers out of range) will be eliminated on grounds of noncooperation. If a respondent states a huge sum (a recreator who personally places high religious value on wilderness experiences, a citizen who wishes to protect the rights of those who do, or an Earth citizen who holistically values ecosystems), will this make it into the cost-benefit equations, or be tossed out as a monkey-wrench answer? The citizen ought not in principle be asked to couple sufficient money with his nonmarket policy preferences; and when he is asked this, he does not in practice reliably know how to answer.

The respondent has no idea how to do any calculations; yet on the basis of his guesstimates, economists do metric calculations, overly refining what are really raw data. All this number crunching creates the illusion of mathematical exactitude covering up what were, to begin with, iffy replies in a cramped hypothetical context. Nor is the use of the respondent's behavior to correct verbal misjudgments of willingness to pay reliable, because behavior is already infected with the inequities in the prevailing distribution of wealth. Meanwhile, it will take considerable intellectual subtlety for the respondent to understand the differences between willingness to pay and willingness to accept payment, between consumer and citizen uses of dollars, between option, existence, and bequest values, between hypothetical and actual markets, to say nothing of reliably attaching dollar amounts to these issues. It is fortunate that most visitors to wildernesses, where these surveys are usually conducted, are college educated!

The wilderness purist thinks the procedure is profane; the ethicist protests that justice is wholly overlooked. How we treat the environment is not always a matter of economics; it is sometimes a matter of conscience. If the psychiatrist Jung is right, some of our emotions toward the land rise out of the collective unconscious; yet we are asked to price them in a few minutes. In psychology, advocates of values clarification argue that we have not identified a person's values until we find options he or she has chosen (1) freely (2) from genuine alternatives (3) after reflection, understanding the outcomes. The person must (4) remain satisfied with the choices, (5) be willing to advocate them publicly, and (6) act upon them (7) repeatedly. Not one of these criteria is satisfied here.

The admission-price-to-nature question could hardly have been asked in any earlier century or in a nonindustrial country, being the product of an economy biased toward production maximizing dollars. The mentality of the methodology by which we seek a solution is what created the problem, decimating the wilds. "Where will you put your dollars?" is as theory-laden as "Where is your center of gravity?" But unlike theories in physics, here we have a value$_{mp}$-laden theory that already purports to know what counts as costs and benefits. What we want to know here (or ought to want to know) are the citizens' *convictions* about goods in nature and their appropriate response to them, their public conscience, and we only confuse those we interview when we ask about their *desire* to pay. The question is about principles, not pocketbooks. They are being asked if an ideology is for sale. Desire-to-pay questions elsewhere in life are kept carefully separate from what we believe to be noble or ignoble behavior. The cash question is incompatible with answers of breadth. To insist on pricing is to insist on a category mistake ("the gold standard") where attitudes are inchoate.[12]

Advocates and even critics can throw up their hands. They can say that the technique is well intended, that there is nothing better, and that we cannot avoid running an economy. Some dollar values are better than none at all, for otherwise these intangible values get lost in the midst of pressures for economic use. Especially as the technique has been lately refined, the results significantly aid wilderness preservation. Environmentalists can fight fire with fire and prevent the burning of their wildlands on the altar of progress. Perhaps. But (to change the figure) a philosopher hates to fly in a conceptually flawed airplane, even though for the time being it is pragmatically flying in the right direction. If the model is a muddle but we use it anyway, being unwilling to face its fallacious reductionism, we are disinclined to admit the complexities of the real world and to look for truth in likelier directions.

WILD DECISION RULES

We do not want to play the game by the old rules, but to rewrite the rules. The point of my narration of levels and types of value (section one) was to display a richer value spectrum than we have reason to believe can be caught by economic valuation (section two). Can we say anything positively (section three) to order decisions? These principles will not constitute a procedural set. Like a compass, they will orient general directions of travel. Specific paths will have to be figured out locally. The rules will only begin to map some presently wild terrain. But they will be more dependable for discovering and protecting wildland values than economic reductions, which as we just found normally lead us astray.

(1) *Use an axiological model.* A diagrammatic schema (figure 1) should guide policy decisions on remnant U.S. wildlands in the contiguous United States. It is applied elsewhere (abroad, Alaska, outside environmental ethics) at your own risk. Above the line is a humanistic sequence, below it is a naturalistic sequence.

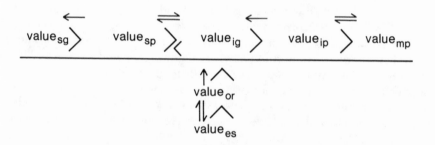

Figure 1.—An ordering of levels of value.

Social goods ordinarily override ($>$) social preferences, although the latter routinely produce ($\leftarrow$) such goods. In turn, this combination overrides individual goods, though these feed and determine social preferences, which reciprocally also promote ($\rightleftharpoons$) individual goods. A caveat, the small wedge checking the larger one ($\gtreqless$), specifies that some individual goods, few but crucial, veto some social preferences. Murder is not justified to obtain wilderness, even supposing society preferred this. Individual goods trump those individual preferences that commonly produce them. Individual preferences are what produce ($\longrightarrow$) market prices, and the existence of a market produces in turn ($\longleftarrow$) the satisfaction of individual preferences so that there is a two-way arrow ($\rightleftharpoons$).

On remaining wildlands, all this valuing overrides market value. The social drama is superimposed on the underlying ecosystem, and the diagram suggests the shrunken wild domain. Organismic value, as a populational form of life (e.g., endangered species, not individuals) ordinarily trumps what (usually minor) social or personal goods compete with it, though organisms ordinarily contribute social values. Pileated woodpeckers are good in themselves and also enrich human experience. Ecosystemic value is more basic than the life-form level, though biosystems are naturally selected to interfit (⫟) the two. Both contribute to serial human goods.

The diagram yields *prima facie* rules. For exceptions, the burden of proof is on the dissenter. On remnant wildlands the odds are that the sacrifice of wild values will not both contribute to long-term human goods and be justified. The wilder and rarer the land, the lower the probability that any consumptive economic use will override other values. Virgin forests will stay intact. The demand for wilderness is increasing quite as rapidly as the demand for timber; although the latter can be satisfied on private lands, the former cannot.

I am advocating a kind of *maxi-min* principle following the ratio of continental domestication to wildness so that a minimum level (2 percent, 4 percent) of wildland values (intrinsic and human instrumental) is maximized (at 98-2, 96-4 odds), opposing a *maxi-max* principle (maximum consumption increasing from 96 percent to 98 percent to 100 percent our available acreage to raise our already high standards of living). That two to four percent surfeit is a "consumers' surplus" we do not need. It is a few more pounds on already fat people, who need the rigorous leanness that disciplined exposure to wildness can give. Considering probable economic productivity, rather than acreage, there is no reason to think that, on average, U.S. citizens would be even one percent better off if all wildlands were sacrificed. From this viewpoint the odds are 99-1 that the sacrifice of wildness makes sense in order to achieve economic gain at the cost of values 2-12 lost.

The areas richest in resources have long since been domesticated, and sacrificing the remaining wildlands is scraping the bottom of the barrel, a matter of diminishing marginal returns (notwithstanding newly developed technologies), although from other points of view the destruction of noneconomic value would be enormous. Public lands, often left over from the public domain in the West or reacquired after marginal use in the East, tend not to be economically productive in agriculture, timber, or minerals.

(2) *Maximize noncompeting value types.* The twelve types of natural value are incommensurable, but are also largely noncompeting in all cases but the first. Although they cannot be commensurated, they do not have to be. There is no translation unit by which A + B - C = D. Genetic diversity (indicated by species counts, low extinction rates) cannot meaningfully be added to, or subtracted from, recreational benefits (visitor days). But we can easily add together and simultaneously enjoy multiple noncompeting incommensurables. Historical, character-building, or therapeutic uses of wildlands will seldom interfere with scientific and religious uses, and nowhere are science and religion more congenial than here. The cultural value carried by eagles requires the preservation of a

flourishing wild population. Aesthetic uses (measured on preference scales) do not upset the life support value (indexed by energy flow?) in an ecosystem. So we are not forced to prefer only one value. The commensurability of values is, thus far, a pseudoproblem, because these nonconsumptive values reinforce and need not be traded off against each other.[13] They do not use up wilderness in the ordinary resource sense at all, making it into something different from what it spontaneously was.

Only economic uses tend to consume wildlands. The question faced here is not whether the past economic reduction of the continent was justified, but whether it is enough. How much more of the goods (values$_{ip}$, $_{sg}$) we already amply have (fiber, timber, energy) can we obtain by consuming the surviving wildlands, and do we want these as economic benefits (value$_{mp}$) by trading away the nonconsumptive set of values? Although this seems to pit market value against some or all of values 2-12, for a wider public it only pits a little more extracted from the 2 percent wild (the 4 percent half wild) of what we have extracted already from the 98 percent (96 percent) in impressive amounts. Yet this "more" could as easily and efficiently be extracted from nonwild lands, which are far and away already the richest ones economically. If we ask who are the chief beneficiaries (a few operators, perhaps more workers) and who are the trickle-down beneficiaries (the public), we may find that this gains a few concentrated, short-term values$_{ip}$, $_{ig}$ (profits, jobs perhaps unobtainable elsewhere) traded against values$_{sg}$ and diluted but extremely widespread, long-term value$_{ip}$ (recreational benefits, religious experiences). Do we have enough consumption? If more is needed, need it come by sacrificing wildlands?

On remaining wildlands, economic use is typically consumptive, and that gives preferential treatment to one class of users and uses (value type 1) at the cost of depriving other users of their alternate uses (value types 2-12). The nearest that policy can come to nonpreferential treatment is by nonconsumptive use. Everyone can use wildlands, but no one ought be allowed to use them up. Sometimes disparagingly called a "lockup" use, that use treats all users alike, even though (indeed, just because) the would-be economic user is prohibited from "takeover" use. "Lockup" only prevents "takeover." It is more likely to result in gradually unlocking an equal distribution of benefits of the other types over time. It simultaneously protects organismic and ecosystemic value, leaving wildlands in a spontaneous natural state.

If basic needs were at stake, or if the continent were not already 98 percent developed and developable, this might be unjustly prohibitive. But it is not unjust on the last 2 percent, where only more of already abundantly possessed goods is at stake. While any economic use is somewhat consumptive, since it sacrifices primordial wildness to some degree, some economic uses are more consumptive than others. A clear-cut takes the forest out of other uses for a century, and the second-growth forest is never the equal of the virgin forest. A cut by selection leaves half the original wildness and may only halfway destroy values 2-12.

Beyond this, however, values of the sort here defended tend not to aggregate additively, even when noncompeting. They integrate into a gestalt in which a calculus is irrelevant. A single value change may throw the whole pattern into a different light. Colored floodlights on Old Faithful, illuminating it for night viewing, would add tourist revenue, and yet break the picture of wildness for most park visitors. A small-scale, out-of-sight logging operation returns economic benefits; while the noise of the chainsaw carried around the valley may subtract only a little from the solitude of some wilderness travelers, it destroys it entirely for others. Various thresholds of perception and value experience are crossed, which are not incorporated in aggregating procedures.

(3) *Keep remaining public wildlands off the market.* The military, police, courts, schools, museums, churches, scientific societies, historical parks—all cost money and have budgets, but are not businesses expected to produce income in any cost-efficient sense, not even when they capture (by fees, admission charges, or contributions) part of the value of their services. Though we sometimes decide how much they are worth in dollars, their purposes are to produce nonmonetary values. Wildness costs something to preserve, though only the minutest fraction of what these other social activities cost. Costs are largely opportunity costs forgone, so far as these cannot be achieved on the 98 percent of the continent on the market.

Even on semiwild lands, it is a category mistake to compare market efficiency in a Weyerhaeuser timber tract with a national forest. Where national forests are quasi-market operations, and little more, they should be sold or leased to private entrepreneurs, who will operate them better. On truly "national" forests we protect other values, and here market-style questions are awkward because what we want on wildlands is what the market never sells—a hiking trail, a trout stream, a scenic view, a wilderness experience. No one invests in land to lease it for bird watching or butterfly collecting. That is economic nonsense. The purpose of public wildlands is to provide benefits that we cannot expect on the market.

The point of a value analysis should not be to translate all or as much as possible of values 2-12 or levels 1-7 into an economic common denominator, but to display the wide spectrum of types and levels and give decision makers and citizens a strengthened persuasion where these really do (or do not), in aggregate or gestalt, beat economic considerations on the fractional remaining wildlands. We want a policy to protect these value dimensions not because they are covert economic values, but because they are not economic values at all.

(4) *Do not use remaining wildlands nonrenewably or consumptively to satisfy the basic needs of a minority in society.* The way to feed the hungry is by a redistribution of produce from lands in private hands, not by further exploitation of the fractional public wildlands. Very few will be put permanently to work by wildland exploitation, and these can surely as well be employed elsewhere in the enormous American economy. In a free economy, left otherwise

unchanged, it is impossible to assure that the benefits from sacrificing wildlands will go to the poor; indeed, they probably will not. What the disadvantaged (or the middle or upper class) think about trading wildland values to help the disadvantaged becomes irrelevant when considered apart from whether in the prevailing economy this transfer can reliably be expected to take place.

Nor will the individual economic gains of the poor (value$_{ig, mp}$) overcome the social losses (value$_{sg}$) in value types 2-12. Poverty problems should be solved where they arise: in the mainstream economic sector, not on wildlands. To pit the trivial pleasures of an elite (a few fit, wealthy backpackers) against the needs of the many (starving in the ghettos) is confused. While such a choice may not be spurious in underdeveloped nations, it is in the United States, to which this analysis is applied. Even elsewhere, unjust social structures will often prevent goods obtained by sacrificing wildlands from benefiting the poor in any long-term way. It is everywhere futile to sacrifice wildlands to benefit the disadvantaged unless the social structures are just enough to make it probable that this transfer will take place. Failing that, the issue is a smokescreen that merely protects vested interests; it sacrifices almost every kind of value type and level only to delay needed social reforms, keeping in place a social disvalue. The basic needs of all can be met, and would already be, if the system were just. Social injustice condoned, does not justify destroying natural values, as yet unappreciated.

(5) *Increase options.* By this we increase our possibilities to actualize preferences (value$_{ip}$) and so increase freedom and the quality of life. Most Americans are oversupplied with market artifacts and undersupplied with sites for experiencing pristine nature. They live in an urban or rural environment 99 percent of their time, in a wild environment 1 percent or less. We should, therefore, manage wildlands to meet needs that are unmet and unmeetable elsewhere (desires for a temporary exit from society or to see bighorn sheep). This is more true when these needs are intense, even in a minority, and if society's meeting these needs involves doing little or nothing. Also, there is truth in the adage that one should manage for the specialized user (the fly fisherman, the backpacker) rather than the general user (the picnicker, car camper), since it is likely that the interests of the former will be keener, resulting in higher quality experiences for which there are no substitutes. Economic uses that consume wildlands destroy our liberties here. Although society as a whole should increase all sorts of options, in remnant wildland decisions we increase options in wildness alike for ourselves and future generations. The pluralist model of "multiple use" here means such multiple uses as are noncompeting and nonconsumptive. Competitive and consumptive use is provided for elsewhere in the market sector. All this optimizes social diversity.

(6) *Make explicit the latent value judgments in quantitative models.* The numbers look hard—11,176 visitor days, $4,175,000 timber sales, willingness to pay $2.32 per person, discount rate 6.7 percent, preference 7.3 (scale of 10) in age group 25-35, with 12+ years of education. Although some will say that quantification makes values explicit, remember that the numbers are no harder than the

theories out of which they come, as limited as the concepts which generate them. Unless the theories and concepts are explored and remain visible in the discussion, the numbers can deceive. All numbers in science are theory-laden, in environmental and social science often laden with soft theories. When used to persuade, they arise from value-laden theories. They contain large empirical margins of error and value judgments that need to be made manifest. To take visitor days as a value indicator concentrates on the value$_{ip}$ level, value type 3, and leaves unanalyzed all other levels and types. To use any discount rate prefers the present over future generations.

Quantitative techniques, when ineptly or mechanically used, can obscure important value relations, and even when used at their best can never substitute for judgment, intuition, scope of understanding, and verbal assessment. Only the latter skills can suggest, at the start, what values are worth quantifying and how to try to quantify them, and in the end, only the latter can interpret the numbers that emerge. Dollar signs give the impression that a host of problems have been overcome interrelating value$_{sg}$ to value$_{mp}$. The "number values," nevertheless, are meaningless except in the context of an interpreted narrative of values. Numbers may disguise, rather than expose, value judgments. Indeed, the numbers are sometimes little more than tropes, used for the sake of giving life or emphasis to an idea. They are used in a different sense from the way numbers are usually used, not to count empirical things exactly at all, but only symbolically to stand for values when they are felt to be real but the amount present, though important, is unverifiable. We should distrust any numbers for which there is only one indicator, since there is no cross-checking and the cramped value judgments are less easy to expose.

In the end, wildland decisions are not a data-driven process; rather the data is caged by a value-driven theory. The data seldom changes anyone's mind, but is gathered and selected to justify positions already held, and ignored or reinterpreted if it is in conflict with favored positions. We should decide first about the latent ideology, only secondarily about the number analysis.

(7) *Protect minority interests, especially where this is nonconsumptive and requires doing nothing.* Consumptive minority interests, especially if they require expensive action (building a road to keep a local mill going) should not override nonconsumptive majority interests. On the other hand, nonconsumptive minority interests (mountaineering, bird watching) which can be satisfied by doing almost nothing are cheap and easy to protect and are noncompeting between values 2-12. The protection of such minority interests is a long-standing majoritarian American value. Nothing is actually taken away from the majority in protecting these interests, although opportunity costs may be forgone. These may be significant to a few, but are not likely to be great to the community as a whole.

Opportunity costs forgone (value$_{mp}$) make sense as real social costs (value$_{sg}$) only when these opportunities are available only on the site in question. From the perspective of value$_{sg}$, the timber lost on a wilderness site is no irretrievable disvalue if by better management techniques an equal amount might have been grown elsewhere, although managers are too inefficient or uninterested to attempt this.[14] Similarly, in assessing the costs of the Cranberry Wilderness in West Virginia at $30.77 per visitor day, it makes little sense to count as by far the largest factor $223,609 per year in opportunity costs of coal left underground and unmined, since there is a three-hundred year supply of coal elsewhere in the Appalachian coal strata, and no reason to think the Cranberry coal should be mined soon or needs to be in order to meet national needs.[15] Nor should one forget, when development takes place and these opportunity costs become dollar benefits instead, that a spectrum of other opportunity costs (values 2-12) appears, opportunities lost perhaps forever.

Any delay, moreover, brings opportunity to see whether even the majority do not gain in values 2-12 more than they lose in opportunity costs. We gain benefits for the minority and the benefits of waiting for the majority. This rule protects against a danger in what otherwise seems so democratic—settling things by referendum. One purpose of government is to see that the fully considered will of the majority is done, where there is no injustice; another is to see that this is not imposed on the minority unjustly. A strategy for insuring this might be, for instance, to prefer nonconsumptive minority interests over consumptive simple majority interests, and furthermore, to require a two-thirds majority, on grounds that consumptive use of relict wildlands requires more caution and a quite unequivocal demonstration that this is in fact the considered majority view—that it is a use worth imposing at irreversible sacrifice on the minority and with irreversible loss of option to the majority.

Policy here should favor nonconsumptive minority interests over consumptive minority interests, since those who want to "lock up" the land delay but do not irrevocably destroy the option of developing it, while developers who "use up" the land irrevocably erode the original set of wild values carried by it.

(8) *Do not underestimate diffused values.* Although lots of persons may be hurt by a decision, they are not hurt very much (a diminished vacation vista), while a few (the mill operators who clearcut) have a lot to gain. We can expect the latter to lobby full force; the former, however, will be disorganized, slow to realize what is at stake, and ill-represented in the public participation process. Yet, the aggregate loss of value—now to the majority—can be much larger than the gain to the minority. The scenery is marred for a century. Even when the amenity values are accurately represented, they are intangible.

Sometimes the agenda can determine the result. The hard values, considered first, are thoroughly assessed; the soft values, held in abeyance to be considered last, are only loosely (and wearily) thrown in, after the hard values are already massively in place. If the agenda is the other way around, with as much attention given to specifying the soft values, and only afterward considering whether economic benefits override these, the results could be different. The path by which the choice is made can bias the choice.

All this tends to stunt the attention given to soft values, that is, to under-represent the widespread, low-level intangibles and overestimate the concentrated, intense tangibles. Even the use of willingness to pay, well-intended though it is, routinely underappraises the soft values, for reasons we have examined. More-over, one needs to identify the changes in value distribution over different populations, always an ethically relevant consideration even beyond aggregates, to avoid unjustly benefiting the few while burdening the many.

Some contend that a preservationist policy imposes concentrated costs (the few, local timber companies who lose a lot) and diffuse benefits (the public, who gain slight recreational benefits). Such policy is rarely implemented not only because it is difficult to maintain legislatively, but even more because it is ethically unsatisfactory. The better gestalt is to turn the picture around and say that a development policy, at least on relict wildlands, permits concentrated benefits (the timber sellers and buyers) and diffuse costs (intangibles over a larger public). The latter is the more logical and ethical gestalt, because the public, which is the present owner and has its benefits of wildness taken away, is the loser. The timber operators, who do not now own the timber but who buy it for profit, are the gainers.

Furthermore, if the timber companies do not pay the full costs, or if they destroy what money cannot buy, then they (and their customers) are subsidized at the public loss, a situation that is even more ethically unsatisfactory. The ideal in a democracy is for the majority to have their well-considered way, provided there is no injustice to the minority, and provided that there is a full counting of the production and distribution costs and benefits. The concept of opportunity costs forgone should not be applied to minority would-be exploiters of the land, who are not now its owners, but to the present owners, the public. If this public uses wildlands as one kind of resource, it must consider its opportunity costs forgone, especially if such opportunities cannot be had elsewhere. But oppor-tunity costs forgone need not apply to consumptive opportunists on public lands. That is why we should not pit concentrated costs against diffuse benefits, but turn the issue around and pit concentrated benefits against diffuse costs.

(9) *Recognize that wildland decisions must be one place where the model (myth?) of the perpetually expanding economy is broken.* Four hundred and fifty years ago Europeans began to enter what they naively called an empty continent. Abetted by the industrial revolution in the last two hundred years and the explosion of science and technology in the last hundred, the American economy has been on a growth trip unprecedented in the history of the world. A national tradition conflicts with the preservation of wildland values. Many people cry, "More!" Wildland managers, aside from the natural values they positively protect, negatively have to say, "Enough!" It will always be possible to increase the GNP a bit by sacrificing wildlands. But now is the time, here is the place, to draw the line at the boundaries of the wildland remnants and say: this far, but no farther with expanding economy.

Expand it, if you must, on nonwild lands. It is futile to sacrifice the relict wildlands and to confront the collapsing growth myth only after they are gone. To confront it now saves so much in values 2-12. This policy also helps us anticipate the steady-state economy and not tumble into it by default and catastrophe. We have no reason to think that the last fraction exploited will leave us any nearer to satisfied consumer desires in a system designed ever to escalate those desires. Americans are already rich and need to learn when enough is enough. In this sense, wildland decisions are not peripheral "recreational" matters but frontline challenges to a governing paradigm. Wildland managers are not simply supplying values additionally to those generated in the domestic economy; they are confronting the slowdown, and, at wildland boundaries, the breakdown of a traditional economy in favor of noneconomic values. Wildland decisions are rewriting history, terminating and reevaluating the transcontinental growth trip. At the wilderness boundary, we should post a sign: "Enter the wilderness. Abandon the GNP rat race here. Learn to be wilderness rich."

In this context one frequently hears proposals that developers and preservationists ought to meet each other halfway. Compromise is frequently a necessity and often moral in policy decisions, but there is no logic by which fairness is always meeting each other halfway or by which conflicting values are usually optimized by compromise. There is even less reason to believe this in wildland disputes, where 98 percent of the continent is developed, 2 percent remains wild, and developers propose to preservationists that they should meet halfway over the remaining 2 percent.

(10) *Expect wildland decisions to awaken previously latent and newly emerging values.* Environmental values are among those things until recently taken for granted, naively appreciated, or unappreciated. Not until developers threatened the mountain on the skyline did we realize what it meant to us. Not until they proposed to drain the marsh could we say that we would rather have it left alone, and even now it is difficult to articulate why. We never miss the water until the well runs dry. We learn what is at stake only when we learn that it is at stake. We awaken to goods when their opposites threaten, or awaken to inconsistencies in our value sets when we cannot have our cake and eat it too. In these matters we can hardly expect a congressional mandate ever to be as groundbreaking as it ought to be, though we can reasonably expect it to express social preferences over economic interests. One cannot get anything through Congress that is very complex or controversial. The earliest growth in value awareness comes somewhere back in the grassroots, but decision models need to help it along. Deciders should find the trend, not the mean; they should lead, not just follow. They should set principles, not just sum preferences.

I close with a factual claim and a plea. A trend approximating this axiological model (above the solid line) and these rules can be found in congressional legislation over the last twenty years (the National Environmental Policy Act; the Endangered Species Act, the various Wilderness Acts, the Wild and Scenic Rivers Act), usually expressed vaguely as a desire to protect "environmental," "ecological," or "amenity" values from economic usurpation. The Federal Land

Policy and Management Act of 1976 "declares that it is the policy of the United States that" there be "a combination of balanced and diverse resource uses . . . without permanent impairment of the productivity of the land and the quality of the environment with consideration being given to the relative values of the resources and not necessarily to the combination of uses that will give the greatest economic return."[16]

What is novel here is adding the understory of natural value, which, while not explicit in the legislation, is permitted by and consistent with it, and more ethically advanced (nonanthropocentric) than can yet be expected of congressional legislation. What we still need is a kind of emancipation proclamation for the wildness that remains, which can be issued with the full assurance that the benefits to the emancipators will outweigh their costs, with these to be added to the benefits to the emancipated (as was true with the Emancipation Proclamation of 1863). This is a call for humans to respect the plenitude of being, once so vast and now so quickly vanishing, which surrounds us in the wild world.

Can humans genuinely gain by exploiting the fractional wilds that remain? What does it profit to gain the whole world, only to lose it—to gain it economically, only to lose it scientifically, aesthetically, recreationally, religiously, as a wonderland of natural history, as a realm of integral wildness that transcends and supports us—and perhaps even to lose some of our soul in the trade-off?

NOTES

This paper was written under Research Contract No. 28-K2-259, USDA Rocky Mountain Forest and Range Experiment Station. The author thanks Dennis Donnelly and J. Baird Callicott for stimulating criticism.

1. William Wordsworth, "Lines Composed a Few Miles above Tintern Abbey" (1798).

2. J. V. Krutilla and A. C. Fisher, *The Economics of Natural Environments* (Baltimore: Johns Hopkins University Press, 1975), p. 124; J. V. Krutilla, "Conservation Reconsidered," *American Economic Review* 57 (1967): 777-86.

3. For contingent valuation of aesthetic, scenic visibility, see: Alan Randall, Berry C. Ives, and Clyde Eastman, "Bidding Games for Valuation of Aesthetic Environmental Improvements," *Journal of Environmental Economics and Management* 1 (1974): 132-49; Alan Randall, Berry C. Ives, and Clyde Eastman, *Benefits of Abating Aesthetic Environmental Damage from the Four Corners Power Plant, Fruitland, New Mexico,* New Mexico State University Agricultural Experiment Station Bulletin 618 (Las Cruces, 1974); David S. Brookshire, Berry C. Ives, and William D. Schulze, "The Valuation of Aesthetic Preferences," *Journal of Environmental Economics and Management* 3 (1976): 325-46; R. D. Rowe, Ralph C. d'Arge, and D. S. Brookshire, "An Experiment on the Economic Value of Visibility," *Journal of Environmental Economics and Management* 7 (1980): 1-19. For contingent valuation of wildlife experiences see: Judd Hammack and

Gardner Mallard Brown, Jr., *Waterfowl and Wetlands: Toward Bioeconomic Analysis* (Washington, D.C.: Resources for the Future, 1974); David S. Brookshire, Alan Randall, and John R. Stoll, "Valuing Increments and Decrements in Natural Resource Service Flows," *American Journal of Agricultural Economics* 62 (1980): 478-88; David S. Brookshire, Alan Randall, et al., *Methodological Experiments in Valuing Wildlife Resources: Phase I Interm Report to the United States Fish and Wildlife Service*, 1977. For contingent valuation of option, existence, and bequest value in wilderness preservation see: Richard G. Walsh, John B. Loomis, and Richard A. Gillman, "Valuing Option, Existence, and Bequest Demands for Wilderness," *Land Economics* 60 (1984): 14-29. For a sensitive overview, cautiously advocating contingent valuation, see: William D. Schulze, Ralph C. d'Arge, and David S. Brookshire, "Valuing Environmental Commodities: Some Recent Experiments," *Land Economics* 57 (1981): 151-72. See also George L. Peterson and Alan Randall, eds., *Valuation of Wildland Benefits* (Boulder, Colo.: Westview Press, 1984).

4. U.S. Water Resources Council, "Principles and Strategies for Planning Water and Related Land Resources," *Federal Register* 38, no. 174 (10 September 1973): 24, 778-866, citation on p. 24,804; U. S. Water Resources Council, *Procedures for Evaluation of National Economic Development (NED) Benefits and Costs in Water Resources Planning*, Subpart K, *Recreation*, *Federal Register* 44, no. 242 (14 December 1979): 72, 950-65.

5. J. F. Dwyer and M. D. Bowes, "Benefit-Cost Analysis for Appraisal of Recreation Alternatives," *Journal of Forestry* 77, no. 3 (1979): 145-47, with comment by A. A. Dyer and J. G. Hof, 147-48, and vigorous discussion by others, *Journal of Forestry* 78, no. 1 (1980): 21-28.

6. Consumer's surplus is "the maximum a consumer will pay for a given amount of a good, less the amount he actually pays" (E. J. Mishan, *Cost-Benefit Analysis: An Introduction* [New York: Praeger Publishers, 1971], p. 31).

7. See I. M. Gordon and J. L. Knetsch, "Consumer's Surplus Measures and the Evaluation of Resources," *Land Economics* 55 (1979): 1-10; Randall, Ives, and Eastman, *Benefits*, pp. 19, 24; Shultze, d'Arge, and Brookshire, "Valuing Environmental Commodities," p. 166; Rowe, d'Arge, and Brookshire, "Experiment," p. 9.

8. Subsidized public recreation is not at issue here. On-site wildland users may be enjoying benefits that have maintenance costs (upkeep of roads, trails, game supervision, ranger salaries) and which taxpayers at large are bearing. Questions about whether on-site recreators should bear more of the actual costs are plausibly subject to willingness-to-pay evaluation, although the lack of a realistic market context troubles answers here too. The unspecified mix of recreational with other benefits preserved on public lands (life support, genetic diversity), which taxpayers do enjoy, complicates the issue. But should-users-bear-the-maintenance-cost questions are conceptually different from willingness to pay to prevent economic development, pollution, species extinctions, scenic despoilations, which impinge on recreational opportunities.

9. Walsh, Loomis, and Gillman, "Valuing Option, Existence, and Bequest Demands," p. 25.

10. Contingent valuation needs to be distinguished from citizens' referendums. In April 1981 Larimer County, Colorado, citizens voted for a half-cent sales tax over six months to purchase the Soderberg Ranch containing Horsetooth Mountain, on the skyline of Fort Collins. Following public debate, a local jurisdiction voted to use mutual coercion to buy something on the market, which they did not own, in order to preserve

wild recreational, aesthetic, and cultural embodiment values. There is nothing hypothetical and nonmarket here, and no victim-must-pay-for-what-he-already-owns overtones. They were buying a working ranch, with the owner using the proceeds to relocate, competing with offers from real estate developers. They were not separately bidding, but had a corporate target figure, translated into a tax, on which they were voting yes or no. That is a citizen choice using votes to allocate dollars. By contrast wildlands are already public lands, and citizens (if they so regard themselves as respondents) are being asked about a hypothetical willingness to pay to protect what they already own, with nothing traded that bears any relationship to actual markets.

11. Those who value the mere existence of wildlands, though they never expect to visit them, are often called "off-site users," a term revealing the utilitarian, anthropocentric coordinates of this value-mapping system, made worse by contingent valuations treating them as off-site consumers. Such categories lie in an alien reference frame from that of those trying to report convictions about intrinsic values in nature. "Off-site users" grotesquely illustrates the extent to which a nonnegotiable paradigm ("resource use") can be twisted to accommodate anomalous phenomena. It exactly reverses what those so categorized would say of themselves: that wildlands are valuable when left alone, apart from questions of human use.

12. M. Sagoff, "At the Shrine of Our Lady of Fatima, *or* Why Political Questions Are Not All Economic," *Arizona Law Review* 23, no. 4 (1981):1283-98.

13. Some counterexamples: Sioux and Cheyenne Indians lost a legal bid to halt recreational development at Bear Butte State Park in the Black Hills, a conflict of religion with recreational value; other kinds of recreation would have been nonrival. In a Maine referendum on moose hunting, the aesthetic, recreational, cultural symbolization (the state animal) values of environmentalists, as well as their respect for intrinsic organismic value, clashed with the differing recreational, aesthetic, character-building, and historical values of the hunters. In Florida, fishermen sought, unsuccessfully, to have the park service relax restrictions on fishing in the Everglades, restrictions protecting the endangered crocodile. The Defenders of Wildlife protested regulations that allow the twilight shooting of game birds, on grounds that the low visibility makes it difficult to distinguish common from endangered species. These involve clashes of forms of recreational value with scientific, genetic diversity, organismic, ecosystemic, and alternate forms of recreational value. But such conflicts are minimal beside economic conflicts on wildlands. Though they are not handled by the rules proposed here, willingness-to-pay surveys are even more irrelevant.

14. Julie F. Gorte and W. Wendell Fletcher, analysts for the Office of Technology Assessment, find that simple management practices (such as thinning) on only 30-40% of the U.S. commercial forestland base could double the current harvest levels, and at the current levels, Americans already consume more wood than people in any other nation. "Technology, Timber and the Future," *Renewable Resources Journal* 2, nos. 2 & 3 (Autumn 1983 & Winter 1984): 16-19.

15. R. W. Guldin, "Predicting Costs of Eastern National Forest Wilderness," *Journal of Leisure Research* 13 (1981): 112-28.

16. *Federal Land Policy and Management Act of 1976* (Public Law 94-579), Secs. 102, 103. (90 STAT. 2743) There is similar language in the *Multiple Use Sustained Yield Act of 1960* (Public Law 86-517), Sec. 4(a). (74 STAT. 215)

10

Duties to Endangered Species

In the Endangered Species Act, Congress has lamented the lack of "adequate concern [for] and conservation [of]" species.[1] But neither scientists nor ethicists have fully realized how developing this concern requires an unprecedented mix of biology and ethics. What logic underlies duties involving forms of life? Looking to the past for help, one searches in vain through 3,000 years of philosophy (back at least to Noah!) for any serious reference to endangered species. Among present theories of justice, Harvard philosopher John Rawls asserts, "The destruction of a whole species can be a great evil," but also admits that in his theory "no account is given of right conduct in regard to animals and the rest of nature."[2] Meanwhile there is an urgency to the issue. The *Global 2000 Report* projects a massive loss of species, up to 20 percent within a few decades.[3]

DUTIES TO PERSONS CONCERNING SPECIES

The usual way to approach a concern for species is to say that there are no duties directly to endangered species, only duties to other persons concerning species. From a utilitarian standpoint, summarized by Hampshire, the protection of nature and "the preservation of species are to be aimed at and commended only in so far as human beings are, or will be, emotionally and sentimentally interested."[4] In an account based on rights, Feinberg reaches a similar conclusion. "We do have duties to protect threatened species, not duties to the species themselves as such, but rather duties to future human beings."[5] Using traditional ethics to confront the novel threat of extinctions, we can reapply familiar duties to persons and see whether this is convincing. This line of argument can be impressive but seems to leave deeper obligations untouched.

Persons have a strong duty not to harm others and a weaker, though important, duty to help others. Arguing the threat of harm, the Ehrlichs maintain, in a blunt metaphor, that species are rivets in the Earthship in which humans are flying.[6] Extinctions are maleficent rivet-popping. In this model, nonrivet species, if there are any, would have no value; humans desire only the diversity that

Reprinted by permission from *BioScience* 35 (1985): 718-726.

prevents a crash. The care is not for particular species but, in a variant metaphor, for the sinking ark.[7] To worry about a sinking ark seems a strange twist on the Noah story. Noah built the ark to preserve each species. In the Ehrlich/ Myers account, the species-rivets are preserved to keep the ark from sinking! The reversed justification is revealing.

On the benefits side, species that are not rivets may prove resources. Thomas Eisner testified to Congress that only two percent of the flowering plants have been tested for alkaloids, which often have medical value.[8] A National Science Foundation report advocated saving the Devil's Hole Pupfish, *Cyprinodon diabolis,* because it thrives in extremes and "can serve as useful biological models for future research on the human kidney—and on survival in a seemingly hostile environment."[9] Myers further urges "conserving our global stock."[10] At first this advice seems wise, yet later somewhat demeaning for humans to regard all other species as *stock.*

Destroying species is like tearing pages out of an unread book, written in a language humans hardly know how to read, about the place where they live. No sensible person would destroy the Rosetta Stone, and no self-respecting persons will destroy the mouse lemur, endangered in Madagascar and thought to be the nearest modern animal to the relatively unspecialized primates from which the human line evolved. Still, following this logic, humans do not have duties to the book, the stone, or the species, but to ourselves, duties of prudence and education. Humans need insight into the full text of ecosystem evolution. It is not endangered species but an endangered human future that is of concern. Such reasons are pragmatic and impressive. They are also moral, since persons are benefited or hurt. But are they exhaustive?

One problem is that pragmatic reasons get overstated. Peter H. Raven testified before Congress that a dozen dependent species of insects, animals, or other plants typically become extinct with each plant that goes extinct.[11] But Raven knows that such cascading, disastrous extinction is true only on statistical average, since a plant named for him, Raven's manzanita, *Arctostaphylos hookeri* ssp. *ravenii,* is known from a single wild specimen, and its extinction is unlikely to trigger others. Rare species add some backup resilience. Still, if all 79 plants on the endangered species list disappeared, it is doubtful that the regional ecosystems involved would measurably shift their stability. Few cases can be cited where the removal of a rare species damaged an ecosystem.

Let's be frank. A substantial number of endangered species have no resource value. Beggar's ticks, *Bidens* spp., with their stick-tight seeds, are a common nuisance through much of the U.S. One species, tidal shore beggar's tick, *B. bidentoides,* which differs little in appearance from the others, is endangered. It seems unlikely to be a potential resource. As far as humans are concerned, its extinction might be good riddance.

We might say that humans ought to preserve for themselves an environment adequate to match their capacity to wonder. But this is to value the *experience* of wonder, rather than the *objects* of wonder. Valuing merely the experience seems to commit a fallacy of misplaced wonder, for speciation is itself among the wonderful things on Earth. Valuing speciation directly, however, seems to attach value to the evolutionary process, not merely to subjective experiences that arise when humans reflect over it.

We might say that humans of decent character will refrain from needless destruction of all kinds, including destruction of species. Vandals destroying art objects do not so much hurt statues as cheapen their own character. But is the American shame at destroying the passenger pigeon only a matter of self-respect? Or is it shame at our ignorant insensitivity to a form of life that (unlike a statue) had an intrinsic value that placed some claim on us?

The deeper problem with the anthropocentric rationale, beyond overstatement, is that its justifications are submoral and fundamentally exploitative even if subtly. This is not true, intraspecifically, among humans, when out of a sense of duty an individual defers to the values of fellows. But it is true interspecifically, since *Homo sapiens* treats all other species as rivets, resources, study materials, or entertainments. Ethics has always been about partners with entwined destinies. But it has never been very convincing when pleaded as enlightened self-interest (that one ought always to do what is one's intelligent self-interest), including class self-interest, even though in practice genuinely altruistic ethics often needs to be reinforced by self-interest. To value all other species only for human interest is like a nation's arguing all its foreign policy in terms of national interest. Neither seems fully moral.

Perhaps an exploiting attitude, and the tendency to justify it ethically, has been naturally selected in *Homo sapiens,* at least in the population that has become dominant in the West. But humans—scientists who have learned to be disinterested and ethicists who have learned to consider the interests of others—ought to be able to see further. Humans have learned some intraspecific altruism. The challenge now is to learn interspecific altruism. Utilitarian reasons for saving species may be good ones, necessary for policy. But can we not also discover the best reasons, the full extent of human duties? Dealing with a problem correctly requires an appropriate way of thinking about it. What is offensive in the impending extinctions is not the loss of rivets and resources, but the maelstrom of killing and insensitivity to forms of life and the forces producing them. What is required is not prudence but principled responsibility to the biospheric Earth.

SPECIFIC FORMS OF LIFE

There are many barriers to thinking of duties to species, however, and scientific ones precede ethical ones. It is difficult enough to argue from the fact that a species exists to the value judgment that a species ought to exist—what philosophers call an argument from *is* to *ought*. Matters grow worse if the concept of species is rotten to begin with. Perhaps the concept is arbitrary and conventional, a mapping device that is only theoretical. Perhaps it is unsatisfactory theoretically in an evolutionary ecosystem. Perhaps species do not exist. Duties to them would be as imaginary as duties to contour lines or to lines of latitude and longitude. Is there enough factual reality in species to base duty there?

Betula lenta uber, round-leaf birch, is known from only two locations on nearby Virginia creeks and differs from the common *B. lenta* only in having rounded leaf tips. For thirty years it was described as a subspecies or merely a mutation. But M. L. Fernald pronounced it a species, *B. uber,* and for forty years it has been considered one. High fences have been built around all known specimens. If a greater botanist were to redesignate it a subspecies, would this change in alleged facts affect our alleged duties? Ornithologists recently reassessed an endangered species, the Mexican duck, *Anas diazi,* and lumped it with the common mallard, *A. platyrhynchos,* as subspecies *diazi* U.S. Fish and Wildlife authorities took if off the endangered species list partly as a result. Did a duty cease? Was there never one at all?

If a species is only a category, or class, boundary lines may be arbitrarily drawn. Darwin wrote, "I look at the term species, as one arbitrarily given for the sake of convenience to a set of individuals closely resembling each other."[12] Some natural properties are used to delimit species—reproductive structures, bones, teeth. But which properties are selected and where the lines are drawn vary with taxonomists. When A. J. Shaw recently "discovered" a new species of moss, *Pohlia tundrae,* in the alpine Rocky Mountains, he did not find any hitherto unknown plants at all, he just regrouped herbarium material that had been known for decades under other names.[13] Indeed, biologists routinely put after a species the name of the "author" who, they say, "erected" the taxon.

Individual organisms exist, but if species are merely classes, they are inventions. A. B. Shaw claims, "The species concept is entirely subjective," and, concluding a presidential address to paleontologists, even exclaims, "Help stamp out species!"[14] He refers, of course, to the artifacts of taxonomists, not to living organisms. But if species do not exist except embedded in a theory in the minds of classifiers, it is hard to see how there can be duties to save them. No one proposes duties to genera, families, orders, or phyla; everyone concedes that these do not exist in nature.

But a biological "species" is not just a class. A species is a living historical "form" (Latin: *species*), propagated in individual organisms, that flows dynamically over generations. Simpson concludes, "An evolutionary species is a lineage (an ancestral-descendant sequence of populations) evolving separately from others and with its own unitary evolutionary role and tendencies."[15] Mayr holds, "Species are groups of interbreeding natural populations that are reproductively isolated from other such groups."[16] He can even emphasize, though many biologists today would deny this, that "*species are the real units of evolution,* they are the entities which specialize, which become adapted, or which shift their adaptation."[17] Recently, Mayr has sympathized with Ghiselin and Hull who hold that species are integrated individuals, and species names proper names, with organisms related to their species as part is to whole.[18] Eldredge and Cracraft find that "a species is a diagnosable cluster of individuals within which there is a parental pattern of ancestry and descent, beyond which there is not, and which exhibits a pattern of phylogenetic ancestry and descent among units of like kind." Species, they insist with emphasis, are *discrete entities in time as well as space."*[19]

It is admittedly difficult to pinpoint precisely what a species is, and there may be no single, quintessential way to define species; a polythetic or polytypic gestalt of features may be required. All we need for this discussion, however, is that species be objectively there as living processes in the evolutionary ecosystem; the varied criteria for defining them (descent, reproductive isolation, morphology, gene pool) come together at least in providing evidence that species are really there. In this sense, species are dynamic natural kinds, if not corporate individuals. A species is a coherent, ongoing form of life expressed in organisms, encoded in gene flow, and shaped by the environment.

The claim that there are specific forms of life historically maintained in their environments over time does not seem arbitrary or fictitious at all but, rather, as certain as anything else we believe about the empirical world, even though at times scientists revise the theories and taxa with which they map these forms. Species are not so much like lines of latitude and longitude as like mountains and rivers, phenomena objectively there to be mapped. The edges of all these natural kinds will sometimes be fuzzy, to some extent discretionary. We can expect that one species will slide into another over evolutionary time. But it does not follow from the fact that speciation is sometimes in progress that species are merely made up, instead of found as evolutionary lines articulated into diverse forms, each with its more or less distinct integrity, breeding population, gene pool, and role in its ecosystem.

At this point, we can anticipate how there can be duties to species. What humans ought to respect are dynamic life forms preserved in historical lines, vital informational processes that persist genetically over millions of years, overleaping short-lived individuals. It is not *form* (species) as mere morphology, but the *formative* (speciating) process that humans ought to preserve, although the process cannot be preserved without its products. Nor should humans want to protect the labels they use, but the living process in the environment. Endangered "species" is a convenient and realistic way of tagging this process, but protection can be interpreted (as the Endangered Species Act permits) in terms of subspecies, variety, or other taxa or categories that point out the diverse forms of life.

DUTIES TO SPECIES

The easiest conclusion to reach from prevailing theories of justice, which involve tacit or explicit "contracts" between persons, is that duties and rights are reciprocal. But reciprocally claiming, recognizing, exercising, and enjoying rights and duties can only be done by reflective rational agents. Humans have entered no contract other species; certainly they have not with us. There is no ecological contract parallel to the social contract; all the capacities for deliberate interaction so common in culture vanish in nature. Individual animals and plants, to say nothing of species, cannot be reasoned with, blamed, or educated into the prevailing contract.

But to make rights and duties reciprocal supposes that only moral agents count in the ethical calculus. Duties exist as well to those persons who cannot argue back—to the mute and the powerless—and perhaps this principle extends to other forms of life. Morality is needed wherever the vulnerable must be protected from the powerful.

The next easiest conclusion to reach, either from rights-based or utilitarian theories, is that humans have duties wherever there are psychological interests involving the capacity for experience. That moves a minimal criterion for duty past rational moral agency to sentience. The question is not whether animals can reciprocate the contract but whether they can suffer. Singer thinks that the only reason to be concerned about endangered species is the interests of humans and other sentient animals at stake in their loss.[20] Only they can enjoy benefits or suffer harm, so only they can be treated justly or unjustly.

But species, not sentience, generate some duties. On San Clemente Island, the U.S. Fish and Wildlife Service and the California Department of Fish and Game asked the Navy to shoot 2000 feral goats to save three endangered plant species, *Malacothamnus clementinus, Castilleja grisea,* and *Delphinium kinkiense.* That would kill several goats for each known surviving plant. (Happily, the Fund for Animals rescued most of the goats; unhappily they could not trap them all and the issue is unresolved.) The National Park Service did kill hundreds of rabbits on Santa Barbara Island to protect a few plants of *Dudleya traskiae,* once thought extinct and curiously called the Santa Barbara live-forever. Hundreds of elk starve in Yellowstone National Park each year, and the Park Service is not alarmed, but the starving of an equal number of grizzly bears, which would involve about the same suffering in psychological experience, would be of great concern.

A rather difficult claim to make under contemporary ethical theory is that duty can arise toward any living organism. Such duties, if they exit, could be easy to override, but by this account humans would have at least a minimal duty not to disrupt living beings without justification.

Here the question about species, beyond individuals, is both revealing and challenging because it offers a biologically based counterexample to the focus on individuals—typically sentient and usually persons—so characteristic in Western ethics. In an evolutionary ecosystem, it is not mere individuality that counts, but the species is also significant because it is a dynamic life form maintained over time by an informed genetic flow. The individual represents (re-presents) a species in each new generation. It is a token of a type, and the type is more important than the token.

It is as logical to say that the individual is the species' way of propagating itself as to say that the embryo or egg is the individual's way of propagating itself. We can think of the cognitive processing as taking place not merely in the individual but in the gene pool. Genetically, though not neurally, a species over generations "learns" (discovers) pathways previously unknown. A form of life reforms itself, tracks its environment, and sometimes passes over to a new species. There is a specific groping for a valued *ought*-to-be beyond what now *is* in any individual. Though species are not moral agents, a biological identity—a kind of value—is here defended. The dignity resides in the dynamic form; the individual inherits this, instantiates it, and passes it on. To borrow a metaphor from physics, life is both a particle (the individual) and a wave (the specific form).

A species lacks moral agency, reflective self-awareness, sentience, or organic individuality. So we may be tempted to say that specific-level processes cannot count morally. But each ongoing species defends a form of life, and these are on the whole good things, arising in a process out of which humans have evolved. All ethicists say that in *Homo sapiens* one species has appeared that not only exists but ought to exist. But why say this exclusively of a late-coming, highly developed form? Why not extend this duty more broadly to the other species (though perhaps not with equal intensity over them all, in view of varied levels of development)? These kinds defend their forms of life too. Only the human species contains moral agents, but perhaps conscience *ought not* be used to exempt every other form of life from consideration, with the resulting paradox that the single moral species acts only in its collective self-interest toward all the rest.

Extinction shuts down the generative processes. The wrong that humans are doing, or allowing to happen through carelessness, is stopping the historical flow in which the vitality of life is laid. Every extinction is an incremental decay in stopping life processes—no small thing. Every extinction is a kind of superkilling. It kills forms (*species*), beyond individuals. It kills "essences" beyond "existences," the "soul" as well as the "body." It kills collectively, not just distributively. It is not merely the loss of potential human information that is tragic, but the loss of biological information, present independently of instrumental human uses for it.

"Ought species *x* to exist?" is a single increment in the collective question, "Ought life on Earth to exist?" The answer to the question about one species is not always the same as the answer to the bigger question, but since life on Earth is an aggregate of many species, the two are sufficiently related that the burden of proof lies with those who wish deliberately to extinguish a species and simultaneously to care for life on Earth. To kill a species is to shut down a unique story; and, although all specific stories must eventually end, we seldom want unnatural ends. Humans ought not to play the role of murderers. The duty to species can be overriden, for example with pests or disease organisms. But a prima facie duty stands nevertheless.

One form of life has never endangered so many others. Never before has this level of question—superkilling by a superkiller—been faced. Humans have more understanding than ever of the speciating processes, more predictive power to foresee the intended and unintended results of their actions, and more power to reverse the undesirable consequences. The duties that such power and vision generate no longer attach simply to individuals or persons but are emerging duties to specific forms of life. If, in this world of uncertain moral convictions, it makes any sense to claim that one ought not to kill individuals without justification, it makes more sense to claim that one ought not to superkill the species, without superjustification.

INDIVIDUALS AND SPECIES

Many will be uncomfortable with this claim because their ethical theory does not allow duty to a collection. Feinberg writes, "A whole collection, as such, cannot have beliefs, expectations, wants, or desires. . . . Individual elephants can have interests, but the species elephant cannot."[21] Singer asserts, "Species as such are not conscious entities and so do not have interests above and beyond the interests of the individual animals that are members of the species."[22] Regan maintains, "The rights view is a view about the moral rights of individuals. Species are not individuals, and the rights view does not recognize the moral rights of species to anything, including survival."[23] Rescher says, "Moral obligation is thus always interest-oriented. But only individuals can be said to have interests; one only has moral obligations to particular individuals or particular groups thereof. Accordingly, the duty to save a species is not a matter of moral duty toward it, because moral duties are only oriented to individuals. A species as such is the wrong sort of target for a moral obligation."[24]

Even those who recognize that organisms, nonsentient as well as sentient, can be benefited or harmed may see the good of a species as the sum of and reducible to the goods of individuals. The species is well off when and because its members are; species well-being is just aggregated individual well-being. The "interests of a species" constitute only a convenient device, something like a center of gravity in physics, for speaking of an aggregated focus of many contributing individual member units.

But duties to a species are not duties to a class or category, not to an aggregation of sentient interests, but to a lifeline. An ethic about species needs to see how the species *is* a bigger event than individual interests or sentience. Making this clearer can support the conviction that a species *ought* to continue.

Events can be good for the well-being of the species, considered collectively, although they are harmful if considered as distributed to individuals. This is one way to interpret what is often called a genetic "load," genes that somewhat reduce health, efficiency, or fertility in most individuals but introduce enough variation to permit improving the specific form.[25] Less variation and better repetition in reproduction would, on average, benefit more individuals in any one next generation, since individuals would have less "load." But on a longer view, variation can confer stability in a changing world. A greater experimenting with individuals, although this typically makes individuals less fit and is a disadvantage from that perspective, benefits rare, lucky individuals selected in each generation with a resulting improvement in the species. Most individuals in any particular generation carry some (usually slightly) detrimental genes, but the variation is good for the species. Note that this does not imply species selection; selection perhaps operates only on individuals. But it does mean that we can distinguish between the goods of individuals and the larger good of the species.

Predation on individual elk conserves and improves the species *Cervus canadensis.* A forest fire harms individual aspen trees, but it helps *Populus tremuloides* because fire restarts forest succession without which the species would go extinct. Even the individuals that escape demise from external sources die of old age; their deaths, always to the disadvantage of those individuals, are a necessity for the species. A finite lifespan makes room for those replacements that enable development to occur, allowing the population to improve in fitness or adapt to a shifting environment. Without the "flawed" reproduction that permits variation, without a surplus of young, or predation and death, which all harm individuals, the species would soon go extinct in a changing environment, as all environments eventually are. The individual is a receptacle of the form, and the receptacles are broken while the form survives; but the form cannot otherwise survive.

When a biologist remarks that a breeding population of a rare species is dangerously low, what is the danger to? Individual members? Rather, the remark seems to imply a specific-level, point-of-no-return threat to the continuing of that form of life. No individual crosses the extinction threshold; the species does.

Reproduction is typically assumed to be a need of individuals, but since any particular individual can flourish somatically without reproducing at all, indeed may be put through duress and risk or spend much energy reproducing, by another logic we can interpret reproduction as the species keeping up its own kind by reenacting itself again and again, individual after individual. In this sense a female grizzly does not bear cubs to be healthy herself, any more than a woman needs children to be healthy. Rather, her cubs are *Ursus arctos,* threatened by nonbeing, recreating itself by continuous performance. A species in reproduction defends its own kind from other species, and this seems to be some form of "caring."

Biologists have often and understandably focused on individuals, and some recent trends interpret biological processes from the perspective of genes. A consideration of species reminds us that many events can be interpreted at this level too. An organism runs a directed course through the environment, taking in materials, using them resourcefully, discharging wastes. But this single, directed course is part of a bigger picture in which a species via individuals maintains its course over longer spans of time. Thinking this way, the life the individual has is something passing through the individual as much as something it intrinsically possesses. The individual is subordinate to the species, not the other way round. The genetic set, in which is coded the *telos,* is as evidently a "property" of the species as of the individual.

Biologists and linguists have learned to accept the concept of information in the genetic set without any subject who speaks or understands. Can ethicists learn to accept value in, and duty to, an informed process in which centered individuality or sentience is absent? Here events can be significant at the specific level, an additional consideration to whether they are beneficial to individuals. The species-in-environment is an interactive complex, a selective system where individuals are pawns on a chessboard. When human conduct endangers these specific games of life, duties may appear.

A species has no self. It is not a bounded singular. Each organism has its own centeredness, but there is no specific analogue to the nervous hookups or circulatory flows that characterize the organism. But, like the market in economics, an organized system does not have to have a controlling center to have identity. Having a biological identity reasserted genetically over time is as true of the species as of the individual. Individuals come and go; the marks of the species collectively remain much longer.

A consideration of species strains any ethic focused on individuals, much less on sentience or persons. But the result can be a biologically sounder ethic, though it revises what was formerly thought logically permissible or ethically binding. The species line is quite fundamental. It is more important to protect this integrity than to protect individuals. Defending a form of life, resisting death, regeneration that maintains a normative identity over time—all this is as true of species as of individuals. So what prevents duties arising at that level? The appropriate survival unit is the appropriate level of moral concern.

SPECIES AND ECOSYSTEM

A species is what it is inseparably from its environment. The species defends its kind against the world, but at the same time interacts with its environment, functions in the ecosystem, and is supported and shaped by it. The species and the community are complementary processes in synthesis, somewhat parallel to but a level above the way the species and the individual have distinguishable but entwined identities. Neither the individual nor the species stands alone; both are embedded in a system. It is not preservation of *species* but of *species in the system* that we desire. It is not just what they are but where they are that we must value correctly.

The species *can* only be preserved in situ; the species *ought* to be preserved in situ. Zoos and botanical gardens can lock up a collection of individuals, but they cannot begin to simulate the ongoing dynamism of gene flow under the selection pressures in a wild biome. The full integrity of the species must be integrated into the ecosystem. Ex situ preservation, while it may save resources and souvenirs, does not preserve the generative process intact. Again, the appropriate survival unit is the appropriate level of moral concern.

It might seem that ending the history of a species now and again is not far out of line with the routines of the universe. But artificial extinction, caused by human encroachments, is radically different from natural extinction. Relevant differences make the two as morally distinct as death by natural causes is from murder. Though harmful to a species, extinction in nature is no evil in the system; it is rather the key to tomorrow. Such extinction is a normal turnover in ongoing speciation.

Anthropogenic extinction has nothing to do with evolutionary speciation. Hundreds of thousands of species will perish because of culturally altered environments radically differing from the spontaneous environments in which such species were naturally selected and in which they sometimes go extinct. In natural extinctions, nature takes away life when it has become unfit in habitat, or when the habitat alters, and supplies other life in its place. Artificial extinction shuts down tomorrow because it shuts down speciation. Natural extinction typically occurs with transformation, either of the extinct line or related or competing lines. Artificial extinction is without issue. One opens doors; the other closes them. Humans generate and regenerate nothing; they only dead-end these lines.

From this perspective, humans have no duty to preserve rare species from natural extinctions, although they might have a duty to other humans to save such species as resources or museum pieces. Humans cannot and need not save the product without the process.

Through evolutionary time, nature has provided new species at a higher rate than the extinction rate; hence, the accumulated diversity. In one of the best documented studies of the marine fossil record, Raup and Sepkoski summarize a general increase in standing diversity (figure 1).[26] Regardless of differing details on land or biases in the fossil record, a graph of the increase of diversity on Earth must look something like this.

There have been four or five catastrophic extinctions, each succeeded by a recovery of previous diversity. These anomalies so deviate from the trends that many paleontologists look for extraterrestrial causes. If due to supernovae, collisions with asteroids, or oscillations of the solar system above and below the plane of the galaxy, such events are accidental to the evolutionary ecosystem. Thousands of species perished at the impingement of otherwise unrelated events.

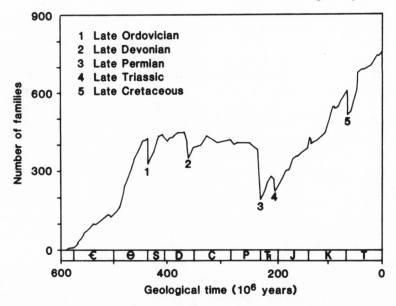

Figure 1.—Standing diversity through time for families of marine vertebrates and invertebrates, with standard geological symbols, and catastrophic extinctions numbered. Source: Raup and Sepkoski (1982); © 1982 by AAAS.

The disasters were irrelevant to the kinds of ecosystems in which such species had been selected. If the causes were more terrestrial—cyclic changes in climates or continental drift—the biological processes are still to be admired for their powers of recovery. Even interrupted by accident, they maintain and increase the numbers of species. Raup and Sepkoski further find that the normal extinction rate declines from 4.6 families per million years in the Early Cambrian to 2.0 families in recent times, even though the number of families (and species) enormously increases. This seems to mean that optimization of fitness increases through evolutionary time.

An ethicist has to be circumspect. An argument might commit what logicians call the genetic fallacy to suppose that present value depended on origins. Species judged today to have intrinsic value might have arisen anciently and anomalously from a valueless context, akin to the way life arose mysteriously from nonliving materials. But in a historical ecosystem, what a thing is differentiates poorly from the generating and sustaining matrix. The individual and the species have what value they have, to some extent, in the context of the forces that beget them.

Imagine that Figure 1 is the graph of the performance of a 600-million-year-old business. Is it not a healthy one? But this record is of the business of life, and the long-term performance deserves ethical respect. There is something awesome about an Earth that begins with zero and runs up toward 5 to 10 million species in several billion years, setbacks notwithstanding.

What is valuable about species is not to be isolated in them for what they are in themselves. Rather, the dynamic account evaluates species as process, product, and instrument in the larger drama toward which humans have duties, reflected in duties in species. Whittaker finds that on continental scales and for most groups, "increase of species diversity . . . is a self-augmenting process without any evident limit." There is a tendency toward "species packing."[27] Nature seems to produce as many species as it can, not merely enough to stabilize an ecosystem or only species that can directly or indirectly serve human needs. Humans ought not to inhibit this exuberant lust for kinds. That process, along with its product, is about as near to ultimacy as humans can come in their relationship with the natural world.

Several billion years worth of creative toil, several million species of teeming life, have been handed over to the care of this late-coming species in which mind has flowered and morals have emerged. Ought not those of this sole moral species do something less self-interested than to count all the produce of an evolutionary ecosystem as rivets in their spaceship, resources in their larder, laboratory materials, recreation for their ride? Such an attitude hardly seems biologically informed, much less ethically adequate. Its logic is too provincial for moral humanity. Or, in a biologist's term, it is ridiculously territorial. If true to their specific epithet, ought not *Homo sapiens* value this host of species as something with a claim to care in its own right?

AN ENDANGERED ETHIC?

The contemporary ethical systems seem misfits in the role most recently demanded of them. There is something overspecialized about an ethic, held by the dominant class of *Homo sapiens,* that regards the welfare of only one of several million species as an object of duty. If this requires a paradigm change about the sorts of things to which duty can attach, so much the worse for those ethics no longer functioning in, nor suited to, their changing environment. The anthropocentrism associated with them was fiction anyway. There is something Newtonian, not yet Einsteinian, besides something morally naive, about living in a reference frame where one species takes itself as absolute and values everything else relative to its utility.

NOTES

1. U.S. Congress, *Endangered Species Act of 1973,* Sec. 2(a)(1) (Public Law 93–205).

2. John Rawls, *A Theory of Justice* (Cambridge, Mass.: Harvard University Press, 1971), p. 512.

3. G. O. Barney, study director, *The Global 2000 Report to the President* (Washington: Government Printing Office, 1980-1981), vol. 1, p. 37.

4. Stuart Hampshire, *Morality and Pessimism* (New York: Cambridge University Press, 1972), pp. 3-4.

5. Joel Feinberg, "The Rights of Animals and Unborn Generations," in W. T. Blackstone, ed., *Philosophy and Environmental Crisis* (Athens: University of Georgia Press, 1974), pp. 43-68, citation on p. 56.

6. Paul R. and Anne Ehrlich, *Extinction* (New York: Random House, 1981).

7. Norman Myers, *The Sinking Ark* (Oxford: Pergamon Press, 1979).

8. "Statement of Thomas Eisner," in *Endangered Species Act Oversight*, Hearings Dec. 8 and 10, 1981 (Washington: Government Printing Office, 1982), pp. 295-97.

9. National Science Foundation, "The Biology of Aridity," *Mosaic* 8, no. 1 (January/February 1977):28-35, citation on p. 28.

10. Norman Myers, "Conserving Our Global Stock," *Environment* 21, no. 9 (November 1979):25-33.

11. "Statement of Peter H. Raven," in *Endangered Species Act Oversight*, pp. 290-95.

12. Charles Darwin, *The Origin of Species by Means of Natural Selection* (Baltimore: Penguin Books, 1968), p. 108.

13. A. J. Shaw, "*Pohlia andrewsii* and *P. tundrae,* Two New Arctic-Alpine Propaguliferous Species from North America," *Bryologist* 84(1981):65-74.

14. A. B. Shaw, "Adam and Eve, Paleontology, and the Non-objective Arts," *Journal of Paleontology* 43(1969):1085-98, citation on p. 1098.

15. G. G. Simpson, *Principles of Animal Taxonomy* (New York: Columbia University Press, 1961), p. 153.

16. Ernst Mayr, *Principles of Systematic Zoology* (New York: McGraw Hill, 1969), p. 26.

17. Ernst Mayr, "The Biological Meaning of Species," *Biological Journal of the Linnean Society* 1(1969):311-20, citation on p. 318.

18. Ernst Mayr, *The Growth of Biological Thought* (Cambridge, Mass.: Harvard University Press, 1982), p. 253; M. T. Ghiselin, "A Radical Solution to the Species Problem," *Systematic Zoology* 23(1974):536-44; David L. Hull, "Are Species Really Individuals?" *Systematic Zoology* 25(1976):174-91.

19. Niles Eldredge and Joel Cracraft, *Phylogenetic Patterns and the Evolutionary Process* (New York: Columbia University Press, 1980), p. 92.

20. Peter Singer, "Not for Humans Only," in K. E. Goodpaster and K. M. Sayre, eds., *Ethics and Problems of the 21st Century* (Notre Dame, Ind.: University of Notre Dame Press, 1979), pp. 191-206, especially p. 204.

21. Feinberg, "Rights of Animals and Unborn Generations," pp. 55-56.

22. Singer, "Not for Humans Only," p. 203.

23. Tom Regan, *The Case for Animal Rights* (Berkeley: University of California Press, 1983), p. 359.

24. Nicholas Rescher, *Unpopular Essays on Technological Progress* (Pittsburgh: University of Pittsburgh Press, 1980), p. 83.

25. G. R. Fraser, "Our Genetical 'Load.' A Review of Some Aspects of Genetical

Variation," *Annals of Human Genetics* 25(1962):387–415.

26. D. M. Raup and J. J. Sepkoski, Jr., "Mass Extinctions in the Marine Fossil Record," *Science* 215(1982):1501–3.

27. R. H. Whittaker, "Evolution and Measurement of Species Diversity," *Taxon* 21(1972):213–51, citation on p. 214.

IV. NATURE IN EXPERIENCE

Nature is a philosophical and religious "resource," if we must use that word. Philosophy gone wild finds rich experiences—perhaps of solitude or serenity, perhaps of awe, mystery, vastness, aesthetic beauty. We confront the struggle for life, its conflict and harmony, the constructive, destructive, and regenerative powers within natural history, the agelong flow over time of kindred and alien forms of life. We love the smells, sights, sounds, surprises there, we learn truth about our sources, not less than our resources.

These are experiences of re-creation as well as of recreation. We gain a sense of proportion, place, identity; we are humbled in some ways, exalted in others. We are drawn into intimate contact with wildness, experiencing the nature within ourselves and the nature transcending ourselves. A paradox in wildness is that, despite its nonanthropocentric intrinsic values, only philosophical humans can know these values for what they are cognitively, ethically, metaphysically. Only humans can experience wildness in this richest, contemplative sense. We search nature, and the search returns upon ourselves.

The essays that follow take the experiential plunge into nature, mixing participatory immediacy and reflective distance, reason and emotion, romance and criticism, nature and spirit. We leave the forum, the debate, the academic argument and classroom, and go out into the field. We go wild. Natural values are in some respects objective, and we have earlier argued this. But that was nowhere meant to preclude but rather to provide the emergence of valued subjective experiences, consequent upon this human arrival in nature. We enter a natural scene, latecomers there. But we ourselves, when educated by our choices and patterns of response, compose spirited experiences that are critically novel in the levels of value attained, though also integral to our surroundings. Humans seek meanings in ways that nothing wild can. We accept commitments. When philosophers enter wild nature, the philosophical experience of nature is the consummating result of a historical, evolutionary, ecosystemic Earth. Such philosophical and religious experiences are not the only values there, but are unequaled and unprecedented ones. Persons are both discoverers and creators of value in their experiences in nature.

These essays are personal, often recounting events and experiences in ways approaching story form, relational narratives of a person living through his environmental places in dramatic particularity. An environmental ethic ought to be incarnated as a way of life. The theory must yield practice. It should drive an individual person to inherit the Earth in historical consciousness. The end of philosophy gone wild is human autobiography on a value-laden, storied Earth.

11

Lake Solitude:
The Individual in Wildness

The lake is guarded round on every side save one by pathless wilderness, and isolated at this nearest point to community by a hard day afoot. Even that route has been abandoned beyond the North Inlet trail; the healing forces of nature, as though to redress an affront to her privacy, have been erasing the track, reducing the hike in to a scramble over blowdowns and brush. Grass grows in the few fire-pits scattered about, and nothing indicates that others have come earlier this season. The lake surface, calm and reflecting the curve of the valley, mirrors the skies—and evenings, the stars. When still and reflective, man too is a mirror of earth and heaven. If the Inlet current is deep, the flow is silent. Unless we are also quieted, our depth is seldom revealed. Loosed anciently from the Ptarmigan massif, a glacial boulder now rests on the valley floor. Let it symbolize this moment of release from the matrix of community. Let the lake offer place and permission to seek a lone ecstasy, an *ek-stasis,* a standing out from the common.

I

As those deprived of one sense have another heightened, to forgo human company frees us to engage the natural order. If another person were along, it would seem odd to address this environment; the human context would restrain such communion. A companion would convincingly banish the mute creatures to the realm of objects. But to the solitary traveler, they reassert a quality of presence; they become subjects. Chancing yesterday upon a purple ladyslipper, I hailed it by name, *Cypripedium fasciculatum,* and rejoiced unashamedly. Again I spoke, softly so as not to alarm, to greet a three-toed woodpecker. We need to voice such recognitions, though the response is a silent one. The stare of the deer

Reprinted by permission from *Main Currents in Modern Thought* 31(1975):121-126. Lake Solitude is in Rocky Mountain National Park.

at dusk, the song of the towhee at dawn, nearly persuade us that the Hebrews were right: each has his *nephesh,* his vital psyche. The single camper must even suppress an instinctive apology to the ants who scatter from beneath the rock he moves to realign his hearth; there seems in them an *anima* he ought to reverence. Indeed, he is cautious; sitting too long at a ring of firestones incurs a strange danger: being haunted by myths of the sanctity of place.

Where a man camps for a spell he roots a little, and this rootage seems increasingly less metaphorical. Despite our mobility, humans, like spruce trees, inhabit a place. We locate; we situate. Even in our transience we are provincial; to be healthy is to have a home range—some landscape, some "field" to which for a season we belong, and which belongs to us. We are proprietary animals; we require property that extends our presence in the world. We disregard this need at our peril; lostness plagues the urban, mobile world. To know oneself is to know where one resides. And alone, one locates sooner.

Does not my skin resemble this lake surface? Neither lake nor self has independent being: both exist in dynamic interpenetration across a surface designed for passage and exchange, as well as for delimitation and individuation. Inlet waters have crossed this interface and are now embodied within me; the conifers and I "inspire" each other. I think, animated by the sacrifice of trout that yesterday swam these waters; their vitality was in turn that of the dancing insect the day before. And, begrudgingly, I host mosquitoes. Though the bannock I bake is provided me by human commerce, it originates in this soil, or from soil once just over the divide, and now washed away to the plains below; though it comes by a longer route, it is not different in kind from the nourishment that is provided by my immediate surroundings. Escape from town reestablishes these organic roots in their proper soil. To travel into the wilderness is to go to our aboriginal source, though our return is too often unawares; it is by homecoming to enjoy an essential reunion with the earth. The waters of North Inlet are part of my circulatory system; and the more literally we take this truth the more nearly we understand it. I incarnate the solar energies that flow through this lake. No one is free-living in these woods; the root fungi that sustain these tiny twayblade orchids or the pine-drops rising from the roots of that great pine tree are better emblems of life. *Bios* is intrinsically symbiosis.

The continuities are not only corporeal and substantive; they are also reciprocal and psychic. Itself a requisite for mind, nature has both permitted and encouraged this development. The fluid environment, exemplified in this lake, awakened life, but higher differentiation was terrestrial. The forest gave primates an erect posture, prehensile hands and converging vision to intensify manual capacities and mental focus. That freed the mouth to speak. But the humanizing and language came with a return to the savannas and meadows, like those across the lake. So, every environment I survey has joined to forge my person. In ontology too, as the individual awakens to his own being—not less than in phylogeny, as the evolutionary process reaches the human—nature evokes mind.

To her teasing, her relentless stimulus, we respond in a "standing out," an *existence,* where the I is differentiated from the not-I. The environment moves; we are moved. But then reaction is elevated into agentive action. Ecological prodding brings forth the ego. "The landscape thinks itself in me, and I am its consciousness." (Cézanne)

Curiously, with this there is a communion, but of opposites. The medium that a person is in and of, he or she is also over and against. When the person encounters a world different from himself, he faces a centrifugal wildness which, if unresisted, will disintegrate his centripetal self, but which, if withstood, may be incorporated and domesticated. To travel into the wilderness is to go into what one is not, so that in returning to and turning from its natural complement, mind grasps itself. I encounter an other of which I have the deepest need. Thus journey here is an odyssey of the spirit traveling afar to come to itself.

The backpack that allows my stay differentiates me. Without it, modern humans cannot come into the wilderness either in comfort or in safety; this fact measures the distance that separates us from the elements. The pack concentrates the arts and sciences of the whole human epoch: shelter, clothing, leather, metals, axe and saw, fire, medicines, plastics, chart and compass—products and skills by which we have covered our nakedness and turned to our advantage the spontaneous activity of nature. Rest as we may upon the bedrock of earth, we also live by industry: our very designs separate us from the artless, virgin earth, even as they involve us more deeply in its possibilities. He who seeks his natural origins discovers that encounter veiled and mediated by an intervening culture that he cannot abdicate.

As is nothing else in sight, this pack is intentional. Elephantellas and monks-hoods simply appear and result, but I did not just happen here. Before me all is driven, like the snow; the scene unfolds. Only I premeditate, observe, and prepare. True, the beaver builds his lodge, the marmot burrows, the hare makes his form, and the cony cuts hay for winter. The swallow hollows the aspen in order to nest. To delete all purposive component from their functional behavior seems to impoverish them hopelessly. Yet we can fall into the opposite error, for their rudimentary mind is cryptically preconscious. Awareness is not yet consciousness. Their instinct is not intention. Beast and flower simply describe the wilderness law. I obey it too, but mine is a singular, considered obedience: that by obeying nature I may command her. Thus I prescribe—and speak a word of separation.

All this life rises in a countercurrent, paradoxically driven by entropy's constant threat. But in humans, for all their continuities with that life, a divide is reached and they flow elsewhere. In this forest I am the lone exhibitor of what nature could not achieve in these paintbrushes and columbines, pipers and porcupines. Transcending these embodiments of herself, she has gifted this human son with what she could not attain elsewhere: self-conscious reflection. The beaver knows I am here, and slaps his tail—but I know that I know I am here. The chickaree notices me, and chatters, but I notice that I notice him. The doe halts to think by what route she may avoid my camp and yet reach the meadow. But I think about her thinking so. If in the prehuman mind, causes are already being supplanted by reasons, the conclusion of that replacement is a mental incandescence: this novel iteration of knowing, and seeing, and thinking. The loneliness here exceeds the absence of a companion; what is wanting is the intentional, the fashioned, the cognitive. The lake surface has an analog in my skin, but the lake has an "antilog" in my pondering mind. *Cogito, ergo sum solus.*

Ought I not to respect this radical otherness? How obviously independent of the transient and latecoming human presence are these violets and bishop's caps! Tomorrow, unobserved, they will be, in their diminutive way, as lovely as ever. The human presence may be the ultimate reach of nature, but here it is superfluous; therefore let it be gentle. It would be rude to sin against these forest folk by disturbing them with that very crowding from which I seek relief. Who deserves a privilege he will not grant? The *Kalmia* and the *Sphagnum* need solitude too. The root of "wilderness," *wild-deor-ness,* is that in it the beasts are without the hand of man.

Myriads of larvae infest the lake. At first this annoyed, for it forced a regular walk to the Inlet for fresher water. But now it refreshes, as each walk prompts a moment of truth. This teeming aquatic life reveals an inexhaustible vigor, and I myself flourish, seeing the spontaneous vitality of the Earth. When I leave, the thrush will still spill its song into the forest, yet I will somehow be richer for the beauty that escapes my hearing. Spruce should rot where they fall, repay the elements, recompose in *Sedums* and *Calthas* appropriated from the humus—and so teach of death and life. If he rises to his name, *Homo sapiens* will leave this place unmutilated. There is a fragile fullness here which, oddly, can be shared only when it is honored. We gain what we give; to be whole, I must leave the Earth whole. Who troubles these waters, troubles himself.

Yet how strange that in the quest to find their limits, humans should rise to a higher nobility! This spectator, this pensioner, is transformed into a protector. The forest is overtaken and baptized by intent. I keep it, and am kept by it. It has at least this need of me: my resolve not to trespass. The Inlet that ran of itself for a million years must of late run by act of Congress. It flows by my leave. These *Potentillas* grow by mysteries I scarcely suspect, but today their life is circumscribed by a critical new phenomenon—my deliberate restraint. All that grows and creeps and runs is impelled by predatory and reproductive desire, limited only by collision with the needs of fellow creatures. Without external constraint, each would possess the globe. But now, in humans, that drive for life pauses in charity. They would have the Earth but cannot; I can, but will not. Paradoxically, in that very act of will and grace I do possess it—not in conquest but in preservation, not in assertion but in tolerance, not in lust but in love. Beyond the plow, the axe, the machine, the brass instrument, there is a virile humility that loves enough to let alone. The meek inherit the Earth. Like the ice that floats on this lake in spring, thawing by day to refreeze at night, the separation between me and the folk of this lake country dissolves, only to recrystallize. There is intercourse, but, lingering, I am isolated and distinguished by even the gentlest dominion. With power comes an apartness from which there is no reprieve. I am lord of this Earth, and how lonely that is! *Praesum, ergo sum solus.*

II

Yet the transcendent aristocracy of humans only reveals itself in the individual as he represents his kind. The same culture that differentiates me from the natural order integrates me into a community. There is no private crossing of the human boundary. The luckless feral children, denied society, have thereby been denied humanity. Indeed, the distance that separates me from this Inlet wildness is the measure of my nearness to civilization. My solitude is communal; my existence, coexistence.

There can be no single self, for consciousness is social. For all his rootage in the earth, the thinking subject differentiates himself from it, knowing himself reflexively from what he is not. Yet this negation, though necessary, is not sufficient to define the person. We are humanized as we are met and answered by a fellow human presence. When in the field of my address I find a response that goes beyond mere action I attend to this *thou*—only to find afterward that this enables me to turn around and attend to myself. The self becomes its own object, and the centered subject appears. The mediation of a companion, communion with another mind, thus lifts pre-consciousness into self-consciousness. To know thyself, know thy brother.

To come alone to this lakeside is to travel into an isolation that no one could support if he did not bring with him, like a carapace, the whole weight of his culture. I but apparently escape and am trailed by memories and public education. A person's flight to nature is always artificial, for our specific essence is indissolubly a corporate humaneness. We may withdraw into the wilderness, but physical distances do not break these mental and intersubjective ties. Subtly, even solitary contemplation is a form of social conversation. Like the logs of my campfire, which only burn together, thought achieves its incandescence only in a gathering of minds. *Cogito, ergo non sum solus.*

Of all life forms, the infant human arrives least finished and most educable. The patriarch of Earth is longest juvenile, so that proportionately as instinct operates the less, society may count the more. Our genetic coding does not suffice to humanize us. We are personalized by our heritage of language. We do not mature by the unfolding of an organic inheritance, as do so largely the coyotes and badgers, but are bequeathed the *logos* of our fathers. In us, nature provides for her own transformation. We are works of art. Mechanism and mutation yield to history and culture. The social context permits ideational heredity. Its medium is novel, for now, breaking a previously stifling solitude, the achievements of an individual need not perish with him but may be transmitted in history to successive generations.

I walk in a wilderness that has been circumscribed, in a measure, by human inheritance. For I understand the landscape, its structures and successions, its fauna and flora—partially and incompletely—but sufficiently to be competent here, though now alone. It remains wild and has its hazards and unknowns. But every knowing is a kind of taming, and I enter a gentler wilderness than did my fathers. As a life form is named and understood, it passes increasingly into human power and—unless our knowledge miscarries—into our love. The Shoshone besought strength from the bear, the wolf, the eagle; now these are justly wary of the strength of man. I come boldly, freed to love what others have delimited and ordered, each increment of their possession accumulating in my behalf.

I may come alone, but I understand with the genius of a multitude of minds, all multiplying and amplifying my solitary enjoyment. I celebrate a primrose by the Inlet; although nothing substitutes for immediate experience, I deceive myself if I forget that my familiarity with Parry's primrose is mediated by the minds of Asa Gray and C. C. Parry, for Gray named it from Parry's collection. The waxflower has grown here since Oligocene times, but James found it, with Long's expedition in 1820, and *Jamesia* was described for me. To let Rydbergia and the Englemann spruce recall other pioneers is to realize that one borrows the vastest part of what he or she knows, and cannot even confront the natural order independent of botanists—or philosophers, or poets. *We* see this place, for though alone, I see nothing except as it has passed through a host of minds. To grasp its meaning and perceive its beauty, I integrate wildness into a vast cultural whole. Only bare awareness is immediate; every natural fact enters at once into a conceptual and attitudinal fabric that, though my own, is the sophisticated logic of a civilization.

To seek an absolute solitude is therefore suicidal, for the exiled self disintegrates. But there is a relative solitude that is essential for personal integration—a separateness complementary to human community, its polar opposite. Nature does not define humans in order that they may be cultured, but neither can humans depend upon society wholly to make us human. Each must finish himself. As an eminently political animal, man has the curious capacity to individualize personal worth. But distance is essential for this individualization. So, paradoxically, unless one can come by a lakeside such as this, and let physical distance loosen the hold of society upon him, he cannot find space and sanity within which to establish and maintain the boundaries of the self. Without such spaces there is no togetherness—merely fusion and homogeneity. Alone we cannot be human. Yet we cannot be human until we are alone.

A shy solitaire sings his territorial call. Even gregarious humans bruise with constant contact, and suffocate without the openness of wind and sky. Like the ravens here, my flight distance is greater than most, and in this I betray my own Appalachian heritage. Yet, though tolerances differ, each has a threshold of crowding beyond which he is crippled, for he has not the space for himself which is emblematic of his person. Aye, the truth is bolder and more literal: the self is territorial. Space does not simply represent individuality; it is a constituent of the psyche. He who reserves no privacy and posts no field of his own violates himself in his charity. Mental health today, say some, is increasingly dependent on the capacity to conform and adjust, replacing outdated, more individualistic virtues. Only a half truth, surely! Maturity is bred in solitude, and tested in its own domain.

Who knows himself or herself merely as he or she is seen by others knows only an image. Conforming, we become actors filling roles; we react, ceasing to act. To whatever extent the personality may be formed by social reflection, the person is realized in those moments of integrity when he lays aside his social masks, his *persona*. One cannot masquerade in the forest; every back-country stride is a return to the self. The elevation gained on the hike in is not simply topographical. I climb against the gravity that pulls down into social conformity. The autonomy thus gained must soon be tried in human commerce, but this will be but the retesting of skills learned through detachment. He who thinks, confronting wind and rain, night and the passing seasons, searches a way into wholeness. If this is in a lofty, montane climate, so much the richer is the being found. Thoughts while climbing have a special authenticity.

With these grasses and herbs, to know genus and species is to know the individual. The alders that line the Inlet are always, if never, the same. Particulars submerge into types less well in vertebrate forms, but accidents, however interesting, are never essential. In humans, individuality is our essence. The hominoid family does not radiate, as do birds and insects, but individuates within a single species. If we could not differentiate between persons, we should be reluctant to call them persons. No person is ever simply synonymous with his or her neighbors. We live collectively, but each of us must distinguish himself—not over against his fellows, but among them. When rightly reciprocal with society, the creative individual is its growing edge. Therefore, that community stagnates which suppresses solitude. Hence the wilderness is as important as the university. All real living is on a frontier.

My presence here violates the admonition not to travel alone. That is a caution to respect, and, sometimes, to obey. Where hazards are high, the life we jeopardize is not simply our own; we owe it to those for whom we are responsible, and those who are responsible for us, to balance the risks against the rewards of solitary travel. But a fellow hiker can be at once a bulwark and a barrier against the unknown, social insurance that one need not genuinely face the mountains. This refuge frees a person to be himself, but the single packer knows how urgently it insists upon personal accountability. This forest is for recreation, regeneration—but it is radically more than a place of leisure. Wilderness plays for keeps. It permits and requires an advance into full-blooded manhood. Society is crucial for one aspect of persons, wilderness for another. Never to plunge into wilderness, never to expose oneself to it, is never to know either forest or self. The fledgling eagle must solo. This month, for a hundred miles afoot, I think what may be the last of every step, and warily concentrate my being.

Though the existential naturalist recalls terrain already secured, he lives for an untried trail, an open present, and strives, and hopes, and fears. Those who love a whole wilderness can cherish its challenges, its howls, its disciplines, its insecurities, even its taciturn indifference; this is the mood that the loner knows best. Here order is proportioned to chaos, uncertainty tempers certainty, warmth alternates with cold, there is majesty and struggle; and the private encounter educates values that culture can neither accumulate nor transmit. There is a chary strength to be had by facing alone the north wind. Even the raw ordeals one shudders to recall—exhaustion, cold, wet, hunger, injury, lostness—are, oddly enough, intense moments of truth. He who has camped alone knows that what is preserved here is not only martens and bighorns, but a stalwart self. Nor is the wilderness dangerous, though it is terribly unforgiving of mistakes.

To pack for a solo trip is a therapeutic experience, paring life to its boundaries. It is a kind of sacramental enactment of how we must appropriate and individuate a culture in order to face a primitive ontological solitude. As the gear is weighed against its contribution to survival, comfort, and frugal pleasures, the packer makes not so much a rejection of culture as a shakedown of what in culture is truly essential. To portion adequate physical provisions is to nourish oneself spiritually as well. Then, at the trailhead, to shoulder this pack is to know that culture but prepares us for the single life, and that finally we each must close with it and walk alone. The hiker recalls the cry of the newborn from the womb. He is weaned; she remembers leaving parents to come of age. He projects the day he must receive the viaticum for his journey into a last unknown. In reckoning with solitariness, a person touches the quick of his or her being. *Cogito solus, ergo sum.*

III

To sit by this lake is to risk becoming a parable of contemporary man, increasingly forlorn in his universe. Paradoxically, his brilliance has at once reduced him to materiality and divorced him from it. We boldly hail an ever-encroaching naturalism, only to find ourselves disconsolate in our time of deepest need. Mornings, we delight in earthiness; evenings, we find wildness as indifferent as it is necessary. Ordered and lovely, and we may homestead in it, yet may not the whole of it be chaos? It is not always safe to stare into the midnight sky, lest its darkness and void plunge us into a disastrous *anomie*. Yesterday, losing my bearings, I wandered for half a day. The forest takes on a different mood when one does not know the way out. Am I lost by this lake, midst these stars? What if all our taming of the labyrinthine wilds be but a clearing in the forest, as ephemeral as this shallow lake which even now is being reclaimed by the elements? What if all the human noetic edifice be but a campfire pushing back the night? Do I walk home to discover myself homeless? Alas, must I breathe the thin air of nothingness?

But how bizarre this surrounding nothingness, which breeds me to slay me, yet slays me to breed me! This fair Earth abandons me to longings she refuses to fulfill. In an anxious solitude, I am separated into self-conscious agency. But with that gift comes this dreaded loneliness, as though her ultimate values can be given only as she withdraws from me. She deserts me, lest I be her object, and thereby promises me a dynamism of my own. It is the cougar that keeps the deer, not less than the browse; and for conscious life this encroaching nothingness is my predator. Is this wildness only unfeeling and unloving? Has it not also granted me life, surrounded me with beauty, and even when wolven, does not its howling threat stimulate me into a higher competence? Wildness is the pressing night, but it is wildness too that with me kindles fires against the night. This is an awful wildness, yet inescapably I find myself, though crying in it, unable to curse it, aye, rather grateful for it. Nature thrust me into an immense solitude, but that is her grandest gift, for this very environmental resistance frees me for and impels me toward centered personality.

Like the Hindu god Shiva, wildness ever destroys yet only to recompose, to purge, to evolve. It is as this wildness besets me that there emerges, from within, the existent self, as though I float on the element that both supports and dissolves me. Midst darkness, there is light. I appear from nothing. *Ex tenebris lux. Ex nihilo sum.* But what enigmatic wildness is this, in confrontation with which my life is ennobled! If I live, an encapsulated ego, in unrelieved oppression by this annihilating wildness, then life is quite absurd. Surely it is nearer the truth to believe that this loneness, like the other solitudes I know, however real, is not absolute but relative: that Earth is not a prison for my solitary confinement, but offers a home where I indeed belong in a natural embrace.

How lovely is this crystal lake beneath Mt. Alice! And this aesthetic experience is neither my invention nor simply my discovery; it emerges in relational encounter. With every climb of a peak such as Long's, the self is rallied against its opponent, but on the summit, exhausted, the mountaineer's primitive emotion is not conquest or estrangement, but embrace and communion. Man is for himself, yet not by himself. Lone though we are, to locate worth in ourselves and deny it to the encompassing wildness is surely to tumble into the fallacy of misplacing values. We who tarry must humbly acknowledge, even in the midst of environmental opposition, that we are respondents and recipients. In our spiritual, not less than our physical life, the energies of these mountains flow through us. Before this lake country, there is both loneliness and complementarity. Never is the individual in wildness more responsible than in his gratitude.

This is a silent place, but it is a poignant silence. Unawares, my soliloquy has become a dialogue—as though there were a veiled presence. Could there be some symmetries in these solitudes I sense? As I, guardian of its integrity, lay upon this Inlet refuge a gentle solitude that it may be secure and whole, can it be that there is laid upon me, in turn, a loneness requisite for my integrity too, and that it is, like my recession before these dippers and gentians, the gift of love?

12

Meditation at the Precambrian Contact

The walk in has carried me backward, ten thousand years at every step, and here I must rest, for I am lost in the plethora of time. Pardee Point shall be an Ebenezer, a *stone of help*. Before me is the inclined contact located in the rock cut; now can I fix my bearings from the Precambrian contact? Inescapably, there has crept upon me a feeling of return, of nostalgia, as though I had been here before. Perhaps it is rather the disquiet one has when he visits an ancestral grave. Or has the journey here let sweep over me the ever dormant yearning to return to the womb of Mother Earth? I am the sentient offspring of this rock; in this evanescent encounter dust shall return and meet in retrospect the dust from whence he came. "In the mother's body man knows the universe, in birth he forgets it." If I can recollect my prenatal past, my gestation in the geological womb, my genealogy, then I shall know who I am and where I am.

One steps into the abandoned tunnels enroute here, lower in the gorge, with an initial shudder. He enters the stone bowels of the Earth as though they were haunted with the jinn of Hades. The darkness is lonesome and alien. Intuitions of the savage persist, modern as I am. But the shudder passes, and, as is the case with one's initial encounter with the sea, there follows a fascination born of the intuition of connection, of reconnection. As the blood in my veins is but an inland sea, so the rock in my bones is but borrowed from the subterranean matrix in which I am reimmersed. Behind the hostility of plutonic depths, and interred with these sediments, and dissolved in the sea, are the nutrient powders of life. The waters of the oceans must, if I judge aright, have escaped juvenile from the Earth. Proto-rock sired the seas. Volatile magmas belched fertile vapors and gases. Rains fell from methane-ammonia laden skies, and fell again to enrich the sea with salts of erosion for a billion years. Out of the lithosphere: atmosphere, and hydrosphere, and biosphere. Earth's carbonate and apatite have graced me with the carbon, calcium, and phosphate that support my frame. The iron of hornblende and augite is the iron of the blood in which courses my life. Those stains of limonite and hematite now coloring this weath-

Reprinted by permission from *Main Currents in Modern Thought* 27(1971):79-83. The Doe River Gorge is in Carter County, Tennessee, in the Southern Appalachian Mountains.

ered cut will tomorrow be the hemoglobin that flushes my face with red. So now would I, this rock parasite, return to praise my natural parents. Ephemeral, anomalous, if so I am, erudite, conscious, proud, I can no longer suppress, but yield to, rejoice in, and humbly confess yet another primitive intution, only enriched by my intellectual sophistication. Here is my cradle. My soul is hidden in the cleft of this rock.

This thin line opposite me indexes the passage of the basal conglomerate of the Unicoi formation across a major unconformity down into the Precambrian plutonic complex—here a pegmatitic and gneissic granite, and a little further up the gorge varied with quartz monzonite and granodiorite. That is a date of reckoning in this rock calendar. Prompted by it, I let these hills dissolve and recompose eastward in Primeval Appalachia. But the crystalline basement remains before me, a relic of those aeonian Precambrian years, now all but irrecoverably erased by the tides of time. These dumb and hoary walls, so void of records from that intriguing eon they represent, still speak of my beginnings—if but cryptically.

A porphyritic basalt float block, dislodged from Fork Mountain above, or perhaps left by the Doe in a forgotten flood, rests now in Cambrian terrain, a quarter of a mile northeastward. Earlier I hammered off a chip to see how the world was made, and how I was made. The secret was there. It crystallizes. It polymerizes. Set in the black groundmass of this chip, rotated now between my thumb and my forefinger, is a gray plagioclase phenocryst, a polysynthetic twin, larger than my thumbnail, the faces 110, 010, 001, and $\overline{1}01$ especially well developed. With a lens I make out the lamellae. The scintillations of sunlight cast off these surfaces hint at the crystalline order beneath: silicon, oxygen, aluminum, calcium stacked and inlaid on a lattice that shames the finest arabesque. This spectacular unit runs through the mountain, and a couple of weeks ago I cut a section from a piece gathered on the other side. It is colored mostly by magnetite needles disseminated through a mass of plagioclase laths; much of the feldspar has long since aged to sericite; and there is, as a harbinger of things to come, a little carbonate in euhedral rhombs. The world crystallizes, and more. For vast potential is latent in that carbon!

The comparative monotony of mineral architecture is so only by comparison with organic structure. Geochemistry has a brother and sequel: biochemistry. The chorus of the patterned silicate tetrahedra, of the rings and strings and planes and cells, has a harmonic vibration in carbon. Only now, like a descant that rises above and enhances a melody in lower octaves, there is openness and novelty, a symphony. Mobile and supple, the molecules concatenate, and the megamolecular chains concatenate again, relentlessly pursuing their one-handed dissymmetry, until the motif becomes richer still: amino acids and proteins. Entropy yields. They replicate. Crystal building passes over into reproduction. With this polymerization came the pregnancy of the Precambrian Earth. Indeed, I suppose that when these rocks that face me were congealed her labor was over.

She already nursed and nurtured her infant brood, their molecular umbilical cord hardly yet severed.

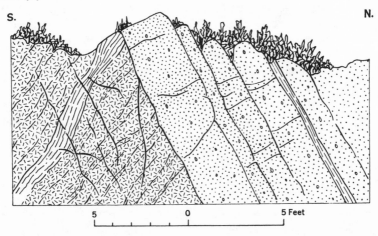

Precambrian contact at Pardee Point in the Unaka Mountains, Carter County, Tennessee. A cut on an abandoned railroad line through Doe River Gorge exposes an unconformity at the base of the Unicoi formation. Conglomerate (right) overlies and truncates complex Precambrian metamorphic rocks (left). From *Geology of Northeasternmost Tennessee,* by Philip B. King and Herman W. Ferguson, U.S. Geological Survey Professional Paper 311 (1960), p. 36.

How much that thin line of contact reveals and conceals! Like an argument from silence, it argues from absence. What is not there is the right half of the rock wall so massively present on my left. Suddenly it terminates, both pegmatite and gneissic granite truncated now by the Unicoi. But the Unicoi came after. That conglomerate was laid on an already truncated surface, a surface that had to be where those great beds of grit and pebble could be laid—submerged at the shallow bottom of a Cambrian sea. I concede that contact's mute argument, pass a dozen million years, and let the Waucobian seas roll inward and over me, filling the Appalachian miogeosyncline. Should I fear the deluge, having carried here with me on my morning hike my own "walking sack of sea water"? Now I shall commune with this face of indurated pebbles, relict skin of sea water in conversation with petrified sea bottom. Besides, the shores are barren and sterile, the hills are naked and silent, and here on the marine stage is where the action is.

Crossing this contact raises the curtain on a drama already in progress. Nature has by now long since reinvoked an ancient tectonic theme, the cell. With that stroke life has exploded. More recently she has armored it, and the armor doubles well as a coffin, and with that innovation this stone manuscript is more legible. The latest newcomer is an arthopod of colossal intricacy and size, colossal, that is, by Waucobian standards—*Olenellus,* whose fossilized remains are found, if not in the gorge, in other Chilhowee beds in the vicinity. My spartailed predecessor's long reign here is appropriately memorialized by the rock sequence from here to Hampton. I reckon myself to have walked through most of the Early Cambrian, and a tombstone of such proportions, a mile and a half long, is a fitting monument for thirty million years or so. By rough equation scratched at my feet, when I am laid in this dust, the length of my own gravestone will serve reasonably well to represent the reign of *Homo sapiens*.

My quartzite stool is solid beneath me (rather too firm; my usual seats are softer), but that stability is a short-ranged deception. When one proceeds as recklessly through time as have I this morning, *terra firma* warps beneath his feet. Else these hills are an illusion. The argument is as impregnable as this rock face with which I converse. The skeptic has only to go round Black Mountain behind me and look at Buckled Rock below Potato Top in the Laurel Fork Gorge. Indeed, there is no need for that. One can see Cedar Mountain from here. The old sea beds crop out where the Doe has cut through them, as they were lifted astride its path. And what else perched them high on Cedar's south side? That orogeny began in the Permian and cast the ancestral Appalachians out of the sea. The ferns of the gorge might remember—*Dryopteris marginalis* and *Polystichum acrostichoides* there; or the *Cheilanthes tomentosa* and *C. lanosa*, and the hauntingly rare *Woodsia scopulina* down in Polly Hollow. Their carboniferous grandparents managed to survive the Permian crisis. And the mountains too have survived by frequent if not continual rebirth. In their long and cyclic struggle with erosion, time and time over again the gnawing rivers have carried them back into the midst of the sea, only to find the peneplained hills reared upward again. The Doe rises on the flanks of the Roan. The river's roar below me I take as a tribute to the massive monarch of the Unakas high above me, longest lived of this generation of these hills, whose pre-Schooley birth reaches back into the Tertiary.

Would that I could hear the venerable patriarch speak, for it, like the Sphinx, knows the riddle of man. While these mountains were last being lofted high, old Mother Earth was lofting upward the most bizarre of her children. Demeter went to work on the central nervous system and the brain. She wrought of rock, polymerized and concatenated a million times over, a personalized dust-up. Morphologically, he is close to his anthropoid cousins. The line is as thin as that between the Unicoi and the granite. Yet the preconscious contact, like the Precambrian, seems to hide a major unconformity. That contact is crossed somewhere in the Pliocene, though no one yet knows precisely where. The earliest strata of the Pliocene are silent and preadamite, but in the next the anthropologist is disconcerted to find signs of his own kind. Another splitter of rocks has preceded him. There are his chipped flints—like these rough chips that I today have made.

As though to invoke his name were to call him to appear, my thoughts had no sooner risen to the coming of man than they were cut short by the coming of man. His earliest sign was the rustle of leaves some distance away and muffled so that one could wonder whether it was just the wind. But no, there again, now the snap of a twig; maybe a grouse or a squirrel. The stir was curiously subdued, like the sounds of stealth. Straining eyes and ears, I next judged that I was eavesdropping on a doe, but shortly I sensed that I had misjudged the encounter. I was being stalked by another of my species, and he was armed with a handgun. At that we met, though he was yet thirty yards away, for there flashed through both the awareness that the presence of each was known by the other. But now he made no effort to conceal his presence, and his weapon was sheathed, so I relaxed as he approached. I was puzzled by him, especially his pistol, he was no less puzzled by me, especially my hammer. Yet it didn't seem quite the mutual estimate of each other's arsenal.

"Seen anybody else around here?" asked the sheriff, for he was close enough for me to see a badge half covered by his leather jacket. I assured him that I had not. On the basis of the specimens in my haversack he deciphered the function of my hammer. There must be some correlation between geology and honesty, even avocational geology—perhaps merely that this gear would be a most unlikely thief's disguise—for his conversation was forthwith level and straightforward. "We are looking for some bootleggers on a tip that they have been working out of a hollow up here." His "we" was more than editorial, for he had mobile support. A carload of deputies crept around the bend, their pace doubly slowed by stealth and the difficulty of travel over the abandoned railroad grade. I was surprised that they had been able to squeeze through the tunnels. His backup squad closed in, but their alarm was a false one. There was no moonshining on the Unicoi; and, after pleasantries, they left to search the metamorphic terrain, the scout advancing about a hundred yards, or a million year's worth of rock, ahead of his fellow lawmen.

How disrespectfully had the sheriff crossed the hallowed Precambrian contact! Having committed his sin of ignorant profanity, he disappeared. Some higher officer of law should arrest and reprimand him for his sacrilege. But the upset that now overshadowed my thoughts went deeper than that. How curious to have watched this *Homo moralis* transgress unawares the boundary between the Cryptozoic and the Paleozoic! It was as though he pursued his moral quest independently of his origins, as though there were now superimposed on the bedrock of Earth a novel, ethical traffic. He came and went preaching and enforcing his "Thou shalt not," as though his sermon and authority were derived elsewhere than from the dust of which he is composed. How out of this naked rock which *is* did there come his *ought?* And from whence did I, who had minutes ago traced my ancestry to the Cambrian, inherit that moral fibre which not less than bone and blood supports my life?

"What a monstrous spectre is this man," wrote Stevenson in a similar mood, "the disease of the agglutinated dust, lifting alternate feet or lying drugged with slumber; killing, feeding, growing, bringing forth small copies of himself; grown upon with hair like grass, fitted with eyes that move and glitter in his face; a thing to set children screaming;—and yet looked at nearlier, known as his fellows know him, how surprising are his attributes! Poor soul, here for so little, cast among so many hardships, filled with desires so incommensurate and so inconsistent, savagely surrounded, savagely descended, irremediably condemned to prey upon his fellow lives: who should have blamed him had he been of a piece with his destiny and a being merely barbarous? And we look and behold him instead filled with imperfect virtues: infinitely childish, often admirably valiant, often touchingly kind; sitting down, amidst his momentary life, to debate of right and wrong and the attributes of the deity; rising up to do battle for an egg or die for an idea; singling out his friends and his mate with cordial affection; bringing forth in pain, rearing with long-suffering solitude, his young. To touch the heart of his mystery, we find in him one thought, strange to the point of lunacy: the thought of duty; the thought of something owing to himself, to his neighbor, to his God: an ideal of decency, to which he would rise if it were possible; a limit of shame, below which, if it be possible, he will not stoop." *(Pulvis et Umbra)*

When first he crossed this contact, he came as *Homo faber* in search of iron to make his tools. The stone chips were far too crude; the native metals much too soft; now he had fire and he knew how to smelt. A nineteenth-century mountaineer with prying eye, given, as am I, to splitting rocks with hammers, found magnetite ore at Cranberry just over the divide from the headwaters of the Doe. Some forgotten whim of Earth had collected enough needles like these in this trap chip I finger to concentrate a workable deposit—as though to hide it—on the inaccessible back side of the Hump, the north end of the Roan group. But how could he get it to the furnaces at Johnson City? A century ago almost to the year the toolmaking animal began to set this track. He subdued his Earth, blasted out the tunnels above and below, and plowed his arrogant way past this watershed of history. A decade and a half later his steaming iron horse, Tweetsie, began to carry out his ore, did so for a half century, and would today had not he cleverly locate other deposits unprotected by so wild a gorge as this. So the sheriff got his gun, and his deputies ride in a carriage of iron. But *Homo sapiens* has crossed this contact again; now he employs his iron, he wields his pistol and he drives his fossil-fueled squad car in the pursuit of an *ought*. If I am wise, as specified in my binomial, I do not now think that in this consists my specific wisdom: that I am *faber*. I cannot exchange the epithet for *sapiens* without loss, for have I not just seen my own brothers doing battle over right and wrong?

On the main road I passed earlier today a shrine in whose name humans have blended reference to this locale and matrix out of which they have risen, to the water, and to this dimension of life that now eludes me: the Doe River Free Will Baptist Church. Never is man more bizarre than when he, *Homo sacramentalis*, washes himself with water from the Doe, celebrates his freedom, and brazenly abbreviates the condition thereby symbolized or attained with f.w.b. And, for all his Tennessean suspicion of my heterodoxy, he is right. Or if he is not right, he unashamedly has hold of the *differentia* of his genus. The mundane parental forces that lofted us upward have cast us high. Like the eagle which is now here so rare, and which we might more wisely have conserved sacramentally, we soar over Roan, noble monarchs of the monarch of the Unakas. We have been thrusted over the Earth that cradled us, thrusted up to an evolutionary critical velocity, aye, an escape velocity, so that whatever telluric forces may yet bind us, we also travel freely. We are doubtless yet obligated ecologically, but this is novel: Earth has sufficiently released us so that now we are more properly beholden deontologically and ontologically. Dust we are, but the dust is excited and animated by the wind, the $\pi\nu\varepsilon\hat{\upsilon}\mu\alpha$, the רוּחַ , and in us wind passes over into spirit. Reason haunts rotted rock. Out of causality emerges intentionality; out of $\phi\acute{\upsilon}\sigma\iota\varsigma$, $\psi\upsilon\chi\acute{\eta}$. Granodiorite pulverizes and personifies. Soma undergoes metasomatic alteration. Stone is transubstantiated into soul.

The rocks that surround me I judge to be *in situ,* for I crossed the Iron Mountain fault at Hampton. But the rock from Elizabethton to Damascus is not autochthonous. In a regional overthrusting that staggers the imagination, the Shady Valley thrust sheet, a couple of mountain counties worth of rock, was imported here from somewhere southeastward. I think now that I also must be allochthonous, liberated from the rock in which I first was emplaced. Pygmalion redivivus, I have sprung from stone and I have sprung loose from stone. Fact surpasses our most riotous and outlandish dreams. Was there ever a fable quite this droll, a myth quite this bold: a man auto-fabricated of mud, and rock, and dust, and wind! *Homo lithospermaticus,* thence *Homo liber* and *Homo moralis!* In a world where what I have recalled and witnessed today has actually managed to happen, anything can happen!

Noblesse oblige. But obligation has commensurate privilege. The sheriff has transgressed this contact and left in quest of his *ought.* I shall linger and wait in wonder. I shall celebrate my geogenesis, my being in freedom, by conversing with this consanguine rock from whence I was hewn. Soul, thou art perched atop these rocks, inconsistently lording it over them and bowing before them. Has this occidental son come home, as those of the Orient advise, to venerate his ancestors? Or has the tail come round to smite the dog? I split that rock; and now I weep over it. Passions return that I knew formerly before the sarsen trilithons and bluestones at Stonehenge; my blood is Neolithic. The Baptist bows at his Doe River altar, confusedly proud of his freedom and yet humble before the mysteries of his origins. The omnipresence of rock must account for the religious bent of the mountaineers; open heights prompt their superstition and spirituality. The heathen were right: temples belong on high places of rock. And the Israelis were born at Sinai. How I too atop the Roan massif have found myself elevated psychically before the mysteries that the stone Roan-sphinx hides! The lifeless granite, this fossil conglomerate inescapably now become charged with a numinous mystique. They address me, alas, they enchant me—the gods have been here—and I succumb again to the naive emoting from which I so deeply disciplined in scientific criticism and positivist analysis, had thought myself to have escaped. Could it be that modernity's ken ignores and suppresses an authentic, primitive organon that now quickens within me? Need I apologize for my wonder? I think I shall rather boast of it. We have crossed this contact as *Homo faber,* we have crossed it as *Homo moralis.* Let now come one to hesitate, to worship here at this sacred line. I come as *Homo admirans.* Knowledge begins in wonder, observed the sage of Athens. But it begets it as well, and, reveling in awe, I am who I am. So find I now my peace, my place as noble and aesthetic scion of stone. In my silence and solitude, is it only the March wind? Or is there an echo down the gorge?—"Look with wonder at that which is before you." "He who wonders shall reign, and he who reigns shall rest." O Rock Face, there does miracle in thee lie. Else thou art a sacrament, a *persona* that outlies and overlies a Presence.

13

Farewell, Washington County

The time has come for me to leave these shale knobs and limestone valleys that somebody, sometime, years ago, carved out of the Appalachians, drew political lines around, and called Washington County. Departure evokes memories, and memories evoke a tribute. One man, at least, has found the boundaries of the county to enclose a region that is broad and wide and rich and deep.

Thoreau wrote in *Walden,* "I have travelled a good deal in Concord." One may travel extensively in Washington County. Louis Agassiz, the consummate naturalist, once remarked, "I spent the summer travelling. I got halfway across my backyard." I think perhaps as the days have flowed into weeks, the weeks into seasons, and the seasons into years, I have travelled not yet halfway across the county.

It was a Monday long since past that I sought out the solitude of the high, tri-county massif of Whitetop and its twin in our sister counties, Mount Rogers. Earlier, my introduction to Whitetop was the panorama from Bear Tree Gap. Then sunny autumn colors of every hue were capped by glistening white. An early snow filled the high crestline meadow. But now she was in a gray, stormy mood. In the blackness of a gathering storm my upward steps were halted by a thunderbolt crashing too near for comfort. The air now saturated with the odor of ozone, I turned to retrace my steps, driven down by the eerie storm, but left with an abiding sense of wonder.

Returning on a Tuesday later, the mute evidence first began unfolding to me of an ancient and far greater violence of mother nature there, the rocks known as the Mount Rogers volcanics. These rocks of Precambrian ages that number into the hundreds of millions of years—rhyolites, basalts, tuffs—remain to testify of nature's wilder moods preceding a hundred times over the arrival of humans. The wonder burned into my soul in microseconds by the fury of the lightning bolt deepened as I held in my hand a fragment of an altered lava from 500 million years ago, speckled with phenocrysts, and thought of the fire and fury in which these Balsam Mountains were born. Who can disentangle the

Reprinted by permission from *Virginia Wildlife* 29, no. 11 (November, 1968): 6-7, 22-23. Washington County is in Southwestern Virginia.

enigmatic red boulder conglomerate west of Konnarock—the whence and the why of rounded granitic boulders and cobbles of aplite and greenstone all frozen in a siltstone matrix? Why is this rock here, anhydrite and gypsum at Plasterco, marcasite at Alvarado, and dogtooth spar in veins along Beaver Creek? How strange to peer into a petrographic microscope at a wafer thin section of rhyolite porphyry from the angular blockfields on Whitetop's slopes and to watch the crystals wink on and off with the rotating stage! What secrets of Earth, her past and present, are hid in her wind and her rocks!

On a Wednesday now and on Wednesday again and again, the chipmunks play outside my study window, scampering after each other when they have their fill of the hickory nuts in the church yard. Easily a sackful of the little striped fellows live within sight of the desk where I am supposed to busy myself with work, placed there either by the Creator to punctuate my studies with amusement, or by the tempter to divert my wandering mind. If Whitetop leaves a sense of antiquity, secrecy, and wonder, the memory of the chipmunks adds to life a pure and instantaneous delight.

Thursday was it?—I cannot quite recall; but the weekday doesn't matter— that I poked amongst the mosses at Sandy Flats, reveling mostly in my ignorance. I collected a dozen to examine more closely, later to learn that I had made a discovery indeed. Not a discovery, to be sure, that would excite the world, but it was discovery enough to etch another permanent memory. Just mosses, they seemed, though what is so uncommon as a common moss—gametophyte and sporophyte, seta, capsule, peristome, operculum, and calyptra. Wherefore was so much labor spent on small things? Just mosses? But wait: the most minuscule of all, half an inch high, the trained eyes of a bryologist, Dr. A. J. Sharp, were to spot as *Campylostelium saxicola,* a rare species otherwise quite unknown in the state of Virginia and collected but once or twice in all the South. And I, only I, had stumbled over it, in a secluded spot known only to me, the moss, and God.

A wintry Friday morning once was quite consumed in business not my own, investigating the clandestine affairs of a fox the night before. I hastened to sort out her string-straight tracks in the light snow, before the warming sun should erase them forever. From the den in the limestone bluff, to the scent post by the creek, thence through the pawpaws and up the hill toward the cornfield she went. The round of the shocks was interrupted by the pursuit of a rabbit. The rabbit, though, had escaped into the brush in a profusion of tracks. Neither I, nor, so I judged, could the cunning of the fox discover into what bush or hole he had found his safety. So it was back to breakfast on an ear of corn. A full morning of travel that was, after a full night, and all in Mobley Hollow. I never knew you could travel quite so far so near home, an itinerary learned from a gray vixen.

It came to pass on a grim Saturday that I stood in the shelter of the church, hardly out of the furious rain, watching a fast moving front drive scud torn from larger clouds through the tree tops. The Whitetop storm the year before was born of thermals generated in the county, but here was a menacing visitor from afar. A Texas-born storm was eddying eastward along the front of a mass of polar air, propagating itself across a thousand miles, driven by energies released a continent and a half away in the Canadian wastes of the Mackenzie River. Now it passed over my head, onward and eastward into the sea. How vast are the powers that range and sometimes rage over and round us in these square miles of home.

Sunday once, again in new fallen snow, early out and on the way to church, I chanced upon a compacted covey of quail, ringed tail to tail, just aside the gravel road. Surely that was a curious place to huddle together for warmth and protection. Suddenly the close knit covey, glimpsed but moments, became forever one of the pictures that I will not forget. A dozen pairs of eyes met mine in an encounter that somehow went right to the nerve of life itself.

So the weeks have flowed on into months, and the months into years.

On a January afternoon, in a pensive mood, I crouched out of a raw east wind in the lee of a tumbledown shack for another unexpected encounter, this time with a tiny chickweed blossom that had found before me the shelter of the southwestern exposure. Foolish flower, this is January! Noxious weed, why must you invade a deserted farmyard? *Stellaria media,* five cleft petals spread wide, was mute, yet in its muteness eloquent enough to stir me anew with lines from Wordsworth's ode:

> To me the meanest flower that blows can give
> Thoughts that do often lie too deep for tears.

A sunny February day I devoted to unraveling the mystery—for I at least did know whither it led—of a forgotten trail up the flanks of Holston Mountain northeastward from where it passes over into Virginia. It ended only not to end, as it linked with the all but interminable Appalachian Trail. Who would have supposed that before its junction on the crest, it would take me by a pond high on a mountain spur? The pond was filled with a hundred—could it have been a thousand?—frogs, all arguing with voices that could be heard a half a mile along the mountainside that spring was bound to come.

But never was I quite convinced of spring until I sighted, inevitably in March, two of our county's humblest weeds and most ambitious harbingers of spring. In the pasture across from where for years I lived, March belongs to the tiny Whitlow-grass, *Draba verna,* and to the Bitter Cress, *Cardamine hirsuta.* Crowded out of the best of the spring by larger plants and grasses, they flourish earlier, doing nobody any good except themselves and me, flourishing in their diminutive way for their own inherent worth in the March wind and sun, and reminding me year after year that the spring simply could not be gainsaid. They disappear the other eleven months, presumably as the microscopic seeds lie fallow in the earth. But return they will March after March after March until the sum is decades of centuries.

Well do I recall my initiation into one of the secrets of ten thousand Aprils on Iron Mountain. I lugged back from the trail up the Cuckoo a lonesome plant, a sizeable clump of narrow, dark green leaves with a simple white flower at the summit of a scape. It had a naked, uncommon look. I, then the newcomer here, found that I had presumptuously uprooted an inhabitant of that locale for a century of centuries. This was Frazer's Sedge, *Cymophyllus Fraseri,* a relict species from geological antiquity. Its structure is primitive. Only a few plants have survived the pressures of competition that evolution has since developed. Reproducing unchanged while all else has changed round about it, Frazer's Sedge has been abandoned and bypassed, reduced to an anachronism, and is now counted among the dozen rarest plants in our area.

The woods come alive in May, and here my every May has been crammed with beauty: the brilliant crimson of Fire Pink, *Silene virginica;* the delicate white of Rue Anemone, *Anemonella thalictroides,* the lacy look of the Foam-flower, *Tiarella cordifolia,* or the dainty but vast profusion of Fringed Phacelia, *Phacelia fimbriata,* a specialty of these southern mountains that finds its northernmost limit along our county's high northeast boundary. The Flowering Raspberry, *Rubus odoratus,* has a purple all its own; an alternate shade belongs only to the violet Wood-Sorrel, *Oxalis violacea.* Orange is monopolized by the Flame Azelea, *Rhododendron calendulaceum,* which resolved to explore the spectrum of all the oranges. Any who become sated with the color of May can ponder the lore of its flora. The Whorled Loosestrife, *Lysimachia quadrifolia,* has opened its little yellow blossoms since our pioneer fathers placed it on the yokes of their oxen teams to make them work in harmony! By May you can predict the weather with the Poor Man's Weather Glass, *Anagallis arvensis,* because the plant reflexively closes its quarter inch scarlet petals with the ap-proach of a storm. The secretive flesh-brown flower of *Asarum canadense* leads to a race of wild ginger. The smell of the Garlic-Mustard, *Alliaria officinalis,* that grows by the North Holston riverbanks is surpassed only by the rank strength of the ramps, *Allium tricoccum* of Whitetop. How often have I pondered the weird, wild loveliness of a Lady Slipper, *Cypripedium acaule,* or plucked from the crevices of trailside stones the exquisite wild Lily of the Valley, *Convallaria montana,* to be plunged, as was Tennyson, down into the depths of being itself.

> Flower in the crannied wall,
> I pluck you out of the crannies,
> I hold you here, root and all, in my hand
> Little flower—But *if* I could understand
> What you are, root and all, and all in all,
> I should know what God and man is.

A hot and sultry June afternoon I spent at the seashore, and that still in Washington County. Sea shells, *Dicellomus,* lie yet buried in the mud in which they fell in the Paleozoic past. Our landlocked county was then the shore of an ancient sea, and these feeble folk were our ancestors here. I unearthed the fossil brachipods one summer day from the crumbling shales where they had slept for a half billion years. The changes of time compacted the sediment to rock, and the rock buckled upward, and the seas receded. The Appalachians rose from the sea. A million million rains washed and washed to strip away the overburden, peeling off the layers above, and exposing the shale. Now and again its marine cargo weathers out so anomalously far from the sea. Fossil sea shells where Mumpower Creek cuts the Nolichucky shale in Big Ridge north of Bristol? Yes, they are there—small but unmistakable relics of a Cambrian fauna, tokens of a remote abysm in time when these hills of home were conceived in a watery womb, subsequently to be brought forth in the labor of the Appalachian orogeny.

Once upon a July twilight I was gifted all undeserved with the loveliest of sunsets. The sun plunged behind the old snag that stood as a sentinel halfway up the western knob on the skyline near home, terminating the day with a blaze of glory that fired an orange-red across half the spacious firmament. It was as though the sinking sun had resolved to exhaust itself in activity and color. Dusk was spent in hues of crimson and violet that lined the deep purple stratocumulus, then to yield to encroaching darkness, but not before a bit of that July became part of me forever.

In August darkness, once, I was meddling again, prowling about the haunts of a screech owl who dwelt in the old big willow on Sinking Creek. Binoculars in hand, I knelt behind an overgrown post in the fencerow, eyes glued to an owl-sized opening well up the trunk. The darkness was falling rapidly now, yet I hoped to spy the little fistful of feathers whose tremulous whinny so disrupted the silence of the night. I could have spared myself the bother of the binoculars, for we soon enough met in closer contact than seemed hospitable. Meddling I was, but I meant no harm; yet the owl misread my intentions, or resented my peeping, and attacked me. Out of hole he (or could it have been a she?) came, a tufted rufous projectile propelled by a silent gunpowder, swooping into my head and hair, wings flapping, talons curled, and finishing with a shriek that must somehow lie behind the rebel yell. The grumpy little night owl dwells yet, for all I know, in the willow in the bend of the creek. That one spot in Washington County has for me an early curfew. It's been off my limits ever since.

The broadwinged hawks fly south over us in September, diurnal birds of prey that have been my symbols of the wild and the free. They, I ought to add by contrast, never seemed to resent my curious watches. September 22, 1962, I lay flat on my back on a rock outcropping in the sunshine of a still day, sprawled across the county line, high atop Clinch Mountain at the Mendota Firetower. The binoculars were necessary now; even with them I strained higher still to mere specks of gray in the blue and white of the early autumn sky. Counting with me was T. W. Finucane, ornithologist and coordinator of the fall hawk count. "Wow, there must be hundreds of hawks up there!" I exclaimed, realizing the size of the flight. I counted rapidly, scanning the open distance ahead to make sure I had spotted the lead hawks. This one was ideal for counting, strung out in a narrow line that followed the mountain crest. Fifteen minutes later, with a chain of hawks, past us a mile long, the flight cut off at 830. Earlier they had come in low, pausing at the tower to circle for altitude. After a lull, more followed. By the close of the day, we had the highest count in the history of observation at the Mendota tower, 2,369 broadwings, which with a handful of redtails, ospreys, and other hawks brought the total to 2,379 hawks. Annually since, a couple or more September days I have reserved as the self-appointed inspector of hawk flights over the Clinch, and I have done my duty well. I remember only one owl, but hawks by the thousands; 4,941 hawks, mostly broadwings, but others as well, Cooper's, sharpies, redtails, ospreys, redshouldered hawks, a few marsh hawks, and a solitary eagle have been my portion of the 25,728 birds of prey counted by observers since 1959 from the wind-swept tower.

October has always converted me into a deerstalker. Just above Shaw Gap in Feathercamp woods I inched upwind through the yellow and red of hickory and oak in the fall. I heard it; then again I didn't—a rustle that seemed something more than just a breeze. An hour of slow motion stealth brought me not a hundred yards. But my quarry was unaware. I had the drop on an old buck, surrounded by three does and a couple of fawns. Would that I had my grandfather's Winchester back home on the rack! But the season was not yet open. Maybe it was just as well, for the longer I watched, the more I had to remember: eight points counted and recounted, the twitch of the tails, their nervous looks, the suckling fawns. After half an hour's intimacy with the stag and his own, a careless step and a snapped twig spooked them all. The memory ends in a snort and a half dozen white tail flags. But on the return there was one reward more. There, on the trail, like a barefoot human, was unmistakably the print of a bear. Shades of Wilburn Waters!

It seemed hardly worth the bother one gray mid-November day to look again at the sterile, thin, cut-over woods in the nearby knobs. Can any good thing come from Mud Hollow? From Mock Knob? I had long since put it down as rotting stumps and brush. Home I came almost empty handed, collecting nothing more than a few tiny mushrooms from inside a doty log. Perhaps because I had so little, I looked more closely. It was the plainest of toadstools, tiny and tan, until that evening late I turned off my study light to discover the weird-green luminescence of *Panus stypticus*. Cap and stalk and especially the gills gave off a soft luminous fire. The faint cold light that braved the winter's dark left me a surviving glow. Who can tell why this uncanny emanation lights a rotting log?

Late in December and late in the day, years ago now, I overlooked from afar the length and breadth and depth of the county in which I have rooted so deeply. The day was spent in the climb up High Knob, visibility zero. Rime ice covered all, and fog covered that. At the summit, the cloud cover thinned; the late evening sun was beginning to set. I stood aloft and clear. At my feet a pillowy cumulus sea filled the intervening miles southeastward, masking all terrain until it washed the flanks of the Clinch. Beyond, everything was crystal clear, the rare visibility of cold winter skies after rain. In a single gaze I embraced Mendota eastward to Beech Mountain and Whitetop. From Tumbling Creek, and the tower on Hayter's Knob, I swept to Brumley and Hidden Valley, then over the county and across the valley to Holston Mountain. A fair landscape indeed! What wonders and pleasures lie in the realm your boundaries enclose, from the majesty of Abrams Falls to the mystery of Ebbing Spring, from limestone sinks to green pastures and templed hills. *De profundis!* What abundance and splendor are compacted here! Lord, bid time and nature gently spare these hills that once were home.

14

Nature and Human Emotions

An Appalachian heritage coupled with life in the West is the personal backing for the argument that follows. The West and the South are landscapes so stimulating in their working on character that some will respond sympathetically, others with suspicion, as I claim that an appropriate exchange between the person and the place is part of our emotional well-being. This argument seeks to be reasoned, but if it is mixed with emotion, that too is intentional.

PASSION IN THE NATURAL ENVIRONMENT

Human emotions have their richest development in a social environment, and many emotions are known only there, such as jealousy or embarrassment. But emotions have a fundamental, "native" expression before the natural world, as with the shudder when staring into the starry night, or the quickened pulse on a balmy spring day. The tears of joy at birth and those of grief at death, though interpersonal, also flow as nature gives and takes away. Goose pimples sometimes rise when persons sing, "America, the Beautiful!" The physiological reaction is to a national heritage, but also before purple mountains' majesties and the fruited plains stretched from sea to shining sea.

Emotions are humane occasions, and some slip into the belief that they only properly obtain between persons, as when disgusted with a sister. But persons do not, or ought not, to curse rocks. They may "give way" to emotions in I-Thou relations, but I-It experiences should be passionless. This view is a mistake, for our encounter with nature is as passionate as it is cognitive. This calls for an ecology of the emotions. At this point, some reply that emotions in primitive man were directed against nature in animism and superstition, but that modern persons have grown out of it. Ecology is not emotional; it is scientific.

Reprinted by permission from Fred D. Miller, Jr., and Thomas W. Attig, eds., *Understanding Human Emotions* (Bowling Green, Ohio: Bowling Green Studies in Applied Philosophy, Bowling Green State University, 1979), pp. 89-96.

That is not entirely so; our argument here is rather that these passions have taken a more calculating form. If we consider Newton and his mechanistic universe, Darwin and his jungle, Marx with his dialectic of man laboring against nature, an existentialist in despair before an absurd world, a technologist craving for dominion over nature, or the ecologist rediscovering his earthen home, fearful of its destruction, we will see that our contemporary thinking often has an understory of concern that is environmental.

Given evolutionary theory, genetics, biochemistry, and more lately, sociobiology, it is difficult to think that our emotions have not been shaped to fit us for the natural environment, and this in ways other than merely providing the cultural life in which we find protection against it. This does not require a perfect fit, for natural selection rough hews its creatures, and some misfitting is required if the system is to move. Also, once they have arrived, emotions may be employed in novel contexts. Still, the prevailing paradigms will hardly allow the anomaly that emotions have no survival value for appropriately judging the world, being a rather ineffective constitutional error. Everyone allows that the hand, brain, and senses have enormous survival value, not denied, but extended in their cultural use, and so too with emotions, as significant as is cognitive thought in directing those hands.

But no single account prevails as to how cognitive and emotional processes are coupled in that brain, and here too the human response to nature is implicated. Some hold that in the bicameral mind the left hemisphere is more linguistic, analytic, and conceptual, the right hemisphere more spatially oriented, perceptual, and holistic, and if so perhaps the more significant not only for our emotional life but for our sense of presence in the natural world. Others find lower, more anciently evolved portions of the mind, followed by intermediately evolved sections, and finally the higher reaches of the mind. The emotional life rises in the visceral intermediate mind, subtending the cognitive mind but governed only in part by it, and if so, our relations with the natural environment reach back into prelinguistic, though by no means unintelligent, foundations of the mind. Humanistic psychologists are not less inclined to find in the unconscious the location of much that drives us, particularly of those deep substructures by which we are oriented toward the natural world. Any particular account may be revised; what is less likely to be revised is what is common to them all, that both our emotions and our attitudes toward the natural world are not formed only, perhaps not mainly, in that part of the mind which is dominantly verbal and cognitive.

Still, a philosopher ought to hope for some veridical unity in the mind, whatever its divisions, and to try to make explicit rationally what is so often tacit. Further, however much is precognitive, everyone knows how much our cultural conditionings—whether superstitious animism, Advaitan monism, romantic naturalism, existentialist nihilism, logical positivism, or Marxism—govern our tempers in the world. Our upsets follow from our mindsets, and we are aroused to act in accord with what we believe. It is in a blending of thought, affection, and willing that the epistemic powers of the mind lie, and we need accordingly a philosophical account of a suitable emotional response to nature.

EMOTIONS OF DISCONTINUITY: THE NATURE WE RESIST AND FEAR

We now suggest the coordinates on which to map these emotions, testing with enough instances to see whether our encounters with nature do go into place on such a framework. Those divisions within the brain are made yet more complex by recognizing that we are not of one mind toward nature. In one sense this is analytic, for any emotions necessarily can be plotted on a graph with positive and negative fields. But in a deeper sense this dichotomy is a synthetic judgment, describing the way the world is, with our minds evolved accordingly. In emotion we are aroused for approach or for withdrawal. The oppositely phased natural world is full of helps and hurts, and hence our ambivalence.

That we should fear nature is axiomatic to the biological essence of life. A countercurrent to entropy, life is a contest where the organism builds itself up against an environment pressing to undo it. Life protests until it loses, and so, at those levels of life where emotions appear, a chary fear is, alas, the only finally relevant emotion. The child is born into the world angry, we leave it in pain, and every intermediate emotion is in a matrix of privations. Hence Dewey held that emotion is always a state of conflict, and psychologists describe us as being "full of defenses." This fear of nature can be pathological and disorganizing, but such upset is the error of the healthy baseline emotion by which we anxiously preserve this discontinuity between the organism and physical nature.

Humanistic psychology adds the notion of a centripetal self maintaining its integrity against the centrifugal wildness. Each species, each individual sets a boundary between itself and the rest of nature, and in humans that discontinuity is enormously greater than elsewhere. The developing child separates his or her "self" as a form disarticulated from the spatiotemporal environment. This *spiritual agency* is the distinctly human genius, wrested from nature, and, except as we insist otherwise, the accidents of external nature will destroy it. Our emotions fence in this ego. That includes much exhilaration in this exodus from nature, in the power to be by being over against nature. We delight in personal narrative as we learn to map and travel through the world. This is the elation of auto/ bio/graphy, not yet intellectual in the child, often not in the adult, but always existential and impulsive from our psychic depths.

The impact of wilderness on the American mind illustrates this psychology as it empowers a society. The pilgrim, the settler, the explorer—all were admired for their prowess against their environment. The wild continent was tamed, forests cleared, roads built, rivers bridged, and often in the name of religion, for the Judeo-Christian faith urged the conquest of nature and redeeming of the fallen world. Scientists and engineers, physicians and farmers, as they have conquered famines, sickness, and natural disasters, remain heir to this hope of gaining security by overcoming a threatening nature. The primary emotion here is a resolute courage. The sagas of the pioneers are spine-tingling, and in Scouting or Outward Bound our youth still seek the outdoor experience as bracing and even therapeutic. An early and provident fear of nature is felt by all roused to work for shelter or to prevent hunger, by all wary of natural hazards, by all who button up before winter. In this, the ego boundary must also be maintained in competition and cooperation with other egos, and so an elaborate superstructure of emotions emerges within culture. But this is always within the fundamental tension of the self against the natural world.

Indeed, we have become modern just as we have become very clear about this struggle and kept our nerve in it. Modernity began when Descartes divorced mind from matter, and the self was already lonesome in Newton's mechanistic universe. In Darwin's jungle that alienation greatly increased, under the variant dualism of the organism struggling against its world. If man has no horns or fangs, he has his hands and brains. Marx dealt with the hands, Freud with the mind, interpreting each as an organ of combat with the environment. As had Darwin, Marx found that man rises up out of nature to be set in dialectical struggle with it by means of his laboring, and such "laboring" always gives Marxist logic an emotional dimension. The class struggles are the cultural super-structure, since the products of labor are inequitably distributed, but the passion with which Marxism opposes social injustice is a function of its underlying conviction that humans have to earn their way against nature.

For Freud too, the self evolves out of nature but is set against it. Because it cannot survive alone, the self consents to the restrictions of civilization, confined to culture because nature poses far more terror. "Nature rises up before us, sublime, pitiless, inexorable." "She destroys us, coldly, cruelly, callously. . . . It was because of these very dangers with which nature threatens us that we united together and created culture. . . . Indeed, it is the principal task of culture, its *raison d'être*, to defend us against nature."[1] But there we find too short-lived a security, and we unconsciously generate the illusion of religion (differently but not unlike the way in which Marx held that frustrated laborers accept the opiate of a heavenly father). Freud hopes to cure this illusion and to leave us rational, with science as our savior instead. But he knows that in the end, "obscure, unfeeling and unloving powers determine men's fate."[2]

The first mood here is one of being resolute against the storm but later we discover that the storm is raging within. We suffer, and lest we suffer the more, we organize ourselves creatively for a while, kept in a broken wholeness by just this apprehension. But afterward we are gripped by loneliness, overcome by pathos as clods fall over the coffin at a mother's grave, or, as in Matthew Arnold's *Dover Beach,* when the cold, gray sea flows over us. Even these emotions belong, for we are not human until we can be uneasy, and we hardly want that "eternal note of sadness" entirely taken from life. Still, there is a breaking point, and, unless there are other emotions to relieve the tragic sense, it alone makes us ill. So the modern mind has become unnerved, for all its boldness, increasingly competent, decreasingly confident, and the strong arm of the laborer becomes a fist flung into nature, protesting with a god-damned scream. Sartre's *Nausea* or Camus' *Sisyphus* portrays this *angst*. The Buddha was right, the natural *samsara*-world is suffering, *duhkha,* a pathetic place through and through, where the self is driven by its thirst, *tanha,* libido. The whole of it, to borrow a place name from the Virginia pioneers, is a "Dismal Swamp." But we have no *nirvana* in which we can put out our passions, we are caught on a wheel of hurt, until a not so distant day when, for the individual, death will extinguish those passions, and a much more distant day when, for the race, nature will put all passions out in that universal heat death that the physicists expect and the biologists fear.

What was earlier a healthy, composing fear of nature seems, under theories that overexplain the offensiveness and underexplain any attractiveness in nature, to have gotten us *lost* on a "darkling plain." Lostness in the wild is, by all accounts, an intensely emotional state which breeds irrationality and disorganization, and in which we become our own worst enemies.

EMOTIONS OF CONTINUITY: THE NATURE WE EMBRACE AND LOVE

That we can be upset when *lost* depends upon a baseline emotion of being *at home.* Our homes are cultural places in their construction, but what we add again is that there is a natural foundation, a sense of belongingness to the landscape. For all those boundaries that we defend against the external world, our emotions are not confined to those of separateness, but we know the bitter ·with the sweet, the rose with its thorns. Is this sheer ambivalence, or can we redescribe that opposition under a larger ecology?

The American settlers found that they had no sooner conquered a wilderness than they had come to love a land. Theirs was a promised land, even though they fought for it, nor are these biblical allusions incidental. After the conquest, there was time to rejoice in the sunshine and the rain, in the seedtime and harvest, in peaks and prairies, in the orchard in bloom, in the smell of the new-mown hay. "We know we belong to the land, and the land we belong to is grand!"[3] Millions learned that chorus, sung in voices not less rousing as it was transposed from Oklahoma to Iowa or the Sierras, though it may not be incidental that it was sung first in the Indian territories. But East or West, and not only transcontinentally but globally, we have never far to seek for such emotional satisfactions.

Few persons want their environments without landscaping, without trees and grass, flowers and gardens, lakes and sky. Of those drawn to the city for livelihood or security, the vastest portion elect the *sub-urbs* so as to remain also near the country, in some place not consummately urban, but where there is more green than anything else, where, with the neighbors, there are fence rows and cardinals, dogwoods and rabbits. For most Americans the ideal life is not so much urban as it is "town and country." We cherish our hills of home, our rivers, our bays, our country drives. Most of us identify so with some countryside that we get a lump in the throat when we must leave it, or when we return after an absence. We have deep affections toward persons and communities, but our affections toward the city, *per se,* are usually exceeded by those which we have toward the landscape.

The notion of evolved fittedness includes congeniality, as well as opposition, but Darwin never quite said this. Nature is not a home ready to hand and we must live in what psychologists call "built environments," urban and rural. Yet this is subtended by the earthen life-support system of which we have again become so aware, and these connections are not only biophysical, they are psychological. If we are emotionally built so as to draw together socially against nature, we also are emotionally built so as to be attracted to skies and plains, pets and flowers, mountains and beaches, waterfalls and meadows. Some may say that this is just a matter of taste and frills, but we have to add that such matters, especially those that influence our moods of well-being and upset, not only have a significant psychological reality but even reveal truth about the world. Why should we ever have evolved the aesthetic sense, if it but makes us freaks of nature? Our emotions defend the organic self, but they also stretch it out to integrate it into its place.

In an analysis of the autobiographies of three hundred geniuses, Edith Cobb concluded that they characteristically recall from their middle childhood a period "when the natural world is experienced in some highly evocative way, producing in the child a sense of profound continuity with natural processes." It is to this encounter that, in the creativity of their adult years, "these writers say they return in memory in order to renew the power and impulse to create at its very source, a source which they describe as the experience of emerging not only into the light of consciousness but into a living sense of dynamic relationship with the outer world. In these memories the child appears to experience both a sense of discontinuity, an awareness of his own unique separateness and identity, and also a continuity, a renewal of relationship with nature as process."[4] We are genetically prepared for this exchange with nature, yet it is so innovative that each individual becomes virtually a species in itself. The child is exalted by a rediscovery of those powers of autonomous agency in which the race has evolved, but the dominant impulse is a sense of immanence in the natural process, more relational than oppositional, more romance than tragedy. To finger a stick, to throw rocks into the creek, to build a fire, to run with a dog across a field, to watch the sparrows—all awaken a sense of wonder at both the natural drama and the part the person is permitted to play in it. Nature is a foil for the self, yet so diversely so across the many cultures and centuries of these geniuses that any environmental determinism is discredited and replaced with an environmental reciprocity.

In his autobiography, Carl Jung recalls being gripped in early childhood by the large stones in his family garden, and returning there to regain those emotions in his adult years. With advancing age, he developed an intricate symbolic relationship with the stone "Tower," a rustic house that he himself built by stages on the scenic upper lake of Zurich. In this rural place, he writes, "I am in the midst of my true life, I am most deeply myself. . . . At times I feel as if I am spread out over the landscape and inside things, and am myself living in every tree, in the splashing of the waves, in the clouds and the animals that come and go, in the procession of the seasons. There is nothing in the Tower that has not grown into its own form over the decades, nothing with which I am not linked. . . . Silence surrounds me almost audibly, and I live 'in modest harmony with nature.' " Later, in retrospect, he concluded, "The world into which we are born is brutal and cruel, and at the same time of divine beauty. Which element we think outweighs the other, whether meaninglessness or meaning is a matter of temperament. . . . I cherish the anxious hope that meaning will preponderate and win the battle. . . . There is so much that fills me: plants, animals, clouds, day and night, and the eternal in man. The more uncertain I have felt about myself, the more there has grown up in me a feeling of kinship with all things."[5]

Perhaps it is enough to set these emotions of continuity and discontinuity, like the *yang* and the *yin,* forever in symmetry and oscillation, cautioning only, to follow that Taoist metaphor, that the nature we oppose is not itself evil, but that the good lies rather in the creative tension of order and disorder. Still, the *yang* and the *yin* tended in the East to cancel each other out and to leave an ultimate nothingness, overcome by that Buddhist *sunyata* before which some rejoice and others recoil. Our Western accounts find more historical development, more novelty, and even hope for progress. The vector is superimposed on the circle so as to form a rising spiral. The person is an evolutionary thesis of nature, set in antithesis to it, and yet drawn toward synthesis with it. But the socialists in their present dialectical struggles have neglected that original thesis and consuming synthesis. Or, for those who prefer scientific to philosophical and religious metaphors, nature offers both resistance and conductance to life, and currents, whether biological, psychological, or electrical, can flow only as aroused and energized in the interplay of both.

Nature is the bosom whence we come and go, and we here want to put in place those emotions that gather round the name "Mother Nature," even if one can make out no Father God, those emotions that Freud thought so misplaced. These emotions cheer for the natural parenting, for those generative, sustentative energies of this earthen home, productive forces strikingly present in the only nature we know in any complexity and detail. Life is something nature hands us, and, given these brains and hands, genes and blood chemistries, life remains nine parts natural for every one part it becomes artificial. We are born clean of culture, for any culture can be emplaced in any newborn, though we are not humanized without such education. But we are not born clean of nature, and in any cultural education we do ill to neglect those emotions that are native to this birth. We are born to die, but it is life rather than death which is the principal mystery that comes out of nature, and our emotions are stirred proportionately. The myth of Antaeus is true: man is an invincible wrestler, but loses his strength if he takes both feet from his Mother Earth. Adam lost his Eden when he spurned it, and fell into labor and pain. Human emotions fit us for defending the self, aloft and transcendent over nature, but they ought still the more to fit us to the natural environment that transcends us. These are emotions that we all live *by,* but they are emotions that some of us live *for.*

NOTES

1. Sigmund Freud, *The Future of an Illusion,* trans. W. D. Robson-Scott (New York: Liverright, 1955) pp. 26-27.

2. Sigmund Freud, "The Question of a *Weltanschauung,*" in *Complete Psychological Works* (London: Hogarth, 1964) 22:158-82, citation on p. 167.

3. Richard Rodgers and Oscar Hammerstein, *Oklahoma!*

4. Edith Cobb, *The Ecology of Imagination in Childhood* (New York: Columbia University Press, 1977). The quotation is from Cobb's synopsis of her book in *Daedalus* 88 (1959):537-48, citation on pp. 538-39.

5. Carl G. Jung, *Memories, Dreams, Reflections* (New York: Vintage Books, 1963), pp. 225-26, 358-59.

15

The Pasqueflower

Earliest among the rites of the western spring is the blossoming of the pasque-flower, which, like the eastern arbutus, precedes by a month the rest of the vernal flora. Its precocious beauty accounts for its name, a flower of the *Pasque,* Easter; and its loveliness, size, and season led Aldo Leopold to introduce his *Sand County Almanac* with the plea that "the chance to find a pasqueflower is a right as inalienable as free speech." Recently, just after the equinox, hiking a meadow in the foothills of the Rockies, I delighted in thousands in finest bloom, with nothing else out save the aspen catkins.

Its finding is a joy immediately in the aesthetic encounter, but beyond that, this windflower is a cherished symbol of the wild for reasons that run deeper. In its annual renewal as the first spirited flowering against the blasts of winter, it is a sign against the eternal storm. Like the daffodil in Shakespeare's England, the pasqueflower dares to "take the winds of March with beauty," and such a brave flower can help us ponder what it means to live in and against the wild. So I venture here to let the meeting of it take a philosophical turn.

Winter in the Rockies is too much a still and lifeless scene, save for, or yet more truly because of, the howling wind. The beauty is of icy peaks, glistening snowfields, crystalline flakes, gaunt aspen, the somber hues of lichens on weathered granite. The seasonal green is gone, and only the conifers preserve it with dark coolness, their branches pruned back by the weight of the snows. Winter is all of frozen beauty, Mother Nature hibernates; by the time of the equinox we tire and hope for the "spring" of life.

The pasqueflower symbolizes all that is missing in the wintry landscape, and should there come a spring without the regeneration it prefigures, the winter would have grown lethal. Wildness without its flora would be only the bleak and conquering storm, and it is this florescence that the pasqueflower helps us to celebrate because it dares to bloom when the winter of which we have wearied is not yet gone. "Flowering" touches values so soon; this biological phenomenon becomes a metaphor for all the striving toward fruition that characterizes the

Reprinted by permission from *Natural History* 88, no. 4 (April 1979):6-16.

psychological, intellectual, cultural, and even the spiritual levels of life.

Flowering adds the splendor of art to our often rather more mean thoughts concerning the evolution of life, for the flowers in the jungle fit their bearers for survival and yet also reveal how life pushes toward a level of living beauty that exceeds all precedent in the nonflowering wilderness. We love the landscape, the sunset, the night sky; yet greatly exceeding the geophysical, mineralogical, and celestial ranges of beauty are those of the emergent structures of life, particularly as these come to their botanical apogee in the flowers of the higher plants, which so marvelously combine function and beauty, as though to mark life's reproduction with a special sign.

Other plants flower more simply, as with the hundred thousand aspen catkins that I passed with the thousands of pasqueflowers, but even these wind-pollinated flowers or the ferns and mosses, which do not properly flower at all, still bear reproductive structures that, when looked at more nearly, amply enrich the phenomenon of florescence. Flowering, whether great or small, is a many-splendored thing, circling round the pageant of life that perennially springs from the latent earth.

The brilliance of this pasqueflower has its simplest explanations in mechanisms for flowering so soon at the winter's end. It must have petals (or, as the botanists prefer, petallike sepals) large enough to attract the few insects that are out so early. The downy surface of transparent hairs on its palmate leaves and stem insulates and also, as do those of the pussy willows, allows a radiation heating to temperatures high enough for development, providing a miniature greenhouse effect. The same coat probably also protects the pasqueflower from unneeded radiation, although it needs much light and cannot grow in the shade, and the hairs help in its water economy.

The energy stored in its root system is drawn upon for its spring growth, and the hollow stem seems to permit its rapid growth and to allow both its bending before the wind and a turning of its floral head to face the spring sun. By the last adaptation it gains enough solar energy to keep the floral parts operating efficiently. Its sap has a low freezing point, and all its parts are soaked with an acrid irritant, which discourages foraging deer and elk. This rose has its poison thorns.

This is survival through winter, to be sure, but the pasqueflower helps me to glimpse something more, the skill of art superimposed on the science of survival. This is exuberance in the fundamental, etymological sense of being more than expectedly luxuriant. Does not such an encouraging beauty speak of that face of nature that overleaps the merest hanging on to life to bear the winds of the storm with vigorous, adorning beauty? Nor is it just the grand petals of delicate purple whorled about the yellow stamens and pistils, for the fingered involucre frames the flower so well, and the villous coat has a sheen that, seen backlighted by the sun, gives a lustrous aura to complement the gentle leafy green.

Butterflies drink its nectar, and if I first reduce them to their pollinating function, I notice soon after their winged beauty. The bees come too, and I must look more closely again, to find in their wing venation still further evidence of the art that emerges with the architecture of life. As when we strip the beauty from the melodies of birds in spring or from human romantic love, laying bare only biochemical reproductive functions, so too here, perhaps when the more is reduced to the less, we refuse to let life's production and rebirth become a window into life's spirited inventiveness. But when released so, what images indeed can the flower build in the mind!

The flower gave our race its first glimpses of paradise, in the Persian walled garden from which the term derives. Flowers hint of Eden to those who deeply appreciate them; but Earth is a natural garden, not entirely, not in winter, but exuberantly enough in spring and summer that its flowering recalls how life persists with appealing grace through the besetting storm. In the legendary days of Noah, the Hebrews took the rainbow for a sign after the Flood that life would not ever be destroyed but would survive its tragedies in blessedness.

The pasqueflower, too, when it bursts forth with the breaking up of the raging winter, is such a reminder of life's survival, indeed of a prospering such that it hopes for paradise. After the flood, the winter, this Earth will aways come round again to its garden season, to bring us somehow nearer to its ultimate natural significance, even to the sacred character of life in its struggling beauty. We begin to see why it is so inalienable a right to be able to find in the dusty earth this draft of beauty.

The natural character that we now celebrate comes through even its scientific name, *Pulsatilla patens*. It is "shaken" *(pulsatus)* by the incessant winds, and of diminutive form *(-illa)*, while yet "spreading broadly" *(patens)* its brandished petals. John Gerard wrote in his 1597 *Herbal* that the "passe floure is called commonly in Latine *Pulsatilla*." Botanists have often placed *Pulsatilla* in the genus *Anemone,* that genus going back to the Greek word for "windflower," but most prefer to separate it out owing to the tails of the achenes, which become so greatly elongated as it sows those villous seeds on the very winds that blast it. Those wisps rising over the prairie gave it another name—the prairie smoke.

The winds have carried it virtually around the north temperate world, for it is found in northern Europe, in the western two-thirds of North America, and in the Siberian Orient. Further, from some ancestral plant there have evolved several closely related species. *Pulsatilla* is everywhere a flower that comes on the heels of winter and is without peer in its own environment. No other flower is able so to endure the cold and, if need be, the dry, and to spread its petals forth so boldly from the plains through the montane and into the alpine. Its taxonomy, geography, and ecology all return to us to its hardy capacity to prosper before the wind and the winter.

The popular name further employs this character, for its prevenient grace has drawn it into association with Easter and the Passover, recalling in Christianity and Judaism alike the passing out of bondage, the passing by of death, and a release into freedom and newness of life. Gerard continues, "They floure for the most part about Easter, which hath mooved mee to name it *Pasque floure*." But long before, it was known in Old English as *passefloure* and in French as *passefleur, passe* being but a half-translated form of Pasch, going back through the Greek *pascha* to the Hebrew *pesach*.

Whatever its antiquity, we might first think, that association has no natural basis; it is entirely fictional. But we later find connections that are so funda-mental—biologically, psychologically, and even theologically—that we are hardly aware of them. It is no coincidence that Easter comes with the spring; the energies of Easter belong with the energies of spring. The vernal lily is more than an artificial symbol, it is a natural emblem of life springing up anew out of a wintry death, and so too with those other symbols of life's reproductive powers—lambs, eggs, rabbits, and even the ladies parading in their fetching dresses and bonnets—that sometimes seem so flippant beside the sobriety of the grave and the hope for more.

The death of Jesus was not incidentally at the Passover, and centuries later, the missionary church, moved by forces it did not wholly understand, super-imposed its annual memorial of the new covenant onto the "pagan" rites of spring that preceded Christianity in Europe. Easter is from an Indo-European root for the East, the rising sun, and the beloved Teutonic goddess Eostre, whose holiday was celebrated at the equinox. By a related insight, hardly less profound or subliminal, the church matched its incarnation with the winter solstice and the pagan rejoicing that the sun would begin its return toward spring, this coinciding with the birth of a Savior.

Whatever meaning the conquering faith added did not so much replace as complement, enrich, and extend the primitive and universal impulse in us to cele-brate the return of the warmth of spring and the resurgence of life that is given by these mysterious powers of the sun. The Hebrew Passover, also with its lambs and eggs, was earlier transposed from a "pagan" pastoral festival as a coming out of bondage in Egypt blended with a deliverance from the grip of winter.

Perhaps it may not be so fanciful but rather entirely realistic that this pasqueflower should in its limited and natural way come to serve as a symbol for what Jesus in his unlimited, supernatural way represents to the Christian mind, a hint of the release of life from the powers that would suppress it. The pasque-flower is of a piece with the rose of Sharon, which blooms in the desert, and the shoot budding out of the stump of Jesse, for here we have an earthen gesture of the powers of resurgent life.

We have become too wise in our own conceits if ever we let a winter solstice go by without a glance upward to rejoice that the sun will sink no lower in the darkening sky, glad that the shadows will not lengthen, glad that the longest night is done. We have become too artificially cultured if ever we let a vernal equinox fail to bring hope in the spring it pledges, glad that there is more of the day than of the night, more of life and less of death. We walk too hurriedly if ever we pass the season's first pasqueflower by, too busy to let its meeting stay us for a quiet moment before this token of the covenant of life to continue in beauty despite the storm. We come too sadly to the autumnal equinox if ever there comes a fall without its thanksgiving, making us glad for the harvest, which, remembering how there is in every root and seed a hope, makes us brave before the returning winter.

Flowers cover our every grave. But is that because they mask death for a moment, before they too fade, their comfort only an illusion adorning death? I think not. They belong there because they somehow betoken to us, at levels more subconscious than we know, this florescence of life, this capacity of the germ plasm to pass through death, to persist in transient beauty over the vortex of chaos.

In one of the earliest burials known to archaeology, in the Shanidar cave in northern Iraq, there lay a man who was congenitally deformed, his bones amidst fossil pollen. His Neanderthal mourners had gathered grape hyacinths and bachelor's buttons, hollyhocks and golden ragwort, and covered him with a blanket of blossoms. They cared for this cripple in life, and then found at death no better symbol than a floral tribute to communicate their hope that life would envelop death.

Their passions at that grave almost make us weep, for they touch so anciently this hope for the "passing over" of death by life, a force that reaches on to the pagan Germanic Easter, on to the Semitic exodus out of winter and Egypt, on to Calvary, on to the medieval naming of the pasqueflower, and on to beset me now.

If the flower has for fifty thousand years served as an emblem of resolution in the face of death, then my thoughts run steady in a natural track as perennial as the springs since Neanderthal times. The flower is a very powerful symbol, it has had a psychologically elevating effect in every culture, and if anyone cares to say that this is not scientific, but romantic, that does not make it any less real. Our recent "flower children" knew this impact when they hung flowers in protest in the guns of destruction.

For longer than we can ever remember flowers have been flung up to argue against the forces of violence and death, because that is what they do in and of themselves, and thus they serve as so ready a sign for any who encounter them in a pensive mood, wearied of the winter, frightened by the storm, saddened by death. This is why it is liberating to find the pasqueflower bearing with beauty the winds of March.

The beauties of winter are heartless, yet there is no deeper mystery than how life flowers because of the agonies that threaten it. Environmental pressures shape life—that is the premise of all biological science. Life is pressed by the storms, but it is pressed on by the storms, and environmental necessity is the mother of invention in life. The winter is a sinister maelstrom against which we fling out our curses, against which we fling up our flowers, yet is it chaos and otherness and nothing more? Or does it too belong in the seasonal economy, as night complements day, almost a sign of the unfathomable dialectic of life with its opposite.

Flowers arose against the adversities of the drought and the cold. We can only speculate about their origins, but it is axiomatic within evolutionary theory that the advanced flowers of the angiosperms conveyed some advantage, perhaps the exploitation of insects for better outbreeding, more experimentation for altered forms, such as the encased seed or the herbaceous habit, the better adapted against the dry or the cold. The seasonal tropical desert was perhaps more significant than the winter in the beginning, but each harshness has much in common, and the subsequent global advance of the angiosperms amply proved their effectiveness for overwintering.

The feat of flowering in the spring is a reciprocal of the defeat of the "fall," and the floral diversification of our temperate climates is very much a product of winters alternating with summers. This pasqueflower springs forth in its particular form of early beauty as much because of the winter as to spite it; it buds and blossoms because it is blasted. Without the wind, there would be no windflowers, and without the advancing of death, there is no advancing of life.

Modern man came out of the Ice Age. Perhaps as the human genetic stock was exposed to the pressures of glaciation, relaxed in the interglacial ages, like winters and summers, we were made modern in this recent flowering of Indo-European civilization. The north wind made not only the Vikings, it made us all. We do not owe every culture to the Pleistocene winter, for archaic civilizations arose in the tropics, but we owe all culture to the hostility of nature, provided only that we can keep in tension with this the support of nature that is truer still, the one the warp, the other the woof, in the weaving of what we have become.

Beyond that, all who live where the pasqueflower flourishes will, when they have searched deeply, find how it was the cold that made our ancestors sew garments and build fires, how it made them fashion an ever more insulating culture, in which dress we proved able not only to survive but to flourish. Our human genus flowered before the winter, much as does this pasqueflower; and once again we find the arts in their beauty superimposed on the science of survival.

This pasqueflower endures the winter in noble beauty; but its suffering is not only the shadow of its beauty, it is among the roots that nourish it. That "suffering" is metaphorical for this insentient flower; still, this natural character is an apt sign to be drawn into association with the passion of Easter and the Pesach. Life decomposes and out of its throes it recomposes; it persists in perpetual beauty while it is perpetually perishing.

The way of nature is, in this deep though earthen sense, the Way of the Cross. Light shines in the darkness that does not overcome it. This noble flower is a poignant sacrament of this, and to chance to find it in earliest spring, and to pause at that meeting, is to find a moment of truth, a moment of memory and promise. Let winters come, life will flower on as long as Earth shall last.

Subject Index

Absolute following of nature. *See* Nature.

Acid rain, 147, 167

Aesthetic value. *See* Value(s).

Agency, human, 32, 223-232, 233-240, 251, 253

Aliens in nature. *See* Nature.

Allied Chemical Corporation, 144

Alligators, 42, 185

Altruism, 20, 22, 63-65, 119-120, 208

AMAX, Inc., 168-169

Anthropocentrism, 22, 58-59, 73, 91-92, 110, 114-115, 145-146, 155, 187, 203, 218, 221

Anthropogenic extinction, 212-213, 216

Artifactual following of nature. *See* Nature.

Aspen, 85, 214, 256

Astronomical nature. *See* Nature.

Axiological following of nature. *See* Nature.

Axiological model, 194

Backpacking, 140, 186, 198, 223-232

Bacteria, 80, 127

Baikal, Lake, 139

Balance of nature, homeostasis. *See* Nature.

Beetles, 126

Beggar's ticks, tidal shore, 207

Benefit-cost analysis, 180-205

Bequest value. *See* Value(s).

Bighorn sheep, 185, 198, 231

Biology, 79-81, 139, 184-185, 206, 214-215, 249, 257-258. *See also* Information.

Biotic community, 18-29, 55, 161-163, 180, 224-227

Birds, bird-watching, 21, 79, 108, 132, 190, 197, 229, 245-246, 254

Bison, 135

Bobwhite quail, 42, 243

Breaking laws of nature. *See* Nature.

Buck-stopping maxim, 165

Burden-of-proof maxim, 168-169

Business and environmental ethics, 144-179, 217-218

Butterflies, 21, 38, 257

Canyonlands, 21, 81, 173

Cardinals, 42, 105, 253

Catastrophic extinctions, 216-218

Category mistake, 193

Character-building value. *See* Value(s).

Chimpanzees, 160

China shop maxim, 159

Christmas, 47, 259

Clear-cutting, 161, 167, 196

CNS maxim, 160

Commanding nature. *See* Nature.

Comprehensive situated fitness, 130, 162-163, 174, 214-215, 217